PEARSON CUSTOM
ANTHROPOLOGY

Managing Editor
Jeffrey H. Cohen
Ohio State University

Associate Editor
Douglas E. Crews
Ohio State University

Contributing Editors–Cultural Anthropology
Randal Allison
Blinn College

Lee Cronk
Rutgers (New Brunswick)

Donald C. Wood
Akita University Medical School

Contributing Editors–Biological/Physical Anthropology
Susan Kirkpatrick-Smith
Kennesaw State University

James Stewart
Columbus State Community College

PEARSON

ISBN 10: 1-256-53003-4
ISBN 13: 978-1-256-53003-9

Table of Contents

Studying Religion through Practice

In late 2009, I took part in a debate in Washington, D.C., about Islam in Europe. A prominent journalist had just published a book in which he deplored the effects of massive immigration of Muslims to Europe. It was a shock to most Europeans, he argued, to have mosques in the cities and headscarves in the schools. I agreed with that part, but not with much else of what he wrote. Muslim immigrants behave unlike other immigrants, he stated, unlike Hispanics in the United States or Europeans moving within Europe, because they follow the teachings of Islam. Those teachings include a command to have many children and a propensity to react violently to events, and so we find Muslims rioting (as in Paris in late 2005), carrying out jihad, and perhaps continuing to have large families. Other prominent news commentators (though not this person) have suggested that Europe will be 50 percent Muslim by 2050, and that Muslims will rise in unison to take over European capitals.

Now, there is a lot to object to in these claims. For one thing, the best demographic information available in 2009 shows that Muslim women born in Europe are having about the same number of children as non-Muslim Europeans—just what the many years of research into immigration and fertility would predict. But I was, and am, more interested in the assumptions many current writers make about the causal force of religious texts in the everyday lives of Muslims. If we assume, as this writer did, that Muslims shape everything in their lives around sacred texts, then we could legitimately read those texts to understand Muslims' actions. But Muslims draw on their scriptures in much the same ways as Christians, Jews, and Buddhists draw on theirs. Some pay close attention to their holy books; others don't read them at all. Some worship frequently; others never do. And, as with Christians, Jews, and others, Muslims interpret their scriptures in varying and changing ways. Moreover, even most highly religious people have a lot of secular aims in their lives: eating well, holding down a job, bringing up children, and so on. These were the issues behind the 2005 Paris riots, which involved many non-Muslims and people of European backgrounds, who all were enraged by problems of unemployment, discrimination, and police harassment; religion was not among their concerns (Bowen 2006).

I begin with this story because of a sense of immediacy I have about the importance of correctly understanding the roles religion does and does not play in modern public life, and the contributions the anthropology of religion can make to this understanding. The issue arises most pressingly with regard to contemporary armed conflicts, from those in the Balkans in the 1990s, through the continuing struggles in parts of the former Soviet Union, Kashmir, Indonesia, and Palestine, to the post–9/11 security debates about Islam in the United States and Europe. Are people fighting because of their religion? Does their religion shape how they think and act? Or is it just a way of mobilizing support? How far can religions be stretched to adapt to new ways of life?

These basic questions are less often posed than are the answers to them simply assumed. In less dramatic ways, many people living in Europe and North America continue to search for new forms of religiosity within or alongside established religious organizations. The fast-rising Christian churches in Melanesia, Africa, and Latin America are posing new challenges to indigenous religions. Muslims are engaging in internal deliberations about how to rethink issues of gender, of the public sphere, and of their religion's place in European and North American societies. Practitioners of smaller-scale religions throughout the world find themselves struggling for recognition or survival.

WHAT IS "RELIGION"?

Discussions of religion are often based on knowledge of only a few familiar religions. Many U.S. politicians and school officials who support a moment of silence for prayer in schools, for example, assume that all religions include the practice of silent individual prayer to a god; and some people find the Islamic practice of five daily prostrations before God disruptive. German officials have declared that Scientology is not a religion. Indonesian officials exclude animist beliefs and practices from the category of religion.

What then is "religion"? I view religious traditions as ever-changing complexes of beliefs (including those authoritative beliefs called "doctrine"), practices (including formalized rituals), and social institutions. But how do we decide which beliefs, practices, and institutions are to be called "religious"?

In most Western traditions, one finds two very common definitions in this context. One emphasizes an individual's beliefs; the other, his or her emotions. The former defines religion as a set of shared beliefs in spirits or gods. The latter identifies religion in terms of a sentiment of awe and wonder toward the unknown. For me, there is no hard and fast definition of religion. This text examines a wide variety of ways in which people in different societies and times have thought about the world beyond the immediate sense-world. Some posit a set of deities; others do not. Some have a distinct sphere of life called "religion"; others do not distinguish religion from the rest of life.

Sufficient for our purposes is that the phenomena we will study—prayer to God, uses of magic, death rituals—all involve the idea that there is something more to the world than meets the eye. This definition is much broader than standard Western usage. What if we said that religion was anything that involves a stated belief in spirits or gods? In those cultures strongly shaped by modern Christianity, people do indeed tend to think of religion in these terms. But the idea of a separate religious sphere is recent even in the West. In other societies, people define the world in different ways, treating as a natural part of everyday life actions and ideas that we would want to include in a cross-cultural category of religion.

Consider the practices of the Azande people of the southern Sudan that ethnographers have labeled "witchcraft." According to the Azande, some people carry in their bodies a substance called *mangu*. This substance is inherited, and it sends out emanations when the person feels jealousy, anger, or other negative emotions toward another person. The substance causes things to happen, and it fits into everyday ways of explaining misfortune: "I tripped at a place where I never trip; it must be witchcraft that caused me to trip."

When the person causing a particular misfortune is discovered (by using oracles), he or she is asked to blow water from his or her mouth and say: "If I was doing harm, I certainly did not mean to, let it be gone." And that is the end of the matter. The Azande do not concentrate on blame or intentions, but on the particular problem at hand and how to solve it. Indeed, they believe the substance sometimes acts on its own without the person's knowledge.

What do we make of these practices? From a Western point of view, they refer to a reality beyond the immediately verifiable, and thus we may legitimately include them in a comparative study of religions. The Azande, on the other hand, see mangu and oracles as everyday, ordinary aspects of reality. Some of the Azande who have converted to Christianity continue their use of oracles and accusations of mangu precisely because they do not see those activities as part of a separate religion, but more in the way that an American Baptist or Catholic might regard the use of an astrological chart.

The diversity of ideas about what constitutes a particular religion places any student of religion in a difficult position. If I write about a particular religion as the symbols, statements, and practices of a particular group of people, I will almost inevitably differ with some of them as to what their religion is. The perspective of an outside observer, who wishes to include a wide array of opinions and activities, may be much broader than that of a practitioner, who may insist on his or her own view of what properly lies within the boundaries of the religion in question.

I have frequently met with objections to the way I define "Islam" when describing certain Sumatran village practices to students in Indonesian Islamic colleges. For example, many villagers gather at ritual meals to ask ancestral spirits for help in healing the sick or in ensuring a good rice crop. These practices may have their origins in pre-Islamic times, but villagers view them as consistent with their understandings of Islam and they explain them in terms of prophets and angels. Much as Catholics ask saints to intercede for them because they are presumably closer to God, these Muslims ask pious ancestors to do so. For this reason, I include them in my own writings about Sumatran Islam. But for the Islamic college students, these practices conflict with proper understandings of Islam. "Those practices are what we try to teach them to throw aside," the students say. For some of them, my own writing could become part of the very problem they are trying to solve, that is, an overly broad idea of Islam.

How do we respond to these challenges? My own response has been to realize that definitions of religion are not just academic matters but part of the very social reality we are studying. I thus refrain from giving too precise a definition for religion or Islam, and instead look at issues and debates among practitioners over the boundaries of religion, recording what they say and what is at stake for them. Baptists and Catholics do not agree about how to interpret Biblical texts, but we nonetheless speak about "Christianity" because both groups do refer to the Bible and do share a history.

Indeed, the boundaries of "religion" are no clearer closer to home. Some people living in the United States would consider modern forms of witchcraft to be a religion; indeed, the Rhode Island state legislature passed a law making it so in 1989. What limits the state should place on religious freedom is also a matter of continued debate, no more so than in cases of Christian Scientists denying medical treatment to their children. (Until August 1996, treatment given by Christian Science practitioners was considered "medical" for purposes of Medicare and Medicaid reimbursements, on grounds that to deny them that category would be to violate their religious freedom.)

I propose to define religion in two stages. First, we can use an extremely broad definition, such as "ideas and practices that postulate reality beyond that which is immediately available to the senses." This broad definition allows us to look at a very wide range of things. Second, for each society we study, we ask how *these* people construct their world. They may have a shared set of beliefs in spirits and deities and thus fit squarely into Western definitions of religion. Or, they may speak about impersonal forces, such as the East Asian idea of a life force or *chi* that permeates the natural and social world. Or, they may not focus on describing beliefs at all, but rather concentrate on carrying out rituals correctly, with a general understanding that the rituals are important. (You may have rituals you carry out in everyday life to ensure good luck; are these practices religious to you?)

What we call *religion* may look quite different from one society to another—in the relative importance of a shared belief system, in the degree to which religious practice involves strong emotions, and in the social functions and contexts associated with religious practices.

AN ANTHROPOLOGICAL APPROACH TO RELIGION

What is the peculiarly anthropological approach to the study of religion? These days, most of us reach across disciplinary boundaries to engage with colleagues in other disciplines. As I work on my own current questions, which in 2010 include debates in Europe and Southeast Asia about religion and politics, I consult the work of specialists from sociology, history, politics, law, and so forth. And yet I find that multidisciplinary research highlights rather than hides the distinctive contributions made by anthropologists. Three closely connected features guide an anthropologist's study of any topic.

First, anthropology is based on a *long-term relationship with people* through fieldwork. We live for a fairly long time, more than one year and sometimes many years, in a particular place. During that time, we develop close friendships with some people and gain, we hope, the trust and respect of many more. I spent about six years in Indonesia, of which four of them were with Gayo people in the highlands of Aceh on the island of Sumatra. My experience is not unusual. I developed a very close and continuing friendship with a Gayo family that has continued through the years, and which is now global in scope. The eldest daughter of the Gayo family now lives in the United States. She began her career with Procter & Gamble in Jakarta, moved to Cincinnati to continue her career, and then, with her Egyptian husband, moved to Sunnyvale, California, where she now works for a large local mosque. After the 2004 Indian Ocean tsunami that devastated much of Aceh, she created a foundation to build orphanages in Indonesia, and then extended her work to Pakistan. My children call her "Cousin Evi"; one of them sometimes babysits her children.

Close relationships are not only the joy of fieldwork but also help us to interpret social life. We trust certain people to report what they think truthfully, and we know enough such people to be able to check our interpretations with people who might be expected to disagree in their views on things. For example, I know people who have very different perspectives on religious rituals, and I can depend on them to disagree with whatever I see. One can compare this source of reliability to that which psychologists obtain by repeating experiments.

Second, anthropologists pursue their study initially through *local perspectives*. Rather than studying the economy by creating a model of what people might do and then seeing whether they do it, or studying religion by reading scripture and then seeing whether ordinary people believe it, we begin with the ideas and practices we learn about in the field: how they grow rice or recite scripture. Then we follow the connections to larger institutions like government agencies, religious schools, or national banks—but we always start from local views of those institutions.

When I study Islamic law in Indonesia, for example, I begin with how Gayo village and townspeople talk about law, how and whether they refer to it when resolving conflicts, and to what extent they make use of courts or religious authorities. Then I study the courts, the universities that educate the authorities, and the national institutions that seek to shape what happens locally, including the Supreme Court and the National Council of Islamic scholars. I learn about colonial law, contemporary civil law, and Islamic codes, but only after studying everyday social life, in order to anchor these codes and institutions in local practices. This feature distinguishes anthropology from disciplines that usually begin with historical, religious, or legal texts, or with national political institutions.

Finally, anthropologists study *connections across social domains*. Rarely do we look only at the economy, or at literature, or at religion. We might wish to focus on one of these domains (indeed, it is required when writing a doctoral dissertation), but when we do, we usually discover that our chosen domain is connected to other domains. Suppose I want to learn about rice cultivation and discover that the planting and harvesting is tied to the performance of elaborate religious rituals and that work on the irrigation system depends on local political structures. I have to investigate religion and politics, then, in order to understand how rice is cultivated.

Conversely, my study of Islam in Gayo society involved learning about how rice is grown, how the major rice-growing regions were allocated among villages, how healing takes place, the origins of political parties, and the short history of a poetic genre written in Arabic script—all because they were part of local practices that people explained by referring to Islam. Indeed, I focused on Islam only as a third project; I was brought to it because the topics I came to study—social structure and oral literature—were interwoven with Islamic ideas about society and history. Even when we work in new kinds of sites, we retain these features in our work. When by 2000, the civil war raging in Aceh had made fieldwork no longer possible, I began working on Islam, law, and politics in France. I began to sit in religious schools along with Muslim students, interview French political actors, and analyze newspaper stories and law review articles. I no longer worked in a village or even in a single neighborhood. Now I am doing similar work on Islam in England. How is what I am doing different from the work of a political scientist? Well, it comes close to the approach of some of my French colleagues in political science—the French version of that discipline having developed more attention to everyday life than has its more behaviorist American cousin—but it retains a critical difference. I focus on how a wide range of

Muslims and non-Muslims talk about matters of importance to them—schools, mosques, political coalitions, and so on—in private and public contexts. The "local" setting in which I work is multiple: a set of institutions and events across France and England in which people deliberate and debate. Starting from these deliberations and debates leads me to look at law, politics, jurisprudence, ethics, the history of immigration, and the perspectives of French and English social scientists on their own society—in other words, the connections across domains. A French political science friend once said to me, her eyebrows slightly raised, "you're studying us, too, aren't you?" That it was so more intrigued than troubled her; it was a way of marking our disciplinary differences and transoceanic differences in perspective, alongside our shared interests in French Islam.

HOW IS ANTHROPOLOGY DISTINCTIVE?

Consider how scholars in different disciplines approach a question about why people believe the (religious) things they do. As I said before, most anthropologists approach the question through fieldwork. Susan Harding (2000), for example, set out to understand how it is that people become "convicted" (that is, convinced) followers of the Reverend Jerry Falwell's Fundamental Baptist community. Her ethnographic approach was to spend a lot of time in the community, listening to what people said and how they said it. She worked to counteract her basic skepticism toward Falwell by "bracketing," as the phenomenologist Husserl put it, her preconceptions and trying to accept his statements as true. This approach allowed her to perceive the complexity and the force of the arguments made by the Baptists. It also gave her a strong, personal sense of what it meant to have a soul and to know that Satan is real. She did not convert but she gained a felt sense of conviction.

Harding's work fits the overall account of the anthropological approach that I offered earlier. She got to know people well enough to be able to discuss a wide range of topics with them and to grasp how they saw the world. She tried to start with their concerns, rather than bringing her own categories and ideas to the field. And she did not limit her study to one specific domain, but investigated ritual, schooling, gender issues, and politics.

Most anthropologists of religion teaching in North America or Europe carry out at least their initial fieldwork outside those areas, reflecting the general anthropological emphasis on grasping the widest possible range of human experiences, practices, and ideas. This centrifugal tendency also means that they must study and explain to their readers the social and cultural context within which they find religion: kinship and marriage systems, local and national political structures, and broad cosmologies and ideologies. One could limit one's reading to the subfield of the anthropology of religion and nevertheless gain a good understanding of all of social anthropology.

Even though many sociologists carry out fieldwork, the fundamental orientation of their discipline is different from that of anthropology, with a greater interest in developing general propositions about social life, but (one might say ironically) less of a concern with broad-based comparative studies. Most sociologists of religion teaching in the United States study the organization of religions, changes in religious attitudes and beliefs, or new religious movements, usually focusing on people and institutions found in the United States. This focus means that they can assume general knowledge of institutions and ideas on the part of their readers, and that they often pitch their writings to generally held concerns, such as the decline in attendance at mainstream churches or the rise in New Age religions.

Penny Edgell Becker's (1999) study of congregations illustrates one sociological approach. She asked how congregations in the United States manage internal conflict. Her concern thus was primarily organizational. She selected a sample of churches in Chicago, choosing her sample to have variation in size, organizational structure, and liberal–conservative orientation. Her concerns were primarily to develop a general model consisting of types of church organizations and concomitant types of conflict resolution. These goals were motivated by a broader theoretical literature in sociology concerning institutions and their cultures in the United States. Along the way, she discovered interesting histories of each church and ways of preaching and worshipping, but each of these miniethnographies was inevitably partial, useful only to the extent that it contributed to her particular question.

Psychologists more rarely study religion, but a few anthropologists have taken up the methods of experimental psychology to pursue research into why people believe certain religious propositions. Pascal Boyer (2000, 2001), for example, observed that people around the world have a strikingly small number of basic ideas about supernatural beings: that they behave much as ordinary beings or objects do except for a slight variation in their properties. Thus, one has supernatural agents who are very much like people except that they can go through walls, remain invisible, hear everything, or live forever. We do not find gods who exist only every other day, or who exist in six dimensions, or who think about everything in the world at once, including the contents of all our refrigerators. Why is this? Boyer and others hypothesized that people have an easier cognitive time working with a limited set of god-concepts. They then tested this idea through experiments with children and adults and found that it held across a number of different cultures. This work resembles that of other psychologists in that it is carried out through controlled experiments and tests some universal propositions about human minds, but it joins long-standing anthropological concerns with the question of what it is that humans share in their religious beliefs.

PRACTICES, CONTEXTS, AND DIVERSITY

I examine religious life from different perspectives: the relations of doctrines to rituals; the role of religions in explaining misfortune, overcoming grief, and extending human powers; the ways that rituals of pilgrimage, preaching, and sacrificing shape religious belief and experience; the ways that images and taboos can be used to organize religious life or change it; and the role of religions in public life.

The emphasis on practice includes the study of doctrines, focusing on how doctrines are embodied in texts or other forms and how they are understood. Religious practices often invoke texts: A person may read, chant, recite, or sing a text. These textual practices are critical in linking local practices to broader religious traditions.

The particular contribution of ethnographic and social historical studies to knowledge of religion lies in the attention to interconnections among domains of social life—among religion, economy, marriage, politics, and so forth—and to the ways that cultural ideas and social institutions shape activities in many of these domains. The importance of such cross-domain connections was underscored by the social theorists Émile Durkheim and Karl Marx, who continue to have a strong influence on many anthropologists. A particular religious practice such as worship may structure communities in particular ways, or lend a religious interpretation to existing social divisions, as when a Hindu priest distributes consecrated foods according to caste standing, or when men and women worship separately in a Muslim mosque, or when church pews are reserved for those who have contributed to the church.

The interpretation of texts and doctrines is strongly shaped by local factors, as Clifford Geertz (1968) showed in contrasting Islam in Morocco to Islam in Java. Comparing two or more cases of a practice can help to highlight these shaping processes.

I consider the diversity of religious understandings and practices even in small-scale societies. Diversity includes both questions of how knowledge and ideas are distributed in the society—between men and women, or adults and children, or across other social groupings—and the debates among people about how best to understand the norms and forms of religious culture. Anthropology has often been insufficiently attentive to diversity. This insufficiency has been due in part to the idea that a "culture" is an integrated whole, an idea inherited from German nineteenth-century cultural studies, and in part due to ways of carrying out research by concentrating on a small number of "key informants"—or even, in some cases, one such informant.

We know that the same practice may be interpreted in myriad and diverse ways. Beginning from particular religious practices and then examining diverse interpretations allows us to capture these diversities, and in some cases explain them in terms of accompanying social differences and changes. Certain religious traditions allow a particularly broad diversity of practices to flourish.

A great deal of misunderstanding and, to my mind, wrong-headed public policy in many countries, but certainly in the United States, has been based on ideas about religion that ignore diversities, debates, and possibilities. For example, particular features of certain strata of Middle Eastern societies (the role of women, views on Islamic law, etc.) are frequently confused with Islam in general. Religious beliefs are all open to debate and transformation; attending to those debates reminds us of a sense of the open-ended nature of religious ideas.

The Twin Transformations
of "Religion"

Sometimes it is useful to regard the broad sweeps of history before we focus in on small-scale processes and specific societies. Here is one such case: A large chunk of the world's people have experienced at least two major transformations in how they practice and understand what we call "religion" today. One occurred about 2,500 years ago along a broad band of civilizations, stretching roughly from Greece to China; the other occurred over the past two centuries, as colonial powers sought to regulate religions and scholars based in those powers sought to classify them.

AXIAL AGE TRANSFORMATIONS

It was the philosopher Karl Jaspers, writing in 1949, who first drew attention to an extraordinary thing: that in a relatively short span of human history, between about 800 and 200 B.C.E., people living across Eurasia radically changed how they thought about divinity and how they acted toward it. He termed this period the pivotal or "axial" age, and saw it as the beginning of our own cultural world. In broad terms, this new age included the early great philosophers of Greece, Iran, India, and China, who began to ask general questions about who we are and what the purpose of our lives might be.

In more specific, "religions in practice" terms, the transformation involved placing less emphasis on sacrifices and offerings, and more on attending to divine commandments. Whereas, before, religion was to a great extent a set of acts one did to propitiate the gods, or God, now people began to question why powerful gods would need burnt offerings. Would not obedience to their word be more in keeping with their strength and our weakness? Prophets and sages began to ask questions about social justice and ethics. Why is there oppression? What does God (or gods, or the Heavens) intend, plan, and create?

We will look at the ideas more deeply later, but let's start from where Jaspers did, by noting who was living and teaching during that time. (Or for a more comprehensive list, visit any one of a number of sites on important dates in world religions, such as the site at http://www.sacred-texts.com/time/origtime.htm.)

From Chapter 2 of *Religions in Practice: An Approach to the Anthropology of Religion*, 5/e. John J. Bowen. Copyright © 2011 by Pearson Education. Published by Prentice Hall. All rights reserved.

On the early side is the Biblical prophet called the second Isaiah, who (around 740–700 B.C.E.) urged the Jews to obey the Law rather than offer up burnt sacrifices. Next in time are three major figures in Asian religions, about a century and a half later: Gautama Buddha in South Asia (563–483 B.C.E.), and Lao Tse (roughly sixth century B.C.E.) and Confucius (551–479 B.C.E.) in China. On the more recent end is Socrates (469–399 B.C.E.), who radically challenged established truths in Athens. What did these figures have in common? Two elements, anyway: the argument that power lay in a transcendent realm (heaven and God), and that truth lay in an ethical code. On an intellectual plane, some people in Greece, Israel, India, and China at this time were engaged in theoretical thinking or what we might call "second-order thinking". How can we prove a theorem in geometry? How do we proceed to know something about the good life? These are questions about how we do and should reason through questions, and these laid the bases for philosophy.

Why were similar questions posed, and a similar emphasis on the transcendent posited, at roughly the same time across this large expanse of societies? Well, in this area people were trading, traveling, and moving—sometimes against their will—much more than before. Specialized agriculture and small craft production gave rise to lively trade, largely managed by small urban structures and small states that remained outside of large empires. Market society was growing and bringing with it new questions about ethics and meaning. Coinage, laws of commerce, and translation across languages and across belief systems were part and parcel of the movements across boundaries that trade encouraged. (Gore Vidal's novel *Creation* concerns fictive encounters among these great thinkers.) The empires in Persia, North India, and China assimilated some peoples and pushed others outwards.

As people began to move around more, and seek points in common with others, they emphasized the more universalistic elements of their religious traditions. Movement and exchange lead people to seek "common denominators." A command to sacrifice a goat on such and such a hill is fine when you live near that hill, but not when you are exiled (as were the Jews to Babylon in the sixth century B.C.E.) or when you travel long distances to trade—for example, along the various segments of what came to be called the Silk Road, expanded through Persia in the seventh and sixth centuries B.C.E., and in Asia Minor under Alexander the Great and his successors in the fourth century B.C.E.

The new philosophies and theologies converged on ideas of a transcendent source of morals and order, but they differed as to how they saw the world. For example, Chinese philosophy does not posit a radical break between this world and another, whereas the Jewish theology found in the second Isaiah does so. But the Chinese idea of the Heavenly mandate does locate power, well, in the heavens. In the Confucian Analects (II.3), we read:

> The Master said: "Guide them by edicts, keep them in line with punishments, and the common people will keep out of trouble but will have no sense of shame. Guide them by virtue, keep them in line with rites and they will, besides having a sense of shame, reform themselves."

When the ruler cultivates virtues, there is social harmony and order in the realm. Religion, *li*, is part of what the ruler dictates for the social good, for when the people worship spirits and keep rites and ceremonies, they will cultivate order in themselves and around them.

Israelites

Let us consider the Jewish case more closely. Unlike in China, at issue here is a personal relationship between a God and his people. Jewish ritual had been organized around sacrifice, first mentioned when God takes Abel's offering and refuses Cain's in Genesis, an event that introduces homicide and guilt to the world. David and his son Solomon united the tribes of Israel into a kingdom during the tenth century B.C.E. and built a Temple in Jerusalem, where sacrifice regularly took place. At least by the seventh century B.C.E., when Josiah forbade sacrifices "in the high places," meaning the scattered local altars, sacrifice had become exclusively centered on the Temple.

But Israelites were also considering other ways of reshaping political and religious society, and at this time we also read emerging criticisms of the notion that God is best worshiped through sacrifice. The prophet known as first Isaiah, writing sometime before the exile, quotes God as wearily castigating his sacrificing flock (1:11):

> What to me is the multitude of your sacrifices?
> says the Lord;
> I have had enough of burnt offerings of rams
> and the fat of fed beasts;
> I do not delight in the blood of bulls,
> or of lambs, or of he-goats.

God then orders his people to stop approaching with hands "full of blood," but instead to focus on their own purity (1:16):

> Wash yourselves; make yourselves clean;
> remove the evil of your doings
> from before my eyes;
> cease to do evil.

Sacrifice was made impossible when the Babylonians destroyed the Temple and sent the Jews in exile to Babylon ("by the waters of Babylon . . .") in the sixth century. Some dreamed of a restored Temple, where sacrifice would once again be carried out—Ezekiel (45–46) speaks in great detail of how the Temple will be rebuilt and burnt offerings made. But after the end of exile, when Cyrus of Persia permitted the Jews to return to Jerusalem, religious practice became primarily about maintaining the laws of ritual purity. Ezra, the chief creator of a post-exile life, was himself a priest and a scribe, not a hereditary king. Furthermore, many Jews continued to live outside of Judea, in the diaspora areas of Syria, Egypt, and Babylonia. If they did not have the Temple close at hand, they did have the Law of Moses as contained in the first five books of the Bible, the Pentateuch. It was in the period after return from exile that this Law was compiled in roughly the form we know it today. The Law, with its emphases on obedience to transcendent commands, reflects the new social reality of a scattered people.

Over the final centuries before the Common Era, Judea passed from Persian to Greek Rule, and the Jewish community itself became more and more internally differentiated. Even as the upper classes moved into the political and cultural world of the Greeks, others emphasized, by contrast, the importance of hewing to the Law. These groups included various pious groups of hasidim, the Maccabees (leaders of a successful revolt against the Greek rulers in 167 B.C.E.), and the later Pharisees, students of the Bible and strict followers of the laws of ritual purity.

Debates ensued over "what is a Jew." Is a Jew anyone who claims to be a Jew, or only those people who maintain ritual purity? The Pharisees held to the latter position, and their answer prevailed: A Jew was someone who observed the Law as it had been handed down from Moses to the authorities of the day.

Religion had shifted from the group's sacrifice of animals, to each individual's avoidance of certain tabooed animals. From destroying life in atonement for sin, religious life was refocused on living according to the Law. This change was further intensified when Roman rulers destroyed the second Jerusalem Temple in 70 C.E. and then expelled the Jews from the city in 135. Gone was the possibility of worship through sacrifice. Religious scholars, rabbis, became the leaders of the community, and sought to rebuild religious life around the idea that by obeying the Law in their homes, Jews could experience the divine without a Temple. A general, shared religious life could be created through the medium of the Law, and observing the proscriptions contained in it would also keep the Jews separate and distinct. Taboos and boundaries became central elements in everyday life.

ENLIGHTENMENT TRANSFORMATIONS

For most of Western Christian history, religion was regarded as an individual's personal piety or faith, not as a set of systems of belief and practice. Current ways of regarding religions and of studying them date from transformations traceable to the European Enlightenment and to the expansion of European power through trade, travel, and colonial rule.

The word *religion* comes from the Latin word *religio*, whose early meaning appears to have been "a power outside the individual, or a feeling relative to such a power." *Religiosus* meant a powerful place and conveyed a sense of mystery. The term also came to refer to the particular pattern of worship, the *religiones*, that was due a certain god (Smith 1978, 19–31).

The early leaders of the Christian Church adopted these usages from the Romans. Roman authorities forced the early Christians to participate in the traditional Roman cultic ceremonies. If they refused, they were often put to death. So, the key issue about religion was how to worship: the Roman way or exclusively the Christian way—the choice was literally a matter of life and death. This focus on one's own religious rituals as opposed to those of other people gave rise to the new idea that there was more than one way to practice religion: our way of worship (*nostra religio*) as opposed to the *religiones* of outsiders. In this context, the phrase "the Christian religion" was often used to mean the Eucharist, the central ritual performed by people considering themselves Christians.

The concept of religion might then have developed its current meaning, as a term used to refer to the system of beliefs and practices of each of a number of societies. But it did not develop in this way, and the word "religion" itself virtually passed out of existence for a thousand years. (An exception is St. Augustine, whose *De Vera Religione* we might translate as "On Proper Piety"; it concerned the bond between an individual and God and not a system of beliefs and practices.) People did not write books about religion, but about faith, on the one hand, and the institutions of the church, on the other.

Despite the general impression, true in many ways, that the European Middle Ages were an age of religion, it appears that no one ever wrote a book using "religion" in the title or as a concept during this period. Not until the fifteenth century, during the Renaissance, was the term taken up again, and then with the sense of a universal capacity for piety and worship common to all human beings. There was to be only one kind of *religio,* but it would exist in different degrees in different people.

The Reformation continued this line of thought; both Martin Luther and John Calvin stressed the importance of individual piety and faith over and against any external religious system, by which they meant the Catholic Church. Luther inveighed against any "false religion," or putting faith in religion rather than in God. Indeed, Luther inaugurated a tradition in the German language of avoiding the term "religion" altogether in favor of *Gottesdienst,* "service to God" (Smith 1978, 35).

Religions as Objects of Study

The idea of religion as a system of beliefs, as opposed to personal piety, did not take hold until the seventeenth century. The change was partly the result of efforts during the Enlightenment to classify and understand the world. It was also because of a growing diversity of religious claims within Europe and the increased awareness, because of trade and travel, of religious traditions beyond Europe. By the eighteenth century, treatises on religions of the world (introducing religious pluralism) began to appear. The plural "religions" is possible only when we think of religion as a cultural system rather than a personal one. There are no plural forms for "piety," "reverence," or "obedience."

As Europeans began to study other religions, they tended to use the religions most familiar to them, namely Judaism and Christianity, as a general model. They assumed all religions would have three central elements: a central *text, exclusivity,* and *separation.* The central text was assumed to be a collection of doctrines or beliefs that all adherents shared, ideally, written in a sacred book that had been inspired by a god or gods. Exclusivity meant that a person was a member of one and only one religion, at least at any one time. Separation indicated that religion constituted an area of social life distinct from politics or economics.

The idea of religion as a separate domain developed in modern Western Europe, partly in response to the destructive religious wars of the seventeenth century. John Locke, writing in the late seventeenth century, advocated the separation of state and religion as a way of ensuring toleration and religious freedom. His argument became the basis for the principle of separation of church and state in the United States; nowhere else was it so fully realized.

While this model of religion may have worked well to meet the changing perceptions and desires of Europeans, it fit poorly with the religions of India, China, and Japan.

In each of these large geographical zones, no single book did or does provide a shared creed for practitioners of religion; instead, people refer to one or more of a variety of teachings on diverse aspects of life, and they choose distinct teachers or organizations. Today we know these collections of texts and teachers under the general rubrics of *Hinduism, Buddhism, Taoism,* or *Shinto,* but these labels are modern inventions.

Nor does the idea of exclusivity fit with norms in these societies. In Japan, for example, people routinely bring offerings to shrines dedicated to local gods (practices associated with the label *Shinto*) and, in the same temple complex, venerate Buddha figures. The same people may marry in a Christian church. The idea of a separate religious sphere is also alien to many other religious traditions. Many Muslims argue that all of life should be conducted in accord with God's commands. Hinduism involves ideas of purity and pollution that permeate all social life.

But despite these problems with the European model of religion, modern European attempts to understand these other religions worked from the European model. By the nineteenth century, books appeared about other religions and they introduced the names that we use today. *Buddhism* was first used in 1801 and *Hinduism* in 1829. (Before then writers referred, more accurately, to "the wisdom of the Japanese" or "Hindu teachings.") The term *Islam* also began to be used in Europe; previously, Europeans referred to *Muhammadenism,* treating Islam not as a religion, but as allegiance to a false prophet (Smith 1978, 51–79).

The nineteenth-century European notions of what counted as a religion have powerfully shaped how other religions and other countries have viewed religion. For, with few exceptions, the creation of terms for *religion* and for particular religions has been the result of Western, Christian influence, transmitted through colonial domination.

Take what we often refer to as Hinduism. In India today, religious practice and the precise formulations of doctrine vary from place to place. Indeed, it is a central tenet of religious teaching in India that one should follow the inspiration derived from one's teacher in pursuit of enlightenment. Thus, there is not, nor is there supposed to be, one single formulation of Hindu Religion.

The word *Hindu* itself was not used by ancient Indians to refer to their religion. It is a word meaning "river," and in particular is used as the proper name for the Indus River. Foreigners—Greeks, then Muslim conquerors—came to designate the people living near that river as "Indian" or "Hindu." Under Muslim rule, the term came to be used to refer to all non-Muslims in the country, including Buddhists and Jains. Only recently has *Hindu* been used as a residual term to designate those people, and their beliefs, who are residents of India but who are not Jains, Sikhs, Christians, Muslims, or animists. But in the 1980s and 1990s, some politicians made the creation of a "Hindu India" their party platform, and they succeeded in rallying large numbers of supporters to their cause. Whatever was once the case, today "Hindu" is experienced by many Indians as a unitary social as well as religious category.

The Chinese too did not have any word corresponding to the Western idea of religion. They eventually borrowed a word from the Japanese, *Tsung-Chiao,* which the Japanese themselves had created to accommodate the Western concept. Nor did Chinese have words meaning Confucianism, Buddhism, or Taoism in the sense of religions that one joined or left. Instead, people were aware of collections of teachings that could be followed in trying to find a path toward truth. These teachings included the sayings of Confucius, Buddha, and Lao Tse (a possibly mythic figure who urged followers to find the true path, or Tao).

In a rather neat exchange of terms, the Japanese borrowed the word used to refer to indigenous traditions, *shinto,* from the Chinese. In fact, the term was first used by foreigners to refer to local practices in Japan. The Japanese today use a translation of the Chinese borrowing—*kami no michi,* or "the way of the spirits or gods"—to refer to these practices (Reader 1991, 23). What are included in the definition of religion are of much public interest in Japan today. At the end of the nineteenth century, the Japanese government declared that the indigenous, or Shinto, worship at shrines was not a religion. But what came to be called State Shinto, to which the cult of the emperor was central, became an ideological pillar of twentieth-century Japanese efforts to modernize society, and for that reason the cult was abolished under the post–World War II occupation.

The boundaries of religion were again debated when the new emperor, Akihito, succeeded his father, Hirohito, in January 1989. According to Shinto creed, the emperor is the descendant of the Sun Goddess, and he performs certain rituals at the goddess's shrine when he takes office. Are these rituals to be taken as religious? If so, they imply his claim to be the chief priest of Shinto and the intermediary to the Sun Goddess. But this status was abolished under the occupation, in the Constitution. Are they just political rituals? There was a fierce debate in Japan over this question, and the matter remains unsettled.

The names for religions were often provided by outsiders—one can add to the preceding examples that the term *Judaism* is Greek, not Hebrew. The name *Islam,* used from the beginning by the religion's adherents, is the major exception. However, the term means "submission to God," not the set of beliefs and practices themselves. Indeed, the religious scholar Wilfred Cantwell Smith (1978, 114) has argued that if one believes in God as a Jew or Christian, and realizes that from an Islamic perspective Muslims, Christians, and Jews worship the same God, then one cannot truthfully say in Arabic, "I am not a Muslim." One submits to God, after all, in whatever language.

SOCIAL THEORY AND THE ANTHROPOLOGY OF RELIGION

As Europeans were beginning to think of "religions" as distinct sets of beliefs and practices, European social scientists and theorists began to ask new questions about these phenomena. The question "why religion" came to be posed within the context of different theories about society, culture, and psychology. Theorists such as E. B. Tylor focused on the distinctive ideas that characterize religions, and asked why people hold certain religious ideas and not others. We continue, today, to ask this question, for example, within cognitive anthropology and evolutionary psychology. Other theorists, such as Émile Durkheim, focused on the social realities (and, he thought, origins) of religious practices and groups. Much of the sociology and social anthropology of religions grow out of the questions asked by Durkheim: Why do people join, and remain part of, organized religions? Other social theorists came to look at religion as part of broader theoretical preoccupations. Karl Marx and Max Weber asked how modern capitalism came to dominate the world. Each had his own approach, and his own ideas of religion fit into the picture: for Marx, as part of the structures that subtended a particular form of economic organization; for Weber, as a source of outlook on life that animated much of what people did in their economic and social lives.

RELIGION AS INTELLECTUAL ACTIVITY

One dimension of religion is the intellectual: What do people think exists, and why do they think those things? These questions are still with us and justify turning to some of the major figures who posed them.

In the mid-nineteenth century, the early years of anthropology as a formal discipline, scholars in most disciplines tried to explain the diversity and complexity of today's religions by postulating a process of religious evolution. They were strongly influenced by German idealist philosophers, who saw human history as the development of a set of human essences. These philosophers understood religion as a unity of thought and feeling, intellect and emotion that had developed historically from initial germs. The philosopher Hegel postulated a universal idea of religion that preceded its particular historical manifestations. As it developed over time from an initial germ, it became increasingly complex. This idea of development or evolution did not concern the history of a particular religion or a particular people, but the evolution across time and space of an idea, independent of particular cultures.

This theory of general human cultural evolution provided the intellectual framework for the early anthropology of religion, as well as for social anthropology more generally. The comparative study of religion in the late nineteenth century was based on two assumptions: that religion progressed from the simple to the complex, and that one could reconstruct the origins of religion by studying "primitive peoples" in the world today. Many students of the origins of religion did not subscribe to the universal truths offered by their churches, and their accounts were more or less subtle ways of discrediting the absolute truth of Christianity. If Catholic or Anglican beliefs evolved from something very simple then they looked much less absolute than if they had been delivered through divine revelation.

E. B. Tylor and the Origins of Religious Ideas

The most famous study along these lines was *Primitive Culture* (1970 [1871]) by Edward B. Tylor (1832–1917). Tylor was the first person to be appointed to a university position in anthropology in England, in 1884 at Oxford. He argued that primitive people acted as proto-scientists when they created religion, constructing concepts to explain what they perceived through their senses. Tylor (1970, vol. 2) asked: "What is true of all religions?" He looked around him and saw that all religions employed a belief in spiritual beings. The higher ones had souls, gods, angels, and so on, while the more primitive ones had spirits and ghosts. The primitive form of this belief he called animism. He saw this belief as basic to religious development.

"Why do people come to hold such a belief?" he then asked, and answered that it might well be because they perceive things that lead them to suppose these spiritual entities. They perceive different states of consciousness (wakefulness, sleep, and death), dreams (and the appearance in them of places and persons), and shadows. Then they think up things to explain these appearances. "Soul" explains the different states of consciousness, because as the soul sleeps, or leaves the body, we lose consciousness or pass into death. "Ghost" or "spirit" explains the phenomenon of dreams, because as we sleep, our ghost or spirit leaves the body and travels to other places, and we vaguely remember these wandering perceptions when we wake. Finally, shadows are one form taken by souls and ghosts.

Tylor was able to amass a large body of evidence to support his claims. Religion was due to "the plain evidence of men's senses" for Tylor, and as it develops, it continues to build on perceptions and logic. People reasoned that because animals, too, have life, they must have souls as well. If they are killed, their souls can follow those of their masters to the world of the beyond, and there do work for them. Burial practices from such diverse civilizations as Egypt and China attest to this belief. Furthermore, because plants also live and die, they must have souls as well. All living things, concludes Tylor's primitive thinker, thus have souls; such is the origin of "animism," the belief that all living things are "animated" by souls.

But how is it, asks Tylor, that such ideas have survived until today? One way is through psychological development. As children, we have the very same experiences, and make the very same inferences, as did primitive people: We have dreams and we attribute life to things and play with them as if they were alive. When we grow up, we are thus prepared to accept as true, because in some sense natural, the claims of the religions we are taught. We do so because—and here is the second way the early ideas survived—the ideas of advanced religions are merely further elaborations of the primitive ideas. Tylor offers the example of the Eucharist, the Christian ritual wherein bread and wine become, or symbolize, Christ's body and blood. This ritual might appear to be far from primitive religion. But, he argues, it is but the further development of the idea of sacrifice, which itself was based on the notion that the soul of the sacrificed animal or person would travel to the world beyond.

Tylor's account of religion captures elements that one does, indeed, find throughout the world. The ideas of soul, spirit, dreams that he described as basic or primitive do indeed animate many religious systems. Tylor's weakness, from our contemporary perspective, is that he emphasized an essential commonality to all religious beliefs and thus played down what most anthropologists emphasize today, namely, the diversity of ways in which humans have constructed their religious beliefs and practices. But by analyzing the logic of a set of beliefs, Tylor did inspire his successors to analyze the different ways people have constructed their understandings of the cosmos, their "world views."

An eminent successor to Tylor in this enterprise was James Frazer (1854–1951) whose massive compendium of religion and myth, *The Golden Bough* (1981 [1890]), first issued in 2 volumes and later expanded to 12, brought together in a readable style much of the knowledge of the day about comparative religion. Frazer followed Tylor in sharply distinguishing among science, magic, and religion as distinct modes of thought. Religion, in their view, involves acts intended to appease deities; magic, like science, assumes impersonal relationships between certain actions and their outcomes. Magic rests on two basic, albeit mistaken, ideas. The first idea is that of similarity, that is, like causes like (a green stone will cure jaundice). The second idea, contagion, implies that contact between two objects allows someone to control one through manipulating the other: a person's hair-clippings can be burned, for example, thereby harming the person. Magic is thus pseudoscience; religion proper involves a qualitatively different kind of activity.

Tylor and Frazer's intellectualist legacy was to focus anthropological energies on understanding how particular people view the world, taking their world view seriously as an intellectual or philosophical enterprise. Most anthropologists continued to pose these questions thereafter. Notably, in the United States, Franz Boas and his students developed cultural anthropology around a twofold approach to studying small-scale societies. On the one hand, they sought to discern the patterns of each culture as they were reflected in art, myth, kinship, and everyday ways of speaking. On the other hand, they traced the historical processes through which people transmit cultural ideas across societies and also change them. This dual focus on both ideas and empirical processes reflects Boas's own German training in both empirical sciences and idealist philosophy.

Claude Lévi-Strauss and the Structure of Mythic Thinking

Boas's complex approach to myths probably was best continued by the French anthropologist Claude Lévi-Strauss. Lévi-Strauss drew from Tylor's analysis of the intellectual operations detectable in myth-making, but he also, following Boas, sought to trace transformations of myths as they have passed from one society to another. Myths, in his analysis, are composed according to intricate codes, each of which concerns a distinct level of local life and awareness: a code of flora and fauna, one of geography, one of social institutions, and so on. These codes are structured as oppositions among categories: cold versus hot, high versus low, mother's versus father's relatives, and so forth. Moreover, neighboring peoples often tell contrasting versions of these myths, and these contrasts across societies indicate that myths reflect differences in local social life, and that they may function to underscore the boundaries between peoples.

In one of his best known analyses, Lévi-Strauss dissects a myth told among several peoples of the Northwest Coast of North America, the "Story of Asdiwal" (1976). The myth is structured around four distinct codes of geography, economy, society, and cosmology. Events often concern all four codes at once: for example, a marriage involves geographical movement, fishing, a particular kind of marriage institution, and movements between earth and sky. Lévi-Strauss argues that the myth depicts in especially salient ways the contradictions that are the basis of Tsimshian society. Marriages among families of chiefs, for example, were supposed to create or reaffirm relations of hierarchy among them, but precisely who was superior to whom was debated fiercely at each marriage. The myths depict such chiefly marriages as ending in death and battle, thus representing in heightened form problems inherent in the social structure. The myths also try out alternative realities, such as trying to inherit from one's father and one's mother, "in order to show that they are untenable" (1976, 173).

Differences between two versions of the myth show how myths, as they are transferred from one place to another, are recast in light of local conditions. One version was collected along the coast, from people who make a great seasonal migration from one region to another to catch candlefish in the spring from one river and salmon in the summer from another. In their version of the myth, characters travel great distances and they engage in very different economic pursuits, as do the humans telling the myth. Lévi-Strauss points out that this version of the myth is characterized by strong oppositions between categories along geographical and economic codes. But oppositions are also strong along the social and cosmological codes (for example, featuring people who are distantly related to each other), as if to follow the oppositions generated by the codes of economic life and geographic movement. This priority of some codes, the economic and geographic, over others is mentioned by Lévi-Strauss in referring to himself as a Marxist.

In the versions of the myth that were collected along a river where the residents made fewer movements in the course of the year—they hunted candlefish but not salmon, for example—the oppositions were weaker, again along all four codes. This comparative analysis thus supports Lévi-Strauss's conclusions that codes of a myth are internally integrated and that they all differ in a systematic way across societies. Others, especially James A. Boon (1990), have used this insight in their own ethnographic analyses of how people structure religious and social life through their use of oppositions and contrasts. In these studies, myths are seen as extended commentaries on the practice of everyday social life.

RELIGIONS IN SOCIAL LIFE

Although neither Tylor nor Lévi-Strauss conceived of religious ideas and practices as divorced from society, they underscored the intellectual dimension of religious ideas. Boas, too, and especially his students, emphasized the ways in which religious and other ideas cohere in patterns. As we will see, this emphasis on the cultural patterning of religion has retained a central role in anthropology.

But certain social theorists argued that religious ideas, sentiments, and orientations had developed out of specific social conditions. Each of the three major social theorists of modern Europe—Durkheim, Marx, and Weber—crafted some distinctive ways of understanding religion's relationship to broader social processes. All three theorists were primarily concerned with explaining features of modern life—the rise of modern capitalism, challenges to social solidarity, and the peculiar nature of rational and legal authority. In the process of developing their theories, they also tried to explain the role of religion in premodern societies.

Émile Durkheim on the Social Origins of Religion

Some scholars continued Tylor's quest for the origins of religion, but sought those origins in social life. The sociologist Émile Durkheim (1858–1917), for example, saw the birth of religion in the ideas and emotions generated out of collective social action. "Religious representations are collective representations that express collective realities," he wrote (1995, 9). Durkheim was not entirely the originator of this general idea. Aristotle, after all, had declared that "men create the gods after their own image." The French historian Fustel de Coulanges (1830–1889) and the Scottish scholar of Semitic societies W. Robertson-Smith (1846–1904) had linked social organization to religious ideas in ancient societies. Robertson-Smith had argued that the earliest societies had been totemic, that is, they had been organized into clans, each of which had a special relationship to a species of animal—"my clan is a wolf." Sacrificing this animal was a way to communicate and commune with the deities, and at the same time it was a means to strengthen the emotional bonds among clan members.

Durkheim drew from these earlier writers to argue that knowledge in general, and religious knowledge in particular, has a social foundation. His argument was philosophical, against Kant's idea that humans had innate categories of the understanding, by which he meant categories such as causality and temporal succession that people apply to everything in the world around them. But it was also social and moral, and grew out of the concerns of the day (Lukes 1973). Durkheim wrote at a time of great social and moral turmoil in France, when older certainties about God and Church had been excised from public and legal life by the Revolution but no alternative moral certainties had yet replaced them. The country appeared to be polarized between urban agnostics and rural Catholics. Battles were especially sharp over the future of the school system: Should it be secular or Catholic, and if secular, what would be its moral content? No wonder that in his first articles, Durkheim was deeply sensitive to the problem of social cohesion in contemporary society: "A society whose members are not bound to one another by some solid and durable link," he wrote in 1886, "would resemble a loose pile of dust which could at any time be dispersed by the slightest wind to the four corners of the world" (quoted in Alexander 1982, 82). But what are these bonds? And how do they unite people in societies that have not undergone the sort of schisms experienced by France?

As one would expect given the evolutionary way of thinking in vogue at the time, Durkheim sought his answer in a study of "The Elementary Forms of the Religious Life," the title of his 1912 book. The book posits an early type of social consciousness in those societies where everyone is for all important purposes alike: everyone has the same statuses, duties, and roles. In such societies, people's feelings are also alike, and thus strongly reinforce each other whenever people gather together. Moral sentiments, religious beliefs, and other cultural ideas are all very strong, and law, religion, and social norms are strong as well.

Durkheim postulated that religious beliefs and sentiments must correspond to something real and that they could not be purely illusory or mistaken, as Tylor and Frazer had concluded. These beliefs clearly were false if taken at face value. The problem then was to go underneath the symbol to the reality that it represents and that gives it its true meaning. Doing so required redefining the very idea of "religion."

Rather than defining it as the belief in spirits, as did Tylor and Frazer, Durkheim viewed it as involving a fundamental division of the world into sacred versus profane things. Religion is thus a collective reality that concerns how the members of a particular society divide up the world, rather than an individual reality consisting of what a person believes. But *how* the world is divided into sacred and profane varies greatly from one society to the next; what determines this division?

Here Durkheim accepts Robertson-Smith's thesis that totemism was the earliest basis for social organization and the wellspring of religion. He turns to the religions of Australian aborigines to prove his thesis. In these societies, specific groups perform rituals at sacred sites that are associated either with ancestral spirits or with mythical beings that lived during the ancient "dream time" that came before the time we know. Each group also has objects made of wood or stone engraved with symbols of these ancestors or mythical beings, and these *churinga* objects themselves have sacred powers.

Each such social group also has a special ritual relationship toward certain species, such as kangaroo, or certain natural phenomena, such as rain or wind. Members of the group may have special rules regulating their activities with respect to these species, the group's *totem,* and the group can carry out rituals that increase the species' numbers. These rituals sometimes involve eating an item of the species, and Durkheim thought that this practice confirmed the theory that sacrifice and communal eating were the earliest, basic forms of religious ritual.

Durkheim argued that the general idea of spiritual force that underlay totemism existed prior to ideas about spirits or souls, and he cited related ideas from other societies, such as the notion of impersonal force or *mana* in Melanesia. (He also could have cited the Chinese idea of life force, or *chi*.) This same force, at later stages of development, gives rise to ideas of souls, ancestral spirits, and God, stated Durkheim.

Durkheim set out his argument on two different levels. First, he explained the variety of religious ideas by arguing that particular features of societies give rise to particular features of their cultures and religions. Religion thus represents society. So, there are "societies in Australia and North America where space is conceived in the form of an immense circle, because the camp has a circular form." The early division of society into two halves or *moieties* gave rise to ideas of the cosmos as dualistic. In societies such as the Australians just discussed, where people were organized into clans, people often postulated an animal, or sacred place, or force, as the totem of that clan. These totems were the projections onto a spiritual place of a sense of belonging together in the clan. As the society grew and spread over a wider area, giving rise to a sense of a broad social group with shared interests that spilled over the boundaries of the clan, totemic representations synthesized into the idea of one or more gods, "the god being only a figurative expression of the society," Durkheim summarily stated (1995, 227).

This level of argument presumes that there already is a general religious idea that can be shaped by society. So arguing at a second level, Durkheim tried to explain the emergence of general religious ideas and sentiments in the first place. People sense a moral force that is exterior to them, he argued. This idea is given social content in those moments when people come together in social assemblies, such as dances, meetings, or festivals. These assemblies create a social effervescence out of which religious ideas are confirmed and given stronger emotional meaning. A qualitative change takes place and people began to feel themselves transported to an altered state.

Religion serves the function of strengthening social solidarity by communicating specific ideas and sentiments and by regulating and strengthening social relationships. A totem, for instance, reminds you what kind of person you are (a member of a certain clan) and thereby regulates relations among individuals. It also gives you a feeling of strength—speaking of one Australian society, Durkheim wrote: "The Arunta who has properly rubbed himself with his churinga feels stronger; he is stronger" (1995, 229).

This functionalist perspective on religion gave Durkheim a way of discussing the place of religion in modern society. Religion is no longer a satisfactory *cognitive* solution to the "problem of meaning," in which science is now the master. But religion continues to be *symbolically* important: Cult and faith are essential to any society's social solidarity, including our own, and that explains its continued hold on us. (This logic is what we mean by "functionalism": The positive social consequences of the beliefs or practices explain why they continue to exist.)

Durkheim emphasized the cognitive, emotional, and social aspects of religious ideas and practices. His *Elementary Forms* focuses on the social origins of religion by way of a theory of collective emotions; but there and in other writings, Durkheim also emphasizes the logical nature of religious classifications. In *Primitive Classification* (1963 [1903]), Durkheim and his nephew Marcel Mauss (1872–1950) compared the symbolic classifications found in Australian, native North American, and Chinese societies. The Zuni Pueblo people of the U.S. Southwest, for example, assign to each of the cardinal directions (plus center, and the zenith and nadir of the sun's apparent motion) a color, a season, and a kind of weather, together with a general force such as creation or destruction, a specific group, and an animal. Durkheim and Mauss claimed that members of these societies have created totalizing religious systems; these systems unite the social, natural, and cosmological realms. Their comparison of logical similarities across these societies inspired later anthropologists to make more detailed studies of symbolic classification.

Durkheim's legacy in the field of religious studies was twofold. First, he connected the religious to the social, leading later anthropologists to look for social origins or functions of specific religious practices and ideas. This strain of his legacy was a foundation of British social anthropology, from A. R. Radcliffe-Brown through Edmund Leach and Mary Douglas. For Mary Douglas, for example, the key to understanding food taboos, whether in the Hebrew Bible or in the societies of central Africa she studied in her fieldwork, is to look for the social functions such taboos may have served. She argued that by separating the sacred from the profane, and then by restricting membership in the community to those who observed the rules, food taboos make group membership sacred.

Durkheim also emphasized the ways that participating in collective religious practices confirm faith, and this insight remains compelling. Consider how many European Catholics find visions of Mary to be central events cementing their faith, or perhaps their hope within their faith. In less spectacular ways, the good feelings of participating in something with friends and neighbors may also make the religion particularly "true." Particularly important is the way in which public ritual generates religious commitment. A religious service in which many people worship together can be a wonderfully compelling context, generating a sense of being together and being in the presence of something else. Such feelings, perhaps most startlingly displayed when Christian worshipers speak in tongues, lay behind Durkheim's claim that coming together as a social group gave rise to the earliest ideas of the supernatural. Most people, however, most of the time, experience their activities of carrying out worship, consulting oracles, or avoiding tabooed foods as routine actions. It may indeed be the case that the routine nature of most of the religions' demands, the integration of religion into everyday life, provides a social and psychological comfort. (Perhaps you can think of moments when a religious gathering provokes heightened feelings of belonging together.)

Second, Durkheim connected the religious to the intellectual, in this respect continuing Tylor's emphasis on the intellect, but inverting it, explaining features of the intellect in terms of their origins in religion, seen as a *social* activity. "The essential notions of scientific logic are of religious origin," he wrote in *Elementary Forms* (1995, 431).

This last statement has broadly echoed in cultural anthropology throughout the world, and most notably by Claude Lévi-Strauss, who saw classificatory systems as the product of intense, imaginative intellectual activity. Rather than seeing totems and totemic social organization as a primitive form of identification that then gave rise to higher forms of society and religion, Lévi-Strauss considered them, in his *Totemism* (1963a [1962]), as one among many ways of classifying the world in order to understand it. Particular plants or animals are chosen to be totems not because they have utility or excite awe in themselves, but because they provide a usable symbolic template through which to make distinctions in the natural, social, and cosmological worlds.

Karl Marx on Religion in Capitalist Europe

Durkheim's approach to religion assumed that society, and therefore religion, was an integrated whole. But what if society is not like that, and instead consists of several groups whose interests and ideas are in conflict? How then ought we to understand the social origins and functions of religion?

This question lies behind the work of both Karl Marx and Max Weber. Karl Marx (1818–1883) emphasized the historical process by which different social groups come to dominate social life. The key to this process was the interplay between the material forces of production and the social relations of production: how things were produced and how their production and distribution was organized. Each historical period in European history has thrown up its own distinctive dominant ideology: politics in classical Rome, the Catholic Church in the medieval period, and capitalism as ideology in the modern period. Marx and his collaborator, Friedrich Engels, saw religion not only as serving ideological functions in all periods, as providing social cement in the face of class divisions, but also as expressing class interests (Marx and Engels 1965 [1946]).

Studies of religion inspired by Marx have looked for the material interests served by movements gathered together under the banner of religion. Engels (1956 [1850]) argued that the religious wars of the fifteenth and sixteenth centuries in Germany, although couched in the language of religious dissent, were motivated by the disparate interests of the nobility, burghers, and peasants. Among these movements were those millenarian Christian movements that prophesied the imminent moment (the "millennium," or thousand years) when the corrupt leaders of the church would face the Day of Judgment. German millenarian prophets combined apocalyptic teachings with calls for the end of the feudal system, supporting Engels's thesis that material interests and religious ideas were intertwined. Engels thus showed the power of religion to subvert as well as to confirm the existing social order. His study launched a distinguished tradition of investigations (for example, Worsley 1968) into the material and religious sources of those radical religious movements whose leaders preach an imminent radical transformation of society, if not the end of the world—"millenarian" in today's general sense of the term.

Max Weber on Religion in Modern Civilizations

Max Weber (1864–1920) also analyzed the relationships between particular interest groups and religious ideas. Weber (1978 [1956]) took the social action of the individual as his unit, distinct from Durkheim's emphasis on social structure and function and Marx's emphasis on changing modes of production. Weber wrote that one can only come to understand social action by, first, discovering the meaning of the action for the individual and, second, by explaining it in terms of the social conditions and actions that preceded it. Social science thus involves both interpretation and causal–historical explanation.

Religion provides one major source of ideas and orientations for the actor, and Weber devoted much analysis to the comparative study of religions. His interest was not religious doctrine per se, but the spirit or *ethos* that was produced in individuals by their adherence to one faith versus another, as well as the social conditions that allowed new types of religious orientation to emerge. Weber saw the development of Western society as the progressive *rationalization* of society, a concept that implies both the increasing differentiation of social life into functionally defined domains or spheres—family, economy, religion, and so on—and the systematic reorganization of each domain around a single set of values or rules. Economy gradually became reorganized around the maximization of profit; family, around the general solidarity of kin; religion, around the worship of God. In Weber's view of Western world history, religion gradually shed its "magical" character and developed a set of universalistic doctrines about a divine order and a set of ethical principles that apply to everyone, everywhere.

Weber's theory of religious history is both sociological and universal. Weber carried out separate studies of India, China, Islam, ancient Judaism, and modern Europe. He saw each of these societies as characterized by a distinctive set of religious beliefs, a particular economic ethic, and a specific set of interest groups; his research concerned the interplay of these three elements. In his study of India, for example, Weber argued that the caste system and the doctrine of *karma*—the idea that one's actions in this or a previous life determined the course of one's life—inhibited the development of a rational economic ethic because it led religious energies away from this world and directed them toward the "other world." Only with the development of Calvinist Protestantism in Europe did there arise a religion-driven energy to rationally remold the world; this energy pushed forward modern capitalism.

Weber traced similar developmental processes within each socioreligious system. In the larger-scale societies he studied, prophets arose to challenge an older way of thinking, often in the name of a universal creed and god. But with the demise of the prophet, followers had to "routinize" the movement, creating a religious community or congregation. The eventual development of a rational, differentiated religious system required the parallel development of a bureaucratic state, whether in India, China, or Europe.

Weber's analysis rested on the "ideal types" he created—the other-worldly mystic and the this-worldly prophet. These types give us an initial, clear sense of the contrasts in dominant ideas among large-scale religions. But they are less useful in analyzing the many ways in which people reinterpret and transform those ideas. Weber's ideal types have been questioned by later students of each society. For example, Weber based his claims that the Indian doctrine of karma would retard economic development on the assumption that the doctrine contained in religious texts was also what ordinary people believed. But popular Indian ideas about fate and action in the world are not the same as the textual doctrines (Babb 1983), and they have not prevented people from engaging in modern industrial development (Singer 1964).

Clifford Geertz and the Ethnography of Civilizations

Although a number of anthropologists began to study large-scale societies, or "civilizations," in the 1950s, probably the best known among them was Clifford Geertz (1926–2006). In his *Religion of Java* (1960), as well as in other works on Indonesia and Morocco, he analyzed the diversity of religious beliefs in large Muslim-majority societies.

Geertz draws from Weber's emphasis on the answers that large-scale religious doctrines provide for life's key questions, such as: Why is there evil in the world? Who gets to heaven and why? But whereas Weber worked largely from the writings of religious figures and other literate men—those who formed what Robert Redfield (1956) was to call the urban "great traditions"—Geertz relies on the testimonies of ordinary village and townspeople, those people participating in what Redfield called the rural "little tradition." Geertz looks at the diversity of ideas in a single society.

Geertz's method in his early writing on Java was to define three "streams" of Islam, each situated in a different institutional context: a set of village understandings that focused on spirits and community rituals; a more scripturally oriented Islam of the religious school and the market; and a focus on status and etiquette among noble Javanese. Although criticized for not emphasizing that people in all three streams were Muslims and that many read works of Islamic doctrine and spirituality, his analysis was able to capture both the variety of ways Javanese men and women talked about religion and society, and the ways that large-scale institutions of politics, economics, and religion shaped their understandings and actions.

Geertz's approach has been especially influential in the anthropology of religion. Today many anthropologists place even more emphasis than he did on the ways that villagers and religious experts ("culture brokers") interpret and reshape the texts and ideas of religious traditions in their societies. For example, Stanley Tambiah (1970) studied the uses that monks and other villagers make of Buddhist texts in northeastern Thailand. Dale F. Eickelman (1985) traced the career of a rural Moroccan judge. In these and other studies, anthropologists have situated large-scale changes in specific towns and villages and with respect to specific people. I also began my work in Indonesia strongly influenced by Geertz's capacities to draw on social theory (largely Weber) as he interpreted events and debates, creating a sense of which ideas and which emotions were central to everyday preoccupations.

THE PSYCHOLOGY OF RELIGION

Cognitive and social approaches to religion sometimes fail to provide a full account of the psychological dimension. The individual as portrayed in works by Tylor and Durkheim, for example, is rather one-dimensional: he or she is a would-be scientist, or simply part of a crowd marked by religious euphoria.

Weber and Suffering

Of theorists considered so far, Weber paid the most attention to the psychological dimension of religion. He wished to explain how different religious orientations toward the world would produce different economic ethics, leading to different kinds of economic organization. In particular, he sought to explain how Protestant ideas spurred on modern capitalism in Europe—most particularly the early Protestant ideas of "unknowable election," that some people were elected to heaven and others condemned to hell, but that no one could know his or her category nor change what God had preordained. Weber argued that this doctrine, taught by the theologian John Calvin, was so unsettling that people worked hard to succeed in this world, grasping at the idea that the material signs of their success also were signs of God's favor. The "Protestant ethic" was thus the psychological consequence of a specific doctrine, and it, not the doctrine itself, was a key element in the rise of modern capitalism.

Weber thought that the idea of predestination also served to affirm the absolute, transcendent power of God over his creations. The idea explains the presence of evil in the world by stating that God's motives are beyond human understanding. The idea is basic to one of the most powerful and enigmatic of the Bible stories, the story of Job. The story concerns how Job retains his faith in God through a series of terrible tests—he loses his family, health, and wealth. God wagers with Satan, allowing Satan to inflict these sufferings, with Job's faith as the prize. Job has done nothing to deserve his suffering, but suffer he does. Others voice to Job their belief in a rule-bound God: "Does God pervert justice?" asks one. But of course God does do precisely that, or, rather, he stands above human norms of justice. It is human self-righteousness that leads people to challenge God: "Will you condemn me that you may be justified?" answers God out of a whirlwind (40 Job v.8). The point of the story is to show the reader or listener someone who loses everything and yet keeps his faith—and finally understands the total power of God and his demand for total submission to him.

The Book of Job offers to those who read it a sense that their own suffering is not to be argued with but accepted. This acceptance may provide a psychologically powerful, perhaps comforting way to survive suffering. One finds similar narratives in other religions. For many Muslims, the story of the martyrdom of Husain at the Battle of Karbala plays this role. The story concerns how Husain, the grandson of the prophet Muhammad, died through treachery in battle. The story is important to those Muslims who believe that Muhammad's descendants are his rightful successors. Every year, these Muslims, called the *Shi'i*, or "Shiites," celebrate Husain's martyrdom as an enacted narrative of their own suffering, and their position today as a minority within the Muslim world. Processions in which Husain rides his horse through large crowds of celebrants, while some beat themselves bloody with sticks or chains, dramatize and religiously contextualize suffering (Waugh 1977).

Some Christians stage similar reenactments of Christ's suffering on his way to crucifixion. In some societies people volunteer to play the role of the crucified Christ, enduring great suffering as they are hung from crosses. These "passion plays," public dramatization of suffering and death, remind the faithful of the human drama captured in the phrase, "he died for your sins."

Each of these stories and reenactments represents suffering as part of a broader framework, one that not only transcends but also adds meaning to human societies. We can see these stories as some responses among many to the general human problem of how to endure suffering. They can enable us to place our own problems "in perspective."

Religion Explained by Emotions

Other social theorists have based their approaches to religion more completely in psychology than did Weber. Although the notion that religion springs from emotions is ancient, an important modern argument along these lines came from David Hume, the philosopher of the Scottish Enlightenment. In his *Natural History of Religion* (1757), Hume argued that religion first came from "the incessant hopes and fears which actuate the human mind." Religion thus offers one way of overcoming anxiety.

This idea was given ethnographic substance by Bronislaw Malinowski (1884–1942), one of the first anthropologists to carry out long-term fieldwork. Malinowski worked in the Trobriand Islands, today part of Papua New Guinea, between 1915 and 1918. He distinguished between the practical, rational knowledge and skills that Trobrianders employ to carry out their everyday tasks and the religion and magic they call on to supplement their knowledge and powers. Ideas about the afterlife help people live despite their knowledge that death awaits them, wrote Malinowski, and funeral rituals add further authority to the idea that something awaits them after death. These rituals and ideas "save man from a surrender to death and destruction" (1954 [1925], 51). Ideas about the powers of spells and prayer to change the world also serve a psychological function; they reduce the anxiety that comes from uncertainty, allowing people to carry on their practical life. Religion and magic are thus not pseudosciences; rather, they arise in response to deep-seated, innate human fears and concerns.

Malinowski was influenced by the psychologist William James (1842–1910). In his *Varieties of Religious Experience* (1972 [1901–1902]), James defined religion in terms of a set of individual human attitudes, as "the feelings, acts, and experiences of individual men in their solitude, so far as they apprehend themselves to stand in relation to whatever they may consider the divine." James advocated *pragmatism* in philosophy and science; in his version of this approach, the experiences one accumulates, whether in the laboratory or in everyday life, are the basis for deciding about truth and falsehood. Since belief in God works toward the general good, it is "true." Religious beliefs are validated when they are shown to have beneficial consequences, such as reducing anxiety and fear.

References today to innate or unconscious psychological impulses usually draw on the writings of Sigmund Freud (1856–1939), the founder of modern psychoanalysis. Freud argued that the psyche was more than the conscious. Powerful drives for self-preservation and pleasure often shape our actions and conscious ideas in ways of which we are only half-aware. These drives in the individual run headlong into societal norms, creating repression and neuroses. Freud's (1930) own views on religion were largely negative. Born of infantile feelings of helplessness and society-caused suffering, religion only keeps us from rationally critiquing and rebuilding our social lives, he wrote. But Freud's ideas about the power of religious symbols have been used by some anthropologists to explain why certain objects—hair, the color white, blood, and so on—have the frequent and powerful positions they do in religious rituals.

Other theorists and historians of religion have taken up the issue of how and why certain symbols have widespread power. Among them are theorists who stress the irreducible nature of religious experience. Carl Jung (1875–1961), a student of Freud, saw religion as an experience of awe at the power of the divine, a submission to a superior power that is later codified into doctrines and rituals. Jung followed William James and the theologian Rudolf Otto in finding the truth of religion in these religious experiences. But Jung then postulated a "collective unconscious" of humankind that contains all religious symbols. These symbols stem from "archetypes" that are innate in every human being and that make possible the translation of religious experiences across persons and cultures. These archetypes—the hero, the earth mother, gods, and so on—form the basis of the universal religious experience.

Also viewing religion in terms of archetypes is Mircea Eliade (1907–1986). Eliade exemplifies the "phenomenological" study of religion, that is, bracketing what we think we know of the external world to focus our study on experience itself as an irreducible phenomenon. For Eliade (1954 [1949]), religious objects, acts, and roles are symbols that have multiple meanings but that eventually come together in a cosmological unity. This unity is mainly about the primordial creation of the universe. Eliade examines myths and rituals from many societies, interpreting each as fundamentally about the creation of life, order, and the world. The view of religion in terms of universal archetypes has become even more popular through the writings of Joseph Campbell (1949) on myth. As with Tylor's intellectualist approach, however, this approach points to broad patterns but is unable to provide an analytical foundation for understanding specificities: how people have come to create and understand particular religious forms in particular times and places.

SYMBOLS BETWEEN SOCIETY AND THE INDIVIDUAL

Among anthropologists seeking to integrate sociological and psychological dimensions of religious practices was Victor Turner (1920–1983), whose work has focused on symbols and meanings. Turner is attentive to unconscious meanings and near-universal symbols, but he emphasizes the ways that ritual and social uses of symbolic objects shape their meanings for particular people.

Turner (1967) analyzes the meaning of symbols from three distinct perspectives. He begins by asking how members of the society explain a ritual or unpack the meaning of a statue. He then asks how objects are used in ritual processes and in interpreting their use. Finally, he examines the place of the object in a system of symbols. The meanings he derives from these three perspectives themselves are arrayed between two poles: one around which cluster meanings that relate to general human emotions and desires, especially those of a natural or physiological sort, and a second pole of social norms and values.

Turner's most famous symbolic analysis illustrates this process. His ethnographic work was done among the Ndembu of Zambia, a society organized around matriliny, that is, the continuity between mothers and children. When a girl reaches puberty, the Ndembu hold an initiation ceremony, during which they wrap the girl in a blanket and place her at the foot of a tree, the *mudyi*, known for its white latex. This ritual is thus known as a "white" ritual.

Turner understood the "native symbolic meaning" of the symbols largely from many discussions with one "key informant," a man named Muchona. Based on these discussions, he concluded that the tree stands for human milk, for the ties between the girl and her mother, and for the principle of ties through women, more generally. These meanings seem consistent with other Ndembu statements and practices, although discussions with a broader range of Ndembu men and women might have introduced a greater diversity of meanings into the analysis.

These symbolic meanings include both physiological and social poles: aspects of the human body and of social institutions. Turner then considers the way the tree is used in ritual practices, and here he finds several distinct meanings: in one event the tree is the center for all-female activities from which the men are excluded (meaning of women versus men); in other contexts it is associated with the girl undergoing initiation.

Finally, Turner examines the broader system of symbols, and finds this tree to be one among several trees that are used in ritual activities, each associated with white, red, or black. Each color calls forth associations with natural substances: black with putrefaction and feces, red with blood, white with milk and semen. Although these associations are "natural" in the sense that blood is indeed red, the values placed on these associations are cultural and relatively arbitrary. Is blood good? Powerful? Polluting? The Ndembu highlight certain values and play down others. Red is linked to power and wealth, black to pollution and disease, and white to purity and life. They can then interpret the value of various ritual and medicinal objects in terms of this color scheme. Medicines made from the "white" mudyi tree, for example, aid a woman having difficulties breastfeeding.

For the Ndembu, then, the three primary colors provide a template for much of social life, just as do the four cardinal directions for the Zuni. Turner's account of religious ritual situates the ritual in its matrilineal social context, analyzes the Ndembu explanations of rituals and symbols, and considers the emotional power of Ndembu ritual associations. Other anthropologists, for example Gananath Obeyesekere (1981), emphasize the ways that personal, sometimes unconscious, meanings of key symbols in a culture shape the lives of individuals. For these and other writers, symbols are studied for their roles in the lives of individuals in particular societies.

Conclusions

The anthropology of religion has drawn from a wide range of social theories but seeks to test them against evidence from fieldwork, where we have the capacity to see disagreements and doubt over key ideas, and to follow change in how people practice what we then call "religion". But we do so in the knowledge that our own analytical categories—religion, ritual, symbol, and myth—derive from a very particular history, a history I have called the twin transformations. In succeeding chapters we shall see some of the rough edges that our predicament produces: one person's religion may be another's science, magic, or simply unremarkable facets of everyday life.

For Debate

Many of the central rituals of major religions have their histories. The Islamic pilgrimage probably emerged as a combination of two older rituals, one involving the harvest. A similar set of combinations and changes lie behind the Jewish Passover. But in their texts both religions treat these rituals as unchanged since their birth, and born out of divine intervention. Do we devalue a religious practice by showing it to have been transformed over time? How can practitioners square the historical study of the practice with a belief in its divine origin? Does this arise for your own religion, or for those of your friends and relatives?

Domains and Boundaries of "Religion"

From Chapter 3 of *Religions in Practice: An Approach to the Anthropology of Religion*, 5/e. John J. Bowen. Copyright © 2011 by Pearson Education. Published by Prentice Hall. All rights reserved.

Domains and Boundaries of "Religion"

Only with the advent of the European Enlightenment, world travel, and colonialism was there the emergence of a notion of religions as distinct belief systems in Western Europe and North America, as well as the emergence of social sciences of religion. But what are the boundaries of "religion"? When does it become politics, or magic, or medicine? And who decides these and other questions? How much do these boundaries shift as we move from one country to another?

Let's begin our exploration with a country that has a lot of practices and ideas that surely we would consider to be religious, but where most people say they do not have a religion—Japan!

COMBINING RELIGIOUS PRACTICES IN JAPAN

In practice, Japanese freely blend elements from indigenous practices, state-inspired Shinto, and the traditions of Buddhism, Confucianism, and Taoism, with a bit of Christianity thrown in from time to time. Few would argue for maintaining boundaries between these religions. Indeed, most people speak of a division of labor among the religions; a common saying sums it up as "born Shinto, die Buddhist," referring to the daily appeals to Shinto spirits during one's lifetime and the Buddhist priest's responsibility for carrying out funeral rites (Reader 1991). Marriages are increasingly conducted in Christian style, and many Japanese consult practitioners of the New Religions for solutions to recurring illnesses. These sects themselves combine ideas and practices from many sources, including Hinduism, Japanese nativist writings about racial superiority, and indigenous healing practices. To take an extreme example: It seemed not at all unusual or striking to Japanese that the Aum Shinrikyo sect responsible for the 1995 nerve gas attack in Tokyo combined Buddhist and Hindu texts.

PRACTICE AND BELIEF

About 65 percent of Japanese people have told survey takers in repeated surveys that they have no religious beliefs (compared to fewer than 10 percent in the United States). Only 20–30 percent say they believe in the existence of *kami* (spirits) or in souls of the dead. But 76 percent of these respondents have in their homes either a Shinto altar devoted to kami, or a Buddhist one devoted to the souls of the dead; 45 percent have both. Eighty-nine percent say they visit the graves of their ancestors to pray for them (Reader 1991, 5–12).

These results are very puzzling to Western readers if we assume that people think of their beliefs as governing their practices. One problem is with the word *religion,* which in Japanese is *shukyo,* a word originally devised to answer pesky missionaries who asked Japanese to state what their religion was. It was taken to refer to a separate set of beliefs, removed from everyday life, and not to some everyday activity like stopping for a moment at a shrine to make an offering. Thus, asking someone in Japan if he or she has a religion or religious beliefs is something like asking a person in the United States if he or she is a member of a religious movement, a question that would elicit denials from many churchgoers.

Many students of Japanese culture have also emphasized that ideas about beliefs and morality are more focused on specific events and situations than is true for European cultures. Anecdotes from World War II relate how Japanese prisoners of war, having just been bent on killing Allied troops, suddenly became model prisoners of war. In their eyes, the situation had changed and so had their responsibilities.

Finally, a pragmatic try-it-and-see attitude underlies the approach taken by many Japanese toward religious ritual. This approach emphasizes the importance of sincerity for the ritual to work, but not a general "belief," and certainly not an exclusive commitment to that religion and no other. It is thus relatively easy, within the Japanese religious world view, to try a new healing religion without abandoning offerings to household spirits and Buddhist deities. This willingness to participate in more than one religion lies behind the common practice of declaring oneself to census takers as both Buddhist and Shinto, marrying in a Protestant church, and attending sessions of a healing sect to seek a cure for an illness. And it is evident in figures about religious membership: The government has classified about 75 percent of the population as Buddhist, 95 percent as Shinto, and over 10 percent as members of New Religious movements (Reader 1991, 6). Japanese do affiliate with religious organizations, and usually with more than one.

Perhaps, then, answers to surveys underplay the extent to which Japanese assume that there are spirits at work in the world. It would appear that the practices of keeping an altar at home and reciting prayers for one's ancestors at graveside imply such a set of beliefs. And yet haven't we all engaged in practices for which we are unsure of whether we agree with the associated doctrines? Modern Western religious culture emphasizes the importance of believing in the doctrines behind practices, in the paramount importance of creeds of faith, and this emphasis may make it quite difficult for some people in the United States, for example, to deny belief in God to a survey taker, whatever their doubts might be. Japanese religious culture does not make this same emphasis; consequently, denying the belief while going along with the practice may be easier for the Japanese person than for the American.

This religious–cultural emphasis on practices over doctrines makes it easier for Japanese to combine elements from different religious traditions, as we see in later chapters. First, we can explore the roles played by two major traditions—Shintoism and

Buddhism—and how people's actions may imply their belief in a proposition about the spiritual world without them directly expressing that belief.

SHINTO AND SPIRITS

Basic to the Japanese Shinto tradition are spirits, or *kami* (Earhart 1982), which are located in specific places in the empirical world: in a boulder, or a house, or a shrine. One Japanese estimate is that there are "eight million spirits"—meaning they are innumerable. When foreigners asked Japanese to name their religion, in order to distinguish it from Buddhism, they called it "the way of the *kami*," although it came to be called Shinto in the West (Reader 1991).

The term *kami* refers both to the sense of power felt in things of the world and to particular spirits. A waterfall is a powerful kami; calling it a kami communicates the sense an observer has of its immense power. Space may also contain kami and may be demarcated by rocks, or by a shrine with boundaries and a gateway. One sees these *torii*, Shinto gateways, with two pillars and one or two crossbeams, throughout Japan and in many U.S. cities. A Japanese rock garden works similarly, demarcating a sparsely filled space rather than, as in European-style ornamental gardens, featuring a dense collection of plants. Although kami can be anywhere, they are not everywhere; these boundaries serve to separate the sacred from the profane.

Perhaps the most important spirits are those in the house. They occupy particular places and protect the members of the household when in those places: the god of the kitchen lives in the kitchen, the latrine god in the latrine, and so forth. There is also a guardian deity of the household as a whole; this spirit is made up of many ancestors who have merged to guard the household as a corporate unit that exists over time. The village has a guardian deity, often a fox god or an ancestor of a founding member. The village, like the household, is a corporate group, with control over irrigation, cooperative use of some land, and religious festivals. Villagers will ask the village god for help in their rice harvest or for success in schooling. Village elites once controlled the shrine festivals for the village gods, but today, with many villagers engaged in urban pursuits, their importance has diminished.

Also important to everyday life is the spirit of a rice field. This spirit lives a dual existence, as the figure of Inari, the rice deity, and also as the spirit guarding each particular field. Spirits of the fields and of rice live in the mountains and come down in the spring when the soil is tilled. They guard over the rice, and return to the mountains in the fall after the harvest. They are sometimes represented as fox spirits, probably because foxes, also associated with rice, sexuality, and fertility, were thought to come down from the mountains in spring.

People create new spirits as needed. When the Tennis Players' Association was created in Japan before World War II, someone suggested the creation of a new god, to be named "Heavenly God of Speedy Ball." And in a less individuated way, all equipment, from computer chips to cameras to automobile production machinery, are thought to have a spiritual side. The machines are blessed by a Shinto priest before they are used, and in 1990 engineers met at Tokyo's Chomeiji temple to thank their used-up equipment for the service it had given them. Photographs of the cameras and video recorders were burned as a Buddhist priest chanted verses. Even in the electronics industry, Shinto and Buddhism are mixed (Sanger 1990).

Temple complex near Narita, Japan, with Shinto and Buddhist shrines, and shops selling amulets, books, and other items. (*Courtesy of John Bowen*)

Kami can also be the spirits of deceased persons. Sometime famous people will become deified as kami and have shrines built to them, but for a mixture of reasons. One ninth-century court official, for example, had died at the hands of his rivals for power. As a spirit he wreaked havoc with their lives until they built a shrine to him.

SPIRITS AND SOCIAL CHANGE

Japanese relationships to spirits developed in a civilization centered on enduring social units: the household, the village, and the Imperial House. Household spirits stood for the continuity of the household over generations. Households in a village were protected by community spirits. And everyone was under the protection of the unbroken imperial line, itself said to come from the Sun Goddess and dating at least back to the seventh century C.E. Although these continuities have been disrupted by massive migrations to cities, older orientations toward spirits of the collectivity—including the emperor and his temples—continue in Japan.

Many kami are venerated in shrines, and some shrines, such as the great shrine at Ise to the Sun Goddess, are the focus of national veneration. The Ise shrine is rebuilt every 20 years as part of a cycle of national renewal of life and fertility; the last rebuilding, in 1993, was widely publicized by banners erected throughout Japan.

Parents routinely take their newborn babies to the local shrine to be placed under the care of the spirit guarding the local community. An offering is placed on the altar, and the shrine priest says prayers requesting these blessings. In the older, agrarian world in which Japanese religions developed, they also carried out rites at this shrine to ensure the fertility of the crops. The shrine also served as the place for community meetings and recreational activities; it was thus the center of social life. Often the community shrine was said to be a branch shrine of a famous national shrine, such as that at Ise. Performing rituals at the shrine thus linked the individual to the community and the nation-state.

Since World War II, Japanese have flooded from country to city and from farming to other occupations. In 1950, 62 percent of all Japanese families lived in rural areas, of which 50 percent were full-time farmers. Just 30 years later, in 1980, only 24 percent of families lived in rural areas, and only 10 percent of these families were still engaged in full-time farming. This rapid shift in population led to the realization that a civilization and a set of religious practices that had developed around stable rural households now had to be modified for urban living. The Shinto shrines, however, have been part of this transformation. People who commute to the city from suburbs or rural areas still visit the shrines to seek blessings for their babies and to seek further spirit protection for young children, though now they may dress in Western-style clothes and record the occasions with expensive video cameras.

People living in the cities may return to their ancestral villages for harvest festivals and for the New Year's festival, when they acquire new amulets from the shrines to protect their homes during the coming year. For two years, Ian Reader (1991, 61–64)

Worship at a shrine, Narita temple complex, Japan. (*Courtesy of John Bowen*)

watched proceedings at the Katano shrine midway between the cities of Osaka and Kyoto in what has become a commuter village. He records that on festival days, hundreds of people took trains from both cities to the shrine to seek blessings and purchase amulets. A shrine priest could call on office girls to work as temporary "shrine maidens" on these occasions; at one festival, Reader found himself being blessed by one of his own students who had been engaged to work as such a shrine maiden during the holidays. Businesses sent rice, or sake, to be placed on the altar for blessings (and afterward quickly consumed by visitors). The same priest was called upon to bless a new university building nearby. He had a temporary altar to the shrine spirit constructed inside the new building for the occasion.

Increased ease of transport has meant that Japanese increasingly visit the more famous shrines in larger cities. Several million people visit these shrines each year, while some rural shrines, those not on commuter lines and unable to afford priests, have closed. The social ties affirmed by attending a shrine are less and less local and increasingly national in scope.

BUDDHISM AND SOULS

Most of the people frequenting these shrines with their newborns, or at festivals, also participate in rituals drawn from Buddhism (Saunders 1964). The Buddhist religion came into existence in the sixth century B.C.E. in South Asia, when the historical Buddha, Siddhartha of the clan Gautama, found enlightenment after long meditation. The followers of Buddha also seek enlightenment; his teachings provide examples and practices to follow rather than creeds to which followers must adhere.

In South Asia, Buddhism diverged into two major streams. One, called "Theravada" (the elders), emphasizes the role of the monastic community in mediating between laypersons and Buddha. This stream spread from Sri Lanka to mainland Southeast Asia. The other stream was called "Mahayana," or "Greater Vehicle," for its universalistic approach to salvation. In this stream, individuals are encouraged to engage in practices that lead to their salvation and to enter directly into contact with Buddhas and other deities.

The Mahayana stream of Buddhism spread northward from India through Tibet and China. Japanese scholars learned about Buddhism in China, and for that reason, Japanese Buddhism adopts the Mahayana orientation. Mahayana Buddhism emphasizes the illusory character of the world and orients the individual toward a transcendent reality in which he or she might achieve salvation. One sees this emphasis in paintings, where individual Buddhas are depicted floating above the world we live in, transcendent of its specific concreteness. These diverse Buddhas— Fudo, Amida, Maitreya—provide multiple sources of divine aid and also multiple paths for individuals to seek salvation.

Each of the several major schools of Buddhism in Japan—Zen, Shingon, Nichiren, and others—combines a set of spiritual disciplines that lead to salvation (Reader 1991). They all evince a special concern for death and treatment of ancestors. Zen Buddhism, the best known in the West of these schools, emphasizes meditation. Indeed, the word *Zen* itself means "meditation." Zen teachers point to the example set by the historical Buddha, Gautama, who achieved enlightenment in this world by sitting and meditating. Zen practitioners may use *koan*, problems that appear unsolvable, as a way of breaking down the barriers that everyday linear thinking places in the path to enlightenment. They practice together in communities of meditators, engaging in strenuous physical labor—scrubbing floors, chopping wood—as additional aids to enlightenment. Laypeople may participate in retreats at Zen temples, and businesses routinely send their employees on special retreats that incorporate some of the austerities of temple life.

Japanese Buddhism's emphasis on individual meditation and enlightenment provides a counterpoint in religious practice to the overall Japanese cultural emphasis on the value and continuity of the group. But Buddhism also adapted itself to those values by assuming responsibility for the care of family ancestors. Even if they have no other contact with Buddhism, and would not state that they believe in Buddha, most Japanese "die Buddhist," that is, their children or other relatives seek out the service of a Buddhist priest to perform a funeral service. The main activity at most temples is in fact not meditation but performing memorial services for the dead. Most Japanese households are affiliated with a particular temple for this purpose.

Before Buddhism, Japanese people considered that each person's soul traveled to a world of the dead, where it continued to watch and intervene in the lives of its relatives. People carried out rituals designed to ease the transition to the other world and to keep the spirits happy. When Buddhism came to Japan, people saw the priests as possessing spiritual powers due to their activities of meditation. They began to call on those priests to perform the funeral ceremonies. Priests added new practices to the rituals, practices designed to guide the spirit toward enlightenment after death. The priest and his associates cremate the body to rid the soul of its impurities and chant Buddhist texts and prayers to lead the soul toward the state of enlightenment. The word for dead soul, *hotoke,* also means a Buddha.

These ancestors continue to affect the lives of their kin, and both Buddhist priests and practitioners of New Religions are concerned with keeping the ancestors happy and resolving problems that occur when they are not.

Buddhism coexists with Shinto in Japan. The temple complex at Nara, which I visited in 1994, contains both Buddhist temples and Shinto shrines, and visitors stop at both. Temples may include images of kami alongside those of a Buddha, although the former are said to no longer contain spirits but only to represent them. The two kinds of entities are represented in clearly contrasting ways. In paintings, for example, kami are depicted in a realistic manner as specific, human-looking personages, sometimes identifiable as historical figures, always standing near or on the place with which they are associated. Buddhas and bodhisattvas, by contrast, are abstract in their appearance and not confined to specific spaces. Often they are painted as floating above the ground or on clouds.

Two other religious traditions have also influenced Japanese ideas and practices. Taoism (from *tao,* the "way" in Chinese) developed in China as an approach to understanding the way of the universe. Taoism includes methods of divining good or bad days by consulting calendars. Japanese adopted some of these practices—there was even a bureau of divination in early Japan—but no Japanese would identify himself or herself as a Taoist.

Confucianism, based on the teachings of the Chinese philosopher Confucius (551–479 B.C.E.), has played an important role in shaping Japanese social and moral values (Smith 1983, 37–67). Confucius taught that social order and welfare depended on maintaining the proper hierarchical relationships between persons, particularly those of father to son and ruler to subject. In Japan, these ideas strengthened the notion of the family as a corporate entity, with succession passing from father to eldest son, and that of the nation as a family-like entity headed by the hereditary emperor.

THE STATE AND RELIGION

Japan's rulers have added to their legitimacy by drawing on Shinto and Buddhism. The state has variously promoted one or the other of these two complexes of religious ideas and practices. In its encounter with outside cultures and in particular with Christianity, the Japanese state has created indigenous alternatives—systems of ideas and practices that looked like religion as defined in the West.

State promotion of religions began between the sixth and ninth centuries with the adoption of Chinese ideas that the emperor is both divine and the active ruler of society. Just as village guardians often were thought to be the ancestors of the village elite, the emperor declared himself (or herself) the descendant of the Sun Goddess. (These borrowings were a major source of Confucian influence in Japan.)

Scholars began to teach Buddhism in Japan during the Nara period (710–784 C.E.), named after the capital city of Nara. Emperor Shomu (reigned 724–749) quickly made Buddhism the state religion. Buddhism appealed to the emperor and his advisers because it came from China, along with the writing system and ideas of the divinity of the emperor, and also because it could be made the basis of a state-centered system of religious temples, with scriptures and priests. The preexisting religious practices were decentralized, with local spirits and shrines. Buddhism offered the possibility of constructing a religious hierarchy under imperial control.

In 728, the emperor built the Todai temple in Nara (just south of present-day Kyoto) as the first national temple. The statue of Buddha inside the temple, called "Lochana," still stands as the largest Buddhist statue in the world. Lochana, or Dainichi, is the Sun Buddha. When he was building the statue, the emperor had to seek approval from his ancestress, the Sun Goddess Amaterasu, at her temple in Ise. Reportedly, the goddess told the emperor that the Sun Buddha was the same as the Sun Goddess and approved building the statue.

The emperor then ordered two temples built in each province, one as a monastery and one as a nunnery. Monks and nuns were recruited to these temples to recite Buddhist scriptures and accumulate merit, and then to pass on the merit to the nation as a whole. This form of mediated merit was not part of the Mahayana tradition imported by the state; it was created by the emperor for his own project of state building. By venerating the Sun Buddha, the emperor managed to link Buddha to his own Sun Goddess ancestor. By constructing a national temple system, he linked acts of individual merit-making to the welfare of the nation as a whole, and forged a religious connection between the people and the state. But the temples and their priests, particularly at Todai temple, grew more and more powerful, and the decision to move the Imperial capital to Kyoto in 784 was in part to establish a separate power base away from the temple.

In succeeding centuries, the influence of state-sponsored Buddhism waned along with the power of the emperor. But in 1600, the warlord (*shogun*) Tokugawa Ieyasu consolidated power throughout Japan, ending the many centuries of political disorder, and reduced the emperor to a figurehead. Ieyasu once again promoted Buddhism as the state religion, building a new hierarchy of temples. All Japanese were required to

Todai temple, Japan, with statue of the Buddha Nyiori. (*Courtesy of John Renard*)

register at a temple, proclaim their religion, and use the services of Buddhist priests for funeral services. These state actions were not motivated by religious piety, but intended to tighten state control and exclude Christianity as a disruptive, foreign ideology. Thus, Buddhism was promoted as the best alternative to Christianity, as "not-Christianity."

In 1868, a coalition of warlords and a rising economic elite took power in the name of the Emperor Meiji and sought to reduce the influence of Buddhism because of its association with the old regime. The Meiji Restoration combined economic restructuring with the creation of a cult of the emperor. A hierarchy of Shinto priests was created, and the result has come to be called State Shinto. Shrines were created to appeal to popular opinion. Foremost among these new shrines were Yasukuni, founded in 1869, where those soldiers who have died for the honor of the state are enshrined and deified, and the Meiji shrine, built in 1920 to honor the deceased emperor. Both produced talismans for people to take home with them, and people were also required to have talismans from Ise in their homes (Hardacre 1989, 79–99).

These efforts were meant to create a religious plane on which individual households would be merged into the state. The Confucian value of filial piety was emphasized, as well as the common descent of all Japanese, as in the following section from a teacher's manual used in the 1930s:

> The connection between the Imperial House and its subjects is thus: one forms the main house and the others form the branch house, so that from ancient times we have worshiped the founder of the Imperial House and the heavenly gods. Our relationship to this house is sincerely founded on repaying our debt of gratitude to our ancestors. (quoted in Smith 1983, 32)

After World War II, the American forces that occupied Japan insisted that the new Constitution remove the aura of divinity from the emperor. The Constitution states that the emperor is not divine, but only "the symbol of the state and of the unity of the people." The Nobel Prize–winning writer Kenzaburo Oe has written of his and others' astonishment when on August 15, 1945, they heard the emperor speak over the radio. "The Emperor speaking to us in a human voice was beyond imagining in any reverie. The Emperor was a god, the authority of the nation, the organizing principle of reality" (Oe 1995, 103).

The Occupation forces also proclaimed Shinto to be a religion and that because people ought to be able to choose their religion freely, it could not be taught in the schools or be supported by state funds. And yet despite this new official ideology, the Sun Goddess Amaterasu continues to be worshiped at the great shrine at Ise. Each time the shrine is rebuilt, the ancient mirror that is thought to embody the Sun Goddess's spirit is moved into the new shrine. Six and a half million Japanese visit the shrine each year. Japanese visit Ise the way that Jews visit Israel and Muslims visit Mecca, as a journey to a sacred place.

The precise status of Ise and the nature of the emperor's relationship to the Sun Goddess (if any) became major political issues when Emperor Hirohito died in January 1989. At Hirohito's funeral the following month, the Shinto rites were performed behind curtains, evidently so that visiting dignitaries would not have to acknowledge them. Yet many in Japan criticized these proceedings as tantamount to worship of the emperor and thus a violation of the 1946 Constitution.

Then, in November 1990, Hirohito's son and successor, Akihito, was enthroned. Part of the enthronement procedure is the "great food-offering ritual," in which the new emperor offers special foods to the deities of the heaven and earth and performs a ritual of union of sorts (left ambiguous in official accounts) with the Sun Goddess. The last time this ritual had been performed was in 1928, when the emperor was still considered a god. At Ise he is still thought of as the chief priest of Shinto. There was a great deal of protest from those who considered the ritual to be religious, and thus to violate the Constitution's mandate that state and religion be separated (Weisman 1990).

Similar controversy continues to surround the Yasukuni shrine to the war dead. Prime ministers regularly visit the shrine, located next to the Imperial Palace in central

Tokyo, to venerate the war dead, sometimes in their official capacity. In August 1985, Prime Minister Nakasone with his cabinet made an official visit to the shrine to pay tribute to the war dead. But here Japan's difficulty in facing its wartime history surfaced, because major ("Class A") war criminals executed by judgment of the 1946–1948 Tokyo Trial are among the two and a half million people listed as gods in the shrine's record book. Furthermore, the Rape of Nanking is among the events celebrated, a fact that led China to protest this attendance. Protests by many Japanese led Nakasone to forgo additional state visits to the shrine. In July 1996, a new prime minister, Hashimoto, tried again, but he too had to back down after domestic and international protests.

Veterans' groups continue to enshrine and deify the spirits of Japanese soldiers, however. In 1988, the Japanese Supreme Court backed up one such group over the objections of the widow of a soldier about to be deified. She was Protestant and protested that the deification violated her religious beliefs, but the Court claimed that her religion had no bearing on the group's freedom to carry out the ritual. The idea of religious exclusivity—that one religion excludes others—is not part of the Japanese legal tradition (Haberman 1988).

Death practices, indeed, have all along been important elements in the state–religion nexus. The eighth-century ascendancy of Buddhism was accompanied by a change from burial to cremation for emperors and empresses, following Buddhist practice. During the 1600–1868 Tokugawa period, Shinto nationalists were gradually able to reduce Buddhism's official status—after 1654, although burial rites for the imperial family continued to follow Buddhist practices, the bodies were interred rather than cremated. Only at the funeral of Emperor Meiji's father, Komei, in 1867, were all Buddhist elements eliminated from the funeral, and thus one could say that the funeral ushered in the new Shinto-dominated Meiji era. The government prohibited cremation entirely in 1873, as part of its effort to drive out Buddhism, but it was forced to rescind the order as people pointed out that Japan already lacked sufficient space to bury intact bodies (*Far Eastern Economic Review,* March 16, 1989, 66–70).

The place of religion in public life, even the definition of what religion is, continues to be the subject of debate in Japan. What *is* clear in Japan is that lines between religions are fuzzy or, rather, that religions are not defined by the individual's exclusive commitment to one set of doctrines as opposed to others. Japan challenges our idea of what religion means for the individual, for the nation, and for the state.

IMPOSED DEFINITIONS OF RELIGION

Many modern states in Asia, Africa, and Latin America have drawn their ideas of religion from Western, Christian, and, to some extent, Islamic models, and often imposed these ideas on local people who think about their beliefs and practices in quite different ways.

Let us turn to Indonesia to consider these problems of state-imposed definitions of religion. Indonesia, the world's fourth largest country, has about 230 million people living on thousands of islands and speaking more than 300 distinct languages. About

85 percent of the people call themselves Muslim, and the remaining 15 percent includes important Christian and Buddhist minorities as well as practitioners of indigenous religions.

The Indonesian government has "belief in one God" as one of the planks of its ideology. The state defines religion as having a sacred book, a monotheistic foundation, exclusive boundaries (such that one person cannot belong to two religions at the same time), and as transcending ethnic boundaries (rather than being essentially an aspect of a hereditary culture).

This model came by way of several large-scale religions. In the early centuries of the present era, rulers adopted the symbols and ideas of Hinduism and Buddhism, sometimes both together. The Indonesian word for religion, *agama*, comes from Sanskrit, and means "text." The agama of a person was the set of texts from which he or she derived teaching and religious direction: the books of Hinduism, Buddhism, Islam, or others. The idea of a central text does not require that the religion have exclusive boundaries; that idea came later, in the fourteenth through sixteenth centuries, when many rulers began converting to Islam. Islam does insist on absolute exclusivity and on the idea of one and only one true foundational text, the Qur'ân. Christianity, brought to Indonesia at about the same time, shares these ideas.

By the time of Indonesian independence, then, the major religions supported this model of religion. The state decreed that everyone should belong to one of five religions: Catholicism, Protestantism, Islam, Hinduism, or Buddhism; Confucianism was recognized, then removed, and re-added in 1998. One might be surprised to hear that Hinduism, with its many vividly represented deities, stood for monotheism; the Indonesian resolution of this problem—supported by some Hindus—was to declare that the various Hindu gods were all manifestations of a single absolute deity.

Today, any Indonesians who practice local religions that do not conform to the official model are pressured to join one of the state-recognized religions, although this pressure has begun to ease since the fall of President Suharto in 1998. Those who do not convert may be accused of being atheists and therefore communists, a dangerous label in this strongly anticommunist state. So defining one's religion is a matter of great concern, and for some a matter of sheer survival (Kipp and Rodgers 1987).

What do people who practice other religions do? Some nominally convert but retain some older practices, such as ways of healing that involve calling on spirits to possess a healer and speak through him or her. Other people work to have their indigenous practices counted as a world religion, usually as Hindu. In one such case, a group of people on the island of Sulawesi did manage to become recognized as Hindus, despite the fact that there were few resemblances, other than a few words of Sanskrit, between their religion and anything practiced in India. A problem arose when one member of this group was elected to the local parliament. Members of parliament need to be sworn in on "their book." So what was this fellow's scripture? Well, because the book had to be Hindu, as the group's practices were called that, the parliament wrote to a Hindu association in Jakarta asking for their book. The association sent along a book in Sanskrit (I could not determine what book it was), and the new member was duly sworn in using it. Appearances were saved, and the religion's credentials established: they had a Book.

WANA PRACTICES AND INDONESIAN DEFINITIONS

Some people reshape their indigenous ideas in response to state pressures to convert. The 5,000 Wana people of Sulawesi, described by the anthropologist Jane Monnig Atkinson (1987, 1989), practice forms of divination and shamanism, and their ideas about spirits and possession surface in many domains of everyday life. They do not have a distinct domain called "religion."

Central to Wana efforts at dealing with the spiritual domain are the perform-ances called *mabolong*. These rituals of possession and healing are performed by shamans, ritual experts who are possessed by spirits. Shamans are called on to perform mabolong when someone is ill and requires supernatural assistance. Often many people attend these performances. The shaman is invited to feast from a tray of food, and he in turn invites his "spirit familiars" to join him in enjoying the food. He then asks these spirits to discover what is ailing a patient, to rid the patient of foreign objects, and to go with him on a spirit voyage to recover souls or dream spirits that the patient has lost.

Shamans have greater inner powers, and they draw on these powers to keep people healthy and to increase their own social standing. They are heroes in their community. Indeed, they often create new social communities as people seek to live near them. It is in these rituals performed by shamans that ordinary humans engage the spirit world. The Wana have no written texts that prescribe doctrines or beliefs, and their narratives concerning the spirit world are many and varied. What brings their diverse ideas and stories together is collective attendance at shamanic rituals.

But Wana also face intense pressure from Muslim officials and from Christian missionaries to convert to a state-recognized religion, an agama. Wana come into contact with Muslim peoples living on the coast and serving as local state officials, and, more recently, with Christian converts living in other upland regions.

As they have come to understand what is meant by agama, some Wana have constructed their own ideas of what their religion must be. These constructions are not about healing and possession, but about what distinguishes Wana from Muslims and Christians: diet, burial practices, and ties to government among them. Most saliently, Wana are people who, unlike Muslims, do eat pork, and, also unlike Muslims, kill chickens by wringing their necks rather than slaughtering them by knife.

Wana have also constructed a set of beliefs along the lines of Muslim and Christian beliefs, but distinct from them. They claim, for example, that they have a single God and that this God is the same as the Muslim and Christian creator. They recently invented a heaven that corresponds to the images of heaven taught to them by Muslims and Christians but reverses those groups' teachings about the destiny of the Wana. In the Wana notions, Wana lead poor lives on earth and there-fore they will have the best places in heaven. Muslims, by contrast, they believe, will live in pig excrement because they avoid it here. Christians will have only scraps of clouds to eat (an idea probably derived from pictures of Jesus in the clouds in Bible schools).

Most Wana have so far resisted conversion, but even in resisting they have trans-formed their religion in accord with the dominant, ultimately Western, model of proper religion.

Wana shaman during possession at a healing session, Indonesia. (*Courtesy of Jane Atkinson*)

THE CASE OF ISLAM

This example suggests that Islam should be the ideal religion for the "standard model" of a religion, with a book, a prophet, and a set of globally accepted teachings. But precisely for that reason, Islam provides a great case study in how difficult it is to define religion—and how the standard model fails to capture much of Muslim religious practice.

We often hear statements to the effect that Islam concerns all of life. And, indeed, Muslims consider that God set out a way or path, the shari'a, that should guide everyone in all that they do. As humans have engaged in interpreting God's revealed signs—they have constructed a set of norms or rules to guide people along that path. These rules cover two broad domains. One is the set of rituals that fit pretty well with the Enlightenment notion of religion, and that include the "five pillars" of Islam: testifying to one's faith, carrying out daily prayer, giving alms, fasting during Ramadan, and making the pilgrimage to Mecca. These acts Muslims perform for the sake of God, and are called the *'ibâdât* (from the root `-b-d, "servant," here, of God). The second domain are acts that concern relations among humans and are for their welfare; these are the *mu'âmalât*.

Although this distinction is important, its meaning is hotly contested. Many Muslims would deny that it separates religious acts from secular or mundane ones, because such everyday activities as running a business, greeting a neighbor, or eating lunch also should be guided by the principles given by God—and they can cite verses of the Qur'ân and statements or exemplary acts by the Prophet Muhammad that bear on each of these activities. Many of these Muslims, indeed, would extend the meaning of 'ibâdât to take in all activities that may be carried out with God in mind. Other Muslims cite a hadîth from the Prophet to the effect that Muslims should follow him with regard to worship and service to God, and follow their own learning in the pursuit of their other affairs. This major disagreement—actually a whole nest of debates about the various ways one should or should not draw lines between "religion" and the rest of life—runs throughout the topics we discuss here and concerns the very nature of a modern Muslim society and individual.

These debates have important consequences for modern Muslim movements. Some of those Muslims who think that there is a divine precept and a Prophetic example for every action in life also believe that they should work toward creating an Islamic state. The Hizb ut-Tahrir (which flourishes in London, Indonesia, and some other countries but is banned in most of the Muslim world), for example, preaches this line and criticizes all efforts to work within any Western—or any non-Islamic—political system. I recall a major meeting held west of London at which some of the thousands in attendance asked if they might work for parliamentary candidates and were told that doing so was forbidden (harâm), because "the Prophet Muhammad did not hold elections." Other Muslims following this general line of thought hold that Muslims should marry in the manner followed by Muhammad and ignore the requirements of civil law.

By contrast, Muslims who hold to a separation between domains where scripture is to be followed and domains where Muslims should look to other kinds of authority—scientific or cultural—work to create ways to live fully Islamic lives in Western countries. They argue that Muslims should look to the purpose of the tenets of scripture, and then ask how best to reach those objectives in the lands where they now live. For example, Muslim teachers in France and the United States argue that Muslims should consider that marrying and divorcing in civil courts already counts as Islamic. If the purpose of religious marriage in Muslim lands is to guarantee that the marriage is carried out with the consent of the husband and the wife, and that it lasts, these purposes are met in Western lands through the laws and procedures enforced by courts. By this logic, a civil marriage is already a religious one, because it does what Islam set out to do.

Muslims disagree, then, over where the boundaries of religion lie: Is a civil marriage religious? Should politics be religious? They also disagree over whether some practices are part of Islam or are superstitions, or magic, or in fact sinful efforts to worship a being other than God. I ran into this problem frequently during my studies of Islam in Indonesia. I recall shortly after one of my books on the Gayo highlands of Aceh was published, it received a favorable review in a Jakarta weekly. I happened to be in town, and a friend who was also the chancellor of the main Islamic university in Jakarta asked me to come in for a chat. Unbeknownst to me, a rather large group of recent graduates and faculty in Islamic studies awaited next door. I was led into the larger room and asked if I wouldn't mind talking about my work. I did, and discussed the ways in which some Gayo took Islam as a framework for understanding how things worked in their world: from how crops grow to why some people remain ill for long periods. They took what probably are pre-Islamic understandings and transformed them in an Islamic idiom, giving names of prophets to various natural spirits or powers.

For me, this process of Islamizing knowledge testified to the capacity of Islam to provide new frameworks for old knowledge, but to some in the room it was hogwash. "We spend years training to combat this sort of superstition," said one teacher. "None of this is Islam; much of it is *shirk* (polytheism)," said another, citing one of the worst things a

Muslim can do, namely worshiping another being alongside of God. Here were two quite opposed ideas of not how to interpret texts but how to decide what Islam is. As an anthropologist, I took at face value local ways of constructing the world on Islamic terms; for me this was "Islam" in one of its many diverse constructions. As students and teachers of the tradition of Islam, my interlocutors saw their task as bringing some conceptual order to a world—that of Indonesian Muslims—full of wrong-headed ideas, superstitions, and also fanaticism. Their Islam was of a sophisticated and "liberal" sort, but not at all imbued with or very tolerant of river spirits and love magic. And nor would I have been had I been in their shoes, in the shoes of an Islamic teacher. We had different roles in life, and it was those roles, not any limitation on either side, that led us to see things so differently.

The issue here is not like that in Japan. There, local ideas of "religion" are unconcerned with boundaries and exclusive membership. With Islam, those charged with teaching and ruling on religious matters are very much concerned with maintaining boundaries: between Muslims and non-Muslims, between the permitted and forbidden things of the world, and between proper and improper understandings of Islam. But there is no single person or body responsible for making those last determinations, so Muslims engage in seeking out knowledge from their local imams, in reading texts on Islam, and now in looking for advice on the Internet. They end up with widely differing understandings about how best to interpret scripture and how best to implement the boundaries that define Islam.

This rather open pluralism of religious knowledge can be puzzling to those on the outside (and often for Muslims as well). After the 9/11 attacks, many who knew nothing of Islam wanted to know what "Islam says" about war, violence, Christians and Jews, and all manner of other topics, as if there was a single set of answers somewhere, perhaps in the Qur'ân. There is no such set. Instead, those who looked for answers on the news saw, often one after the other, calls by terrorists to kill Americans in the name of Islam and statements by venerable gentlemen saying "Islam is a religion of peace." Now, nearly all Muslims would (and do) say that the former is a perversion of Islam. But the second fails to convince anyone: How could this be true at the same time that some Muslims fight for their religion? The platitudes—Islam is for peace; the Qur'ân says you shall not take a life—fails to take account of the rich and complex structures of interpretation that characterize Islam (and which resemble in many ways those of Judaism).

Conclusions

If Japan shows us how the categories that inform social life do not necessarily conform to the modern Western notion of religion, with its requirement of exclusive membership, Islam shows us how difficult it is to agree on the boundaries of religion even for an example of that modern idea. These difficulties occur all around us. We all know that "freedom of religion" is guaranteed for citizens of the United States, France, Britain, and many other countries. But what is it that is guaranteed? France declared that schoolgirls may not wear headscarves to school even if they considered wearing them to be part of their religion, because the state protects something more limited: religion as practiced in places of religion, such as mosques and churches. But in Britain, wearing religious dress is protected in schools and indeed for civil servants, because the state protects the individual's actions in any place. These two countries work from different conceptions of the domain of religion, of what the freedom of religion refers to.

For Debate

In modern Western societies, we have created distinct domains of education, religion, politics, and so on. We believe that institutions in each of these domains ought to have some degree of autonomy in carrying out their missions: schools to teach, religious institutions to transmit their teachings, and politics to represent citizens in public deliberation. We disapprove of interference by one domain in another's affairs. But things are not always clear. Consider the role of education in the United States. What is the proper role of religion in education? Should parents have the right to censure teachings that conflict with their religious beliefs? Should they be able to homeschool their children in a way that exposes them to religion but not to, say, modern biology? If we say that education is to prepare children to be citizens, are there limits on what freedom of religion should permit parents to do? Or, are parents to be the best judge of how to prepare their children for the world?

Films to See

Shinto: Nature, Gods and Man in Japan beautifully introduces the beliefs and aesthetics of the Shinto tradition. *Japan: Past and Present: Buddha in the Land of the Kami* traces the ways in which Buddhism was assimilated into preexisting beliefs.

Rituals of Transition

Now we turn to the analysis of key elements of religions. We start with those fixed sequences of actions that we often call "rituals." People carrying out a religious ritual try to conform to certain rules to get the ritual right. In some cases they are seeking to accomplish a specific end, such as healing, pleasing a deity, or restoring fertility. In other cases they perform rituals out of a sense of obligation. In this chapter we consider rituals that mark transitions of various kinds, and explore the way such rituals shape, or are motivated by, emotions.

In most, perhaps all, societies, people mark transitions or life stages by carrying out certain transition rituals or rites of passage. These rituals often have a religious dimension, and they tend to cluster around several points in the life cycle, particularly birth, puberty, marriage, and death. Rituals that mark the passage into adulthood may involve changes in name, membership in a new society of initiates, bestowal of new social rights and duties, or, in the category of religiously competent persons, conferral of supernatural powers. Death is also ritually represented as a transition in most societies; death rituals are usually intended to ease the passage of the spirit to another social state and possibly to another world. Many other kinds of rituals are also concerned with transitions. The beginning of an agricultural cycle or the succession to an office may be ritually enacted in ways that resemble life-cycle transition rituals.

We find three aspects across many distinct transition rituals. First, they often emphasize the *creation of life*: new persons, life after death, or the soil's fertility. Initiation rituals that move people from an immature to a mature state are of course directly concerned with reproduction and biological fertility. But funeral rituals may also tie death to the regeneration of life, refocusing attention and emotions on life and fertility rather than on death and loss.

Second, the content and sequence of rituals *shape specific emotions* in the participants. Feelings of grief are given well-specified forms of expression, sometimes a prescribed period of mourning followed by a break from mourning, sometimes the reverse: stoicism followed by an emotional release. The promise of new life gives hope after loss, and rituals that structure time support the notion that humans can control natural processes of growth, maturation, and death.

Finally, transition rituals *represent the social order* in a particular way, often an idealized or partial way, and often as if the rituals themselves produce or shape the social order. Relations and differences between men and women, or superiors and inferiors, may be projected onto a cosmic plane, or produced in the ritual itself, especially in initiation rituals that create adolescent or adult males and females. Initiations often reveal secrets, the mere possession of which is the basis for initiates' claims to supremacy over noninitiates. Secrecy creates status and boundaries across a range of social institutions. From members of initiation societies in Africa and New Guinea, to Mormons and Masons, those "in the know" can claim superiority, power, or at least special status. Death rituals often have a different social design—to restore social order after a loss.

RITES OF PASSAGE

The sociologist Arnold van Gennep pointed out in 1909 (1960) that across many societies, transition rituals display a similar sequential structure. Rites marking birth, puberty, marriage, and death, he remarked, as well as many other rituals of initiation or succession, often are structured temporally as three distinct stages.

The first stage separates the person from the ordinary social environment. It may involve rites to purify the body, seclusion, cutting hair, or simulating death. The separation may amount to the social recognition of a natural event, such as the onset of menstruation or death. Separating one group of people from others may create a peer group, such as a group of boys or girls to be initiated. It may define a geographical space, as when Muslims exchange their ordinary identities and clothing for the garb of pilgrims when entering the sacred precincts of Islam in Arabia.

Next comes a stage of marginality, the transitional or *liminal* ("threshold") stage during which the person is outside of normal social life. The liminal person may have to observe certain taboos, be isolated, be subjected to beatings and insults, or be elevated to temporary high status. This stage may be as short as a brief baptismal ceremony in a Christian church or as long as certain New Guinea initiation cycles lasting 10 years or more. It is a period of social work, where the liminal person is transformed in bodily or spiritual status.

Finally comes the reincorporation of the individual into society (or into an afterlife society), now possessing a new status. A girl may have become a woman, or a boy a man; a candidate is now a king; the loose soul of a dead man takes up its place in heaven.

The middle or liminal period has a key importance in this sequence of events. Consider what happens when a signal event occurs: a girl's menstruation begins; a man dies. The event changes the natural condition of the individual in a way that underscores the limits of society's control over nature. Such events are often thought of as polluting. Ritual removes the person from everyday life and provides time for people to define the event and its consequences; to transform the person in body, mind, and status, and then to define the new state—as a fertile woman, or a soul proceeding to the world of the dead.

Of course, some events that are sequenced as transition rituals are not unplanned acts of nature at all: the initiation of a group of 10-year-olds, or a baptism, or a pilgrimage. Yet the liminal stage of these rituals, too, provides the setting for a dramatization of the individual's recasting into a new form, a convincing statement that the old has died and the new is born.

THE PILGRIMAGE TO MECCA

Let us look in some detail at one well-known ritual, the pilgrimage to Mecca. Each year during the pilgrimage month of the Islamic lunar calendar, more than a million Muslims from throughout the world gather in the holy places in and around Mecca. These men and women have traveled to Mecca to carry out their religious obligation to make the pilgrimage. All the pilgrims must carry out a series of very specific actions, moving and worshiping together, before completing their task and returning home. The principal goal of the pilgrimage is to obey God's commands, as they were made clear to humans through his messenger, Muhammad.

Following the Footsteps of Muhammad

Muslims consider the Qur'ân to be God's major gift to humans, and in this respect the Qur'ân's role is similar to that of the Torah for Jews and that of Christ for Christians. But Muslims also consider as divinely inspired the actions of the Prophet Muhammad—not because he was divine himself, but because he spoke and acted as God's messenger. The collection of reports about his statements and actions are called the "hadîth." These reports supplement the Qur'ân as the second basic source for guidance and law in the Muslim community. Much of Islamic ritual as well as everyday life is based on what Muhammad did as contained in these reports, and it is in this way that Muslims developed the pilgrimage, or hajj.

The pilgrimage is meaningful for Muslims in the first place as a repetition and commemoration of the Prophet's actions, "following in his footsteps," as many pilgrims who had completed the hajj said to me. But it was also dictated by God in his revelations to Muhammad. Several years after Muhammad and his followers had fled from Mecca to Medina to escape persecution came the first revelation concerning the pilgrimage, quoted in the last chapter of the Qur'ân:

> *Say: 'God has spoken the truth; therefore follow*
> *the creed of Abraham, a man of pure faith and no idolater.'*
> *The first House established for the people*
> *was that at Mecca, a place holy, and a guidance to all beings.*
> *Therein are clear signs—the station of Abraham,*
> *and whosoever enters it is in security.*
> *It is the duty of all men towards God to come*
> *to the House a pilgrim, if he is able to make his way there.*
> *As for the unbeliever, God is All-sufficient nor needs any being.*

> *(Qur'ân 3:90–92)*

The house mentioned in this passage is the large cubic structure called the "Ka'ba," which is draped in gold-bordered black silk cloth. The Ka'ba is the centerpoint of the religious world for Muslims. It is toward the Ka'ba that Muslims worship five times daily, and it is around the Ka'ba that they walk when they make the pilgrimage. In Islamic tradition, the Ka'ba dates back to the prophet Abraham, who journeyed to Mecca with his son, Ishmael, and Hagar, Ishmael's mother. (In the Islamic version of the sacrificial trial of Abraham, it was Ishmael, not Isaac, whom he was ordered to sacrifice.) Abraham built the Ka'ba on God's command. The angel Gabriel then brought down a black stone to place in its corner. The stone, it is said, was white, but turned black on contact with the sinful world.

By the seventh century C.E., Mecca had become a trading center in the Arabian peninsula, and it was here that Muhammad was born, grew up, and received his first revelations. His triumphant return to Mecca from Medina marked the victory of Islam over the polytheistic Meccan elites, and his first pilgrimage, in 632, the year of his death, became the model for all pilgrimages since (Peters 1994).

Making the pilgrimage is one of the five ritual obligations, or *rukns* (pillars), of Islam. The pilgrimage has always attracted Muslims from all over the world, but the development of steamship travel in the nineteenth century and air travel in the twentieth has led to a boom in pilgrimage activity. By the mid-twentieth century, about 30,000 people made the journey each year; today, over about 2 million pilgrims, from the 60 or more countries with sizable Muslim communities, arrive in Mecca each year. Pilgrims come from near and far: the largest delegations are from Nigeria, Pakistan, Turkey, and Yemen, and then Iran, Indonesia, and Iraq. Some pilgrims stay on to study and teach; most return home bringing new ideas and trade goods. Islam was founded by a trader amid vast networks of desert caravans; the contemporary pilgrimage enlarges those networks of trade and communication to the scale of the entire world.

Precisely because these holy cities occupy such a central place in the Muslim popular imagination, they have sometimes been the targets of political movements. During the 1979 pilgrimage, an armed group seized control of Mecca's Grand Mosque and broadcast denunciations of the Saudi government over a citywide loudspeaker system. Iranian anti-American demonstrations at Medina in 1982 led to arrests and revived debates about whether religion and politics could legitimately be separated in Islam. Since then, the Saudi government has prohibited delegations from making the pilgrimage when they feared political disturbances (or health risks, as in the 1996 ban on Nigerians during an epidemic in Nigeria).

Although the details of the hajj are taken one by one from accounts of that first pilgrimage, the steps can be sorted into the three stages of rites of transition. Indeed, Victor Turner (1974, 182) argues that in larger-scale societies, pilgrimages perform some of the same social functions that are filled by initiation rituals in smaller-scale societies, in providing the place for a religious experience outside the bounds of everyday social life. The pilgrim separates himself or herself from ordinary social life, enters a liminal stage in which distinctive everyday identities are exchanged for the shared identity of the pilgrim, and then returns to the social world. Each transition point is marked by clear religious duties.

Rites of Separation

Although a Muslim may visit the holy places in Mecca and Medina at any time during the year, the pilgrimage itself may be performed only on the eighth, ninth, and tenth days of the last month of the Islamic lunar calendar—the pilgrimage month, Dhu'l-Hijja.

(Because the lunar year is 11 days shorter than the solar year, the pilgrimage season cycles back through the solar year.) Unlike pilgrimages made by Christians, Jews, or Hindus to their holy cities, the hajj is a series of ritual actions performed together, simultaneously, by all the Muslim pilgrims for that year (Ruthven 1984, 23–48).

Weeks or even months before these key days, pilgrims have been gathering and departing from villages, towns, and cities all over the world. In Indonesia, as in many other countries with large Muslim populations, each group receives an official send-off from a local government official. As recently as two generations ago, departing pilgrims from the Gayo highlands received a different kind of send-off. They were fed at a ritual during which prayers for the dead were recited on their behalf, because most people who made the journey were older, and many would not survive the two- or three-month sea voyage. The ritual was held before they left because otherwise they would not receive one.

Travel, whether by land, sea, or air, is for much of the way a secular affair. Only when approaching the port or airfield of Jiddah must pilgrims take steps to enter the state of consecration, or *ihram*. Each pilgrim announces his or her intention to undertake the pilgrimage, renounces shaving, cutting the hair, and sexual intercourse, and changes clothes. The new pilgrim's clothing consists of identical, simple, white seamless garments. Men leave their heads uncovered, and women must not have cloth touching their faces. Some pilgrims even ride roofless buses once they approach Mecca. Each of these measures maintains an unbroken physical link between the pilgrim's head and God, and signals his or her surrender to God.

Moving in the Liminal State

Wearing identical clothing, renouncing normal relationships to their bodies, and concentrating their lives on worshiping God defines the pilgrim's position during the days of pilgrimage. In the liminal state, between their previous lives of various occupations, nationalities, wealth, and status, and their future lives as returned pilgrims, these men and women live and move as equals, sharing some rudimentary Arabic, simple accommodations (for most pilgrims, anyway), and the same daily objectives.

The clothes mark the fact that all pilgrims are religiously equal. As Muhammad's grandson Husayn stated, "The pilgrim offers himself to God as a beggar." Pilgrims mingle with one another even while onboard ship or plane as pilgrims, leaving ordinary social status aside.

Once in Arabia, they gather in groups by country and are led through the pilgrimage steps by a group leader, usually someone from their country. For many pilgrims, this is their first international experience, rubbing shoulders with others whose language they cannot understand. Arabic prayers and a few short greetings are usually the only form of verbal communication across these groups. Even the American black Muslim leader Malcolm X (1973, 339) was shocked by this universalism, as he wrote in a public letter to his mosque in Harlem. "For the past week, I have been utterly speechless and spellbound by the graciousness I see displayed all around me by people *of all colors.*"

Pilgrims arrive steadily at Mecca. As they do, they make seven left-hand circles (tawaf) around the Ka'ba. Indeed, the root meaning of hajj is "to describe a circle." Huge masses of pilgrims move slowly around the silk-draped structure. Each tries to touch or kiss the black stone set into its eastern corner. The Iranian scholar Ali Shariati (1977, 31) described the experience of the tawaf as that of "a small stream merging with a big river. . . . Suddenly, you find yourself floating and carried on by this flood. You have become part of this universal system. Circumambulating . . . Allah, you will soon forget yourself."

The Ka'ba already served as a holy site before Islam, but its guardian was the deity Hubal, whose statue was kept inside the structure. Many other deities were worshiped as well, and the circumambulation was part of worship. Muhammad retained this practice and the veneration of the black stone when he undertook the first pilgrimage, and his followers, though surprised that he did so given the stone's association with paganism, followed suit. The rigorous logic of following the Prophet's actions won out, here as elsewhere.

After the tawaf the pilgrim does the *sa'y*, "running," which does indeed consist of simply running (or, for the older, walking) back and forth, seven times, along a street in Mecca. The running commemorates the time when Hagar was abandoned under a tree at Mecca by Abraham. When her food and water ran out, she began to run wildly between two high points, pleading with God for help. When Ishmael raised his hand, there was a well, which became known as the well of Zamzam. The well marked the spot where Mecca was then built. Pilgrims collect water from the Zamzam well and bring it home with them; often diluted with rainwater, it will be used to heal or bless others. The running covers about two miles, and some pilgrims must be pushed in wheelchairs.

The circumambulation, also called the *'umra*, is sometimes performed separately out of season as the "little hajj." Travel agencies throughout the Muslim world offer 'umra packages—a Muslim may travel to Saudia Arabia at any time of year, circumambulate the Ka'ba, visit the holy sites, and return home.

The Hajj Proper

Pilgrims then begin the events that constitute the pilgrimage proper, the events that are performed only on the prescribed days. They must travel to the plain of 'Arafat by sunrise on the ninth day of the month. It is at 'Arafat, a barren plain about two miles from Mecca, where Adam and Eve were reunited after their expulsion from heaven. Here, too, Muhammad delivered his final sermon in 632, in which he set out most of the details of the hajj. A vast tent city is erected on this plain on the days before to the ninth, and there the pilgrims are assigned quarters.

At 'Arafat the pilgrims spend the ninth day in prayer and meditation, gathering around the Mount of Mercy at the edge of the plain. After performing the midafternoon worship, the millions gathered together stand, awaiting sunset, shouting cries of "God is great." This standing (*wuquf*) is the central event of the hajj proper. The special status enjoyed by this rather unspectacular (relative to the tawaf that precedes it and the sacrifices to follow) event comes from its role in replicating Muhammad's final sermon, and from the shared sense pilgrims derive from it of showing humility before God.

Pilgrims then disperse and return toward Mecca, stopping to spend the night in the city of Muzdalifa, where they are to rid themselves of all resentments toward others. There, too, they collect pebbles, which they use the next day to throw at three pillars near Mina, on the return road to Mecca. This *rajm*, or stoning, of the statues is understood to be a stoning of devils. No mention is made of it in the Qur'ân; as with the veneration of the black stone in the Ka'ba, it is performed solely because Muhammad did it on his pilgrimage. As interpreted by most participants, it commemorates Abraham's resoluteness to obey God, for it was on this spot that he prepared to carry out God's command to him to sacrifice his son. The devil appeared to Abraham, and tried to instill doubt in his heart about the sacrifice. Abraham stoned the devil until he fled. After the crowding and rushing of the previous two days the stoning also undoubtedly releases tensions. Some commentators have harnessed the energies visible during the stoning to religious mission; Ali Shariati urged pilgrims to think of the pebbles as bullets used to kill one's enemies.

Pilgrims then carry out a sacrifice in memory of Abraham's submission to God's will. Usually they buy a goat on the spot and arrange to have its throat cut. The meat is distributed to the poor, much of it immediately frozen on the spot by Saudi authorities. The day after this event is called the *yaum an-nahr,* or day of sacrifice, and it is celebrated throughout the Muslim world by similar sacrifices. The pilgrimage is thus both a duty for all Muslims and the occasion for a worldwide ritual observance.

Reintegration to Normal Life

The pilgrimage proper is complete at this point, and the pilgrims gradually make the return to normal social status. They begin by cutting some of their hair. Women snip off just a bit, but men often have their heads shaved. Now all prohibitions are lifted except for that on sexual intercourse. Pilgrims return to Mecca, perform another circumambulation of the Ka'ba, collect Zamzam well water for the return trip, and now can again engage in sexual intercourse. They are urged to spend several days in "eating, drinking, and sensual pleasure." This urging emphasizes that the pilgrims are now leaving the state of consecration and returning to normal society—the rite of passage has ended.

Those pilgrims who return home immediately find themselves enjoying a new status, that of hajji (male) or hajjiyah (female), someone who has made the pilgrimage and returned to society. Many now wear white for everyday activities or when they attend the mosque to signal this new status. Their status may lead to other achievements: they are probably looked on with greater favor by their local bank; they may be chosen for office. They certainly have much to tell about from their journey. But they also enjoy a sense of religious accomplishment, having fulfilled the most difficult of God's commands.

How Is It Meaningful?

Ordinary Muslims undertake the pilgrimage for a variety of reasons—they are obeying a divine command; they are fulfilling a duty expected of them socially; they may be advancing their own social status. But is this all we can say? In what ways is the pilgrimage with its many component actions meaningful?

The pilgrimage presents a challenge to our usual ideas of the meaning of a religious act. It is not performed with a separate goal in mind, such as atonement or cleansing. The religious historical event that is commemorated in each segment of the ritual is sometimes but not always clear. The only overall, uniting idea of the pilgrimage is that it is made up of actions that were performed by Muhammad on his first (and only) pilgrimage.

Scholars do suggest parallels with earlier rites, either those performed on the same spot as a contemporary ritual and taken over by Muhammad, or parallel rituals within the Semitic ritual tradition that were adopted by Muhammad as properly monotheistic. For example, the wuquf, or "standing," was part of earlier Hebrew practice. Muhammad made the entire plain of 'Arafat a place of standing before God. The 'umra was originally a sacrifice of firstborn livestock and was held in the early spring, much as with Passover, in the month of Rajab (at that time the lunar calendar was made concordant with the solar, so that Rajab always occurred in the spring). The sacrifice was carried out at the Ka'ba. As late as the twelfth century C.E., local Muslims were still carrying out this older sacrificial 'umra in the month of Rajab.

In fact, although the 'umra is thought of as a little hajj, 'umra and hajj were once distinct events. The essence of the 'umra is the tawaf, the circumambulation of the Ka'ba, while the essence of the hajj is the standing before God at 'Arafat. In origins, the one is sacrificial; the other is an act of submission to God. Muhammad then tied them together in one long series of events.

This kind of explanation may provide a historical account for why certain events became part of the overall pilgrimage. They do not account for the meaning of the rite for those people who take part in it. Muslim commentators have offered several broad lines of interpretation.

One interpretation links the performance of the hajj to the overall meaning of Islam as *surrender.* According to the important twelfth-century theologian Al-Ghazali, devotion to God demands self-abnegation, surrender to his will. Therefore, God has imposed on the Muslim actions that in themselves have no emotional or intellectual appeal, such as the running back and forth between two points, or sa'y.

A second interpretation identifies symbolic or iconic meanings for each individual place or object that the pilgrim encounters. The Ka'ba is the House of the Lord. You will meet God in a seamless shroud, so you meet him today wearing such garments. The tawaf resembles the movement of angels that encircle the Throne of God, which itself is situated directly above the Ka'ba in heaven. Ali Shariati (1977) sees the "running" as standing for purposeful activity on the earth.

A third line of interpretation seems to me to be closest to the ways in which pilgrims themselves interpret their experience. This approach locates meaning not in the events but in their historicity, as commemorations of past events. The running commemorates the moment when Hagar was looking for water for Ishmael and Gabriel created the Zamzam well. The stoning marks the moment when Abraham stoned the devil. The sacrifice commemorates Abraham's willingness to sacrifice his son. At the very least, every event commemorates Muhammad's pilgrimage—and this insight returns us to a key element of Islam, that practices and texts constantly refer back to the life of the Prophet for their authenticity.

And what is the specific goal of the pilgrimage? Despite the fact that worship is always done facing the Ka'ba in Mecca, and that "Mecca" has become a shorthand for a central place or goal, in fact, the central event in the pilgrimage, the standing at 'Arafat, takes place outside Mecca itself, as does the sacrifice, both in places that are virtually uninhabited during the remainder of the year. Within the hajj framework, for instance, the pilgrim is never still, but is hurried around the Ka'ba, down the road to 'Arafat, back to Mina and then to Mecca, around the Ka'ba again, and then home. What the pilgrimage is really about is commemoration of Muhammad's actions, not the visit to the holy places (which, one should again note, can take place at any time of the year).

Man returned from the pilgrimage proudly displays his new clothing, Isak, Sumatra. (*Courtesy of John Bowen*)

Pilgrims expand this sense of historicity from particular commemorations to a more diffuse sense of being in the place where their religion was born, being "at the source." "Everywhere," writes the Pakistani religious leader al-Maudûdî of the typical pilgrim, "he sees the relics of those who lived God, and sacrificed their lives for His sake. Every grain of sand witnesses the glory and grandeur of Islam, and every piece of stone declares: 'This is the land where Islam took birth, and whence God's word rose high'" (quoted in Cragg 1980, 60). As the leader of U.S. Muslims Warith Deen Muhammad said in conversations in St. Louis in 1996, "on the pilgrimage you come near to God; you are visiting Him."

DEATH RITUAL AND THE SOCIAL ORDER

If performing the pilgrimage links the Muslim to his or her history, death rituals across societies can be seen as highlighting ideas about the individual's relationship to the collectivity. If an individual leaves society, is he or she to remain part of it? In the answer to that question, people often highlight their picture, real or ideal, of society and of an individual.

In much of China and Taiwan, villagers conceive of the spiritual world as composed of three beings: ghosts, gods, and ancestors. Each is dealt with differently; for example, offered different kinds of food or money. These three beings are also associated with three kinds of humans. Gods are dressed in the garments of officials and they can punish people and be bribed. They keep records; they are clearly bureaucrats. They are worshipped in temples (Wolf 1974). Ghosts, by contrast, are worshiped outside, with large offerings of food or clothing, and they resemble bandits or beggars—strangers, in other words. Ancestors are, well, ancestors. You owe them a debt for your own life and prosperity, and you feed them as you would feed a human visitor to your home. This close correspondence between society and supernatural beings suggests that in different Chinese settings, people would interpret these beings somewhat differently, and they do: The god who is a police official today may have been an influential country gentleman in the past.

FROM SPIRIT TO HOUSEHOLD GOD IN JAPAN

For an extended example of this general idea, let's return to rural Japan. If the living individual is thought of as a member of a household and of a community, at death he or she becomes a spirit (kami) as well as a Buddha (hotoke). Funerals are performed by Buddhist priests, but death ritual also involves pre-Buddhist ideas of pollution and ritual. A long transition stage allows the spirit to progress from an individual's spirit to one element in the household deity. Death ritual thereby reinforces the notion of spirit collectivity (Plath 1964; Smith 1974).

Death begins a three-stage process of transforming the deceased into a part of the spirit collectivity. At death the body may be cremated or buried; urban Japanese inevitably cremate. In either case, bodily death pollutes the spirit (shirei) as well as the close relatives of the deceased. Death ritual helps to separate the spirit from the pollution. The grave receiving the body is located far away from the residential part of a village and is called the "abandoned grave." In some parts of Japan a second, "ritual grave," consisting of a headstone is built nearer the house. This grave may be tended without encountering the pollution of the dead body. Urban Japanese must rely on funeral parlors. (Today the combined expenses of burial, home altar with tablets, and the services of a Buddhist priest can amount to a middle-class family's one-year pretax income!)

The memory of the deceased individual is preserved for the first 49 days after death. The survivors set up a mortuary tablet on the household altar, together with a photo of the deceased, incense, bells, and other objects. Buddhist memorial services are held for the individual every 7 days until the 49 days are completed. The soul also wanders near the house during this period, before leaving on the 49th day.

Sometimes the soul takes some action on its own on the 49th day to settle scores with the living. In an eighteenth-century puppet play called "The Woman Killer and the

Hell of Oil," Yohei murders Okichi, but no one knows that Yohei is the murderer. Yohei arrives on the 49th day of the ritual, just after a rat has run along the rafters of the room, dislodging a scrap of paper with evidence of the murderer's guilt; and the husband of the dead woman exclaims that this was a sign from the dead person: "This I owe to Buddha's mercy," he says.

At the end of this initial period, the family performs a series of rituals to transform the spirit of the dead into an ancestral spirit (*sorei*). The photo is put away and the temporary tablet disposed of, replaced by a permanent tablet, usually an upright wooden plaque four to six inches high, lacquered in black or gold, and inscribed with a special posthumous name of the deceased and the date of his or her death. (Buddhist temples provide these after-death names.) This tablet is placed with the other tablets on the altar.

The altar and tablets stand for the house's history (Smith 1974, 1978, 152–165). The household (*ié*) is thought of as a corporate group, the headship of which passes from father to son over the generations. The tablets are the first objects to be saved (standard newspaper accounts of fires say that "flames swept through the building so rapidly that the residents only had time to carry out the altar and tablets"). The tablets are even more important than the Buddha image. As one man put it, the ancestors need help like anyone else, whereas the Buddha can take care of himself.

But the tablet itself is impermanent. After either 33 or 50 years (depending on the region of Japan) the tablet is destroyed and the spirit becomes a god. The spirit is sometimes transferred to the household god in a noteworthy ritual in which the tablet is cast into a river and then a pebble is picked up from the river bed and placed on the household god's altar. This collection of pebbles represents the spirits merged into the guardian god of the household as a collectivity.

Thereafter, services are held for the collective dead, without identifying them singly, both with daily offerings of flowers and on seasonal occasions, in particular New Year's on January first through third, Obon or the Festival of the Dead or of Lanterns on August 13 through 15, and the equinoxes in late March and September.

The Obon festival, when the ancestors come down from where they live to their villages, has been celebrated at least since the year 606 C.E. One dedicates temples and recites Buddhist verses and makes offerings to ancestors. One category of ancestor is especially grateful for these offerings: Ancestors who committed misdeeds in past lives may end up on the plane of existence called *gaki-do*, or Plane of the Hungry Ghosts. They suffer from hunger and thirst, and they alone out of all one's ancestors may benefit from offerings one makes to a holy or virtuous person.

But Obon generally is the time to make offerings to the ancestors. The ritual grave near the house is cleared and a path is swept leading back to the house. The household altar is cleaned and a dance (today in decline) is held in the village. People return to their ancestral villages to participate in the festival and end the ritual by taking lanterns and small boats to the graveyard or to a mountain or river to see the spirits off on their return to their abode. Japanese overseas also celebrate Obon. In St. Louis, where I live, it is the time for a Japanese festival at the Botanical Gardens, with the lighting of lanterns around the lake in the Japanese garden.

The long transition stage in Japanese death rituals supports the idea of a gradual melding of the individual into the collectivity and thus also supports the general cultural importance of the collectivity.

REGENERATING LIFE FROM DEATH

Death rituals also frequently feature images of journeys to new worlds, enactments of rebirth, or the disinterment and reburial of bones (Bloch and Parry 1982). Images of journeys are sometimes the material focus of religious innovations. As Sumatran Toba Batak people left their ancestral homeland for big cities, they began to use their new wealth to build elaborate family tombs back home. These tombs were carved in the shapes of boats and other images of soul journeys, and the tombs kept alive a sense of attachment to the homeland and a promise of rejoining the family for the journey to the afterworld. In Ghana, a man named Connie Kway began to carve elaborate, painted coffins in the shapes of boats or birds during the 1970s. These coffins sold for the equivalent of a year's average wage and were snatched up by the rich. They were an innovation; Ghanians had not used fancy coffins before, but because they dramatized the comforting and spirit-raising belief that the dead were going to a resting place where loved ones would see them again, they quickly became popular and spawned imitators. (In 1996, a museum tour of the coffins swept the United States, where they were competed for as treasured folk art objects.)

Death is often linked to life and fertility in the transition stages. This linking may take different forms. Bloch and Parry (1982, 7) argue that death rituals tend to revitalize "that resource which is *culturally conceived* to be most essential to the reproduction of the social order." The resource may be the land, human fertility, or some combination of the two. Thus, in four African hunter-gatherer societies compared by James Woodburn (1982), social reproduction was thought to depend most importantly on control over nature, and the ritual response to death was to reawaken the productivity of nature.

For the Merina of Madagascar, studied by Maurice Bloch (1982), reproducing the society requires that members of a descent group have their bones buried together in ancestral tombs. Because these related individuals do not live in the same place, they are initially buried where they die. Their bones are later dug up and moved to the ancestral tomb. The initial burial is attended by sadness and mourning, but the subsequent "regrouping" of the body with the ancestors is full of joy and dancing. While dancing, women repeatedly throw the brittle bones to the ground, smashing them to bits. These actions merge the physical remains of the individual with the ancestral groups as a whole. The ritual also employs the symbolism of birth, entering into and emerging from the tomb as if it were a womb.

ASMAT HEADHUNTING AND BIRTH THROUGH DEATH

Consider in more detail the case of the Asmat, a society of about 50,000 people living in the swampy plains of West Papua in Indonesia. The Asmat are best known in the West for the tall *bis* poles, made out of sago palm, examples of which are to be found in many Western museums (Kuruwaip 1974).

The Asmat (Sudarman 1984) call themselves the "tree people." Their environment is wood; stone or metal for tools must be acquired from elsewhere. Canoes, poles, housing are all from wood. Their staple, sago, is also wood. Every four or five days, the men of a clan will spend an entire day looking for a large (45-foot-high) sago palm tree in the forest, cutting it down, removing the pith, and then pounding, washing, drying, and roasting the pith into large cakes of sago to be pounded into sago flour. Sago is regarded as a human being. The sago palm resembles a woman: life comes from within it, and the white, milky sago resembles breast milk. When an Asmat man carves a sago palm into a pole, he considers his work similar to what he does to help produce a baby. Asmat hold that the father does not cause conception, but molds the child through frequent intercourse into the shape he or she eventually has at birth (Gerbrands 1967).

Bis Pole. Mid 20th century. New Guinea, Irian Jaya, Faretsj River, Omadesep village, Asmat people. Wood, paint, fiber, H. 216 in (548.6 cm). The Michael C. Rockefeller Memorial Collection, Bequest of Nelson A. Rockefeller, 1979 (1979.206.1611). Image copyright © The Metropolitan Museum of Art/Art Resource, NY

Much of the Asmat men's time used to be spent in warfare between clans, fueled partly by their practices and beliefs surrounding death. Asmat believe that deaths are due to malevolent actions by others, that people in other clans kill your own relatives either in an observable way (in a raid, for example) or through sorcery. The spirits of the dead demand retribution or revenge for their deaths (Zegwaard 1959). The Asmat once took revenge for a death by taking a head in a raid on another clan, thus continuing the cycle of death and retribution. The relative taking the head would have carved for him a long, 15- to 20-foot *bis* pole. The clan would then drum and dance to entice the spirit into the pole. The relative would dedicate the pole to the deceased, and cry out (for example): "Oh mother, I have killed a man from [place name]." Then the spirit of the dead person, which would have remained in the village until avenged, would begin its journey out of the village and toward an island somewhere off the western coast, later to be reborn as a new human (Kuruwaip 1974).

Today, headhunting is prohibited, and Asmat seem to have abandoned the practice. But they continue to carve images of deceased relatives onto the long poles, to drum the spirit into the pole, and to erect the pole and publicly dedicate it, calling out for the spirit to leave the village.

Through their myths, the Asmat believe the acts of producing sago from palms, carving wood poles, and cutting heads to be situating their lives in the universe. Taking a head reenacts a sacrifice made at the beginning of time. In a widely told story, a being who was both god and man killed his brother and cut off his head, immediately causing the universe to come into existence, and all of culture with it. (In some versions of this story, the god–man cut off the head of a crocodile in order to create non-Asmat people.) Taking a head thus caused life to emerge (Zegwaard 1959).

In practice, the skulls of the dead help to bring about a new birth. In past times, the skull used would have come from a headhunting expedition, and thus the same skull would accomplish two important functions: first, it would allow the spirit to leave the world and, second, it would bring a new person into it. Today, the skull would come from a relative. A young male being initiated into manhood sits for days in the men's house, contemplating a skull between his legs, pressed against his genitals. Then he is carried out toward the setting sun in a canoe, following the journey made by the spirits of the dead. When the canoe has traveled far enough from the shore, he lies at the bottom of the canoe in imitation of someone who has just died. Then he is thrown into the water, still holding the skull, to resurface as a newly born initiated man.

Cutting the sago is also likened to taking a human head and releasing energy. The palm is thought to have the same spirit as a human. Men attack the palm, throwing spears at it, and butcher the starch. Asmat also draw on these ideas to project human actions onto the animal world. They see an analogy to headhunting in the behavior of the praying mantis. The insect is seen as human in its movements (think of how its stance gave rise to its English name), and the female bites off the head of the male during mating.

Not only is the mantis's cannibalism like taking a head, but it also reminds the Asmat observer of the mock, or part-mock aggression enacted by women toward men in everyday life. For when the Asmat men return along the river with the sago palm, women carry out an attack on the canoes from the village shore. The attack is ostensibly to keep malevolent spirits from entering the village along with the palm, but in practice women throw their spears hard and accurately and, not uncommonly, men are injured.

Drumming the spirit of the dead into the *bis* pole also replicates a mythic event. The very first man on earth was called Fumeripits. He drowned in the sea but was brought back to life by War, the name of the white-tailed eagle, who pressed smoldering bits of wood against his body. Then Fumeripits built a large men's house and carved images of men and women. He began to drum, and they came to life, dancing. The carvers and drummers of today cannot create life, but they can attract spirits through their carving and drumming, thereby reenacting Fumeripits' deed on the spiritual level.

In everyday life, too, Asmat experience the link between heads and the continuity of life. All adults sleep on skulls, usually skulls of close relatives, and report feeling a continued tie to the deceased through this skull-sleeping. Some men will (or did) sleep on the skull of a powerful enemy, claiming that they absorb some of the deceased's power at night. Carving the pole and cutting heads thus not only frees the spirit from the village (and the village from the spirit) but also signifies to the living that the dead will be reborn and life will continue. The ritual also gives the bereaved a concrete way to care for the spirits of their relatives. And since they practice it together as a social group, a single individual's death strengthens the power of their origin myths.

The ritual as it once was carried out allowed the individual to complete a logical and emotional circle: a death, avenged by taking a head, was completed when the skull of the victim was used to release the spirit from the village and then to cause a rebirth. But now the circuit has been shorted at the point of headhunting. The Dutch (when they controlled the territory) had already prohibited headhunting throughout the region, but they had little direct sway over the Asmat. The Indonesian government has been much more direct in its plans to change Asmat lives and religions: it encourages missionaries to promote the adoption of proper religion, with a book, a creed, but no violence. The missionaries offer salvation through communion (which might be interpreted by Asmat as a different kind of cannibalism) and rebirth through baptism (a different path to rebirth through immersion in water).

SECONDARY BURIAL

The "regrouping" of bones practiced by the Merina, and described above, provides one example of a widespread practice of secondary burial, or the removal and reburial of a corpse. This practice is intended to provide material signs of the transition from life to an afterlife in the form of the state of the bones of the dead after decomposition is supposed to have set in. Secondary burial is relatively rare, but it is found in culturally unrelated areas throughout the world—Greece, Africa, Siberia, Indonesia, the Americas, and in early Jewish practice. Medieval Christian burial in Europe often included the display of bones in an ossuary.

Peter Metcalf (1982) provides a detailed description of the practice from the Berawan society in Borneo. In this society, a body is stored in a large jar right after death. After several days, the bones are cleaned of flesh and stored in the longhouse or on a platform outside. Months or years later (Metcalf records a range of 8 months to 5 years), the bones of some of the dead, but not others, are removed and placed in a permanent death monument. For the Berawan, the display of bones stands for the passage of the spirit of the dead outside the community. It confirms that the spirit has reached the land of the dead.

Robert Hertz (1960) wrote a comparative essay on the practice in 1907. Hertz used material from Borneo and Indonesia but also made reference to similar practices elsewhere. Based on his reading of available ethnography, Hertz argued that people take the natural fact of bodily decomposition as the basis for thinking about the process of death, the transition from the loss of soul to the passage to another place. Just as the body decomposes, so the spirit gradually leaves the body, transformed to a new state in which the spirit is definitively separated from the body.

The process of decomposition, then, defines three moments in the death process, each of which serves as a sign of the unobservable process through which the spirit leaves the body and the community. At the moment of death, the spirit has left the body. During decomposition, the spirit is uncertain as to its final home, and during this period it may haunt the living and roam the community. But when the bones are seen to be clean, the spirit has left for its new home.

Hertz noted that people have a horror of the corpse throughout the world, but that it is not a physical repugnance. The same people fear the corpse but wash it, sit with it, even drink the wash water. The fear is for two reasons. First, the death tears a hole in the community, and the social fabric must be mended and order restored. The more important the person, the more ritual work needs to be done, so only some bones are subjected to secondary burial. Second, the soul remains near the corpse and until it has left the community, it will continue to haunt the living. The rites of secondary burial enact the finality of the passage out of the community.

This analysis explains why Berawan people evinced horror at the practice of embalming when Metcalf described it to them. Embalming for purposes of viewing the body in a "lifelike" state is seen by Berawan as delaying the process of decay and thereby retarding the successful separation of the soul from the community.

Similar concerns are found in the official policy on burial of the Greek Orthodox Church. Bodies must not, commands the church, be buried in airtight caskets lest the natural, and God-ordained, process of decomposition be halted. In rural Greece today, relatives exhume the bones of the deceased five years after the body is buried, and remove the bones to the village ossuary (Danforth 1982). If the bones are clean and white, relatives are assured that the soul has passed to heaven. If decomposition has not been completed, villagers wait for another two years and then repeat the process. Meanwhile they say prayers for the forgiveness of the person's sins; it is these sins that have retarded the soul's passage and the body's decomposition.

In these and other cases, people feel ambivalent about the passage of the soul from the community. People may wish loved ones to remain near them, but they also wish for closure in the process of dying and mourning. Death rituals not only demonstrate to the living that the dead have left the community, taking danger with them, but also that they remain close by and that they can be called on to help the living. The soul of a Berawan person remains ready to aid the living in times of illness or other need. Asmat send the spirits of the dead away from the community to an island off the coast, but people continue to sleep with the skulls of deceased loved ones and sense that the person continues to remain with them. For people in many societies, death involves desires for both finality and remembrance; death rituals give those desires a material form.

GRIEF AND RITUAL FORM

Transition rituals marking events such as initiations or deaths are emotional times. Often the emotions are produced by the rituals themselves. The sociologist Émile Durkheim (1858–1917), stressing the social base for much of religious life, argued that ritual action, especially when in a group, channels and determines emotions. Durkheim maintained that although there might be natural emotional responses to death, they are highly subject to social shaping. Is this view correct? How culturally different are those emotions? What role does ritual play in the interior lives, the feelings, and the grieving of the survivors? Do rituals create emotions or do emotions determine what kind of rituals people create?

Consider the contrast between the ways in which two Muslim peoples mourn the loss of a close relative. In Java, where people typically value the control of their emotions, Clifford Geertz (1960, 73) reports a man he knew well, distancing himself from the loss of his wife, describing how he kept his emotions inside him. A girl who wept softly after her father died was told she could not participate in the funeral events unless she stopped crying. And yet, in Morocco, another Muslim society, the expected behavior is just the opposite. People in mourning tear their clothes and hair and wail loudly and publicly (Westermarck 1968 II, 34–42).

These marked differences in public behavior are between two peoples with the same religion. Ritual forms, linked to dominant cultural values, prescribe sharply contrasting patterns of mourning behavior.

But we cannot assume from such publicly observed contrasts that the emotions and the grieving process experienced by the individual are correspondingly different (Rosaldo 1984). Many Moroccans may feel indifference; many Javanese, great sorrow. Yet men and women in each society are expected to act in certain standardized ways regardless of their feelings. Many people in the United States report feeling quite different from what their public mourning behavior would suggest. Some feel guilty at the gulf between their mixed emotions and the expressions of grief that they are expected to display. Others adhere to religions that urge their followers in a different direction, to maintain a hopeful attitude consistent with a strong belief in the afterlife. Mormon services reflect this attitude, and Christian Scientists argue that bereaved people can and should lift themselves out of sorrow through the sheer force of the will. Yet many adherents to these faiths do grieve, and may find their social networks not offering the support they need (Palgi and Abramovitch 1984).

Is Grief Universal?

Perhaps the most devastating loss to an American adult is the death of a child, and here cross-cultural variation is striking. Psychologists (Bowlby 1980) argue that parents in all societies develop attachment to their children and experience grief at the loss of children. The attachment and the grief seem to have a basis in the evolution of social relationships. Both features are found in nonhuman primates as well as in humans. And yet in many societies the deaths of newborns are not accompanied by the same expressions of loss and grief as are the deaths of older children or adults. In many societies, children are not named until some number of days have passed after birth, and a death before that time is treated very differently than later deaths. Do these practices indicate that parents feel the loss less? How strongly does such a cultural practice shape emotions?

Two studies in anthropology have addressed this question but reach distinct conclusions. Nancy Scheper-Hughes (1992) argues that some poor Brazilian parents do feel loss less than do most middle-class parents. She emphasizes the cultural malleability of emotions—cultural practices shape emotional response. Unni Wikan (1990), emphasizing the distance between public expressions and inner emotions, finds that Balinese people feel strong grief emotions, but that they follow culturally prescribed practices of working on their grief through laughter and sociability. These and other studies underscore the emotional importance of rituals and other practices during the transition stage after a death—and also the difficulties in generalizing about "private" emotions.

Nancy Scheper-Hughes lived, worked, and studied in a very poor region in northeastern Brazil in the 1960s and then again in the 1980s. Many in the area had little to eat, and infant death was common. Mothers, fathers, and siblings developed an attitude of "letting go" toward those infants who seemed near death, often drawing on an elaborate catalogue of symptoms that pointed to an inevitable death.

Scheper-Hughes tried to make sense of the families' emotionally flat responses by challenging the Western view about attachment and mourning. In that view, attachment is a basic instinct that structures relationships between all human mothers and their children. The death of a child triggers natural responses of mourning, which must be worked through if the survivors are to be able to carry on in a healthy way. But Scheper-Hughes (1992, 400–445) argues that many mothers in fact have an ambivalent attitude toward their newborns. When the mother–infant experience is positive, and when nurturing all of one's children is possible, parents invest emotionally in their children and feel great loss at a death. But in poor Brazil and some other places, a "lifeboat" ethic leads parents to choose, reluctantly, to nurture only those who have a chance at surviving. Cultural practices reinforce this survival strategy: parents delay naming their infants and hold them much less often than do middle-class mothers.

Death ritual also plays an important part in this survival strategy. In some parts of Brazil, lower-class men and women treat the death of a very young child as a blessing. The child will be taken to heaven, is already a little angel, they say. The wake held for the little child, who is dressed in a white or blue shirt with curled hair and floral wreaths, includes joyous music and samba dancing. Although much more sober in tone in the community where Scheper-Hughes worked, the "angels" were a "transitional object" for these women, she points out (1992, 421), both because the infant is in transition from life to death, and because the dressed-up corpse and coffin allows the woman to let go of her child by giving her an idealized heaven-child to hold onto. Women told Scheper-Hughes: "I feel free" or "I feel unburdened" after the funeral. Grief seemed absent. For some students of Brazilian society, the flat emotional response is a mask, a wall against the unbearable. But Scheper-Hughes takes the responses of these women at face value, arguing that culture and ritual succeed in preventing grief responses. The idea that deaths need to be worked through by a process of open mourning, she says, is applicable only in some societies.

Still, it may be difficult to decide between several possible interpretations of Scheper-Hughes's data—are denials of grief a mask, or are denials accurate reports of feelings? Another study of the same area (Nations and Rebhun 1988) reports very different findings. In many parts of the world, women lose their babies in infancy and yet mourn them deeply and loudly; high rates of infant mortality do not seem to be associated with low rates of grieving. Finally, we should note that arguments for a universal attachment structure are based on cross-cultural research: the major early empirical work (Ainsworth 1967) was not from the West but from Uganda!

Emotions and Their Expressions

Scheper-Hughes's argument was intended to counter universal theories of death, emotions, and ritual. By contrast, anthropologist Unni Wikan draws on her fieldwork in Bali to oppose culturally relativist theories about the malleability of emotions. In Bali, as in neighboring Java, people are expected to preserve a "face" of equanimity at loss or disaster. Anthropologists had long understood the grace and composure of Balinese as a cultural style that focused on beauty and on distancing oneself from emotions. Balinese selves, wrote the anthropologist Clifford Geertz (1966), are quite different from Western ones; they live in a "dramatistic" world composed of masks, roles, and a stage.

Wikan (1990) argues instead that Balinese think and feel their way through the world in ways that are much closer to European ways than earlier anthropologists believed. She describes several months in the life of one woman who lost her fiance in an accident. Her friends laughed and joked with her, insisting that she laugh too. During the following months, she appeared bright-faced and happy, even to her friend Wikan. After several months Wikan did see her cry, and then the woman began to tell of how devastated she had felt through the whole experience. About the same time, her friends began to change their ways of being with her, sympathizing out loud with the distress she must have felt. Her emotions, and their understanding of them, were not all that different after all.

But why did she laugh her way through the first few months, and why did her friends insist that she do so? The key lies in a distinctive set of ideas about the relationship between one's "face"—appearances and behavior—and one's "heart"—emotions and thoughts. For the Balinese with whom Wikan spoke, emotions of sadness and sorrow weaken one's life force. A weak life force opens up the body to all sorts of invasions, but most particularly to attacks from sorcerers. These attacks are always near at hand; half of all deaths are attributed to sorcery. Moreover, these sad feelings can spread from one person to another, endangering the community, so one has a social as well as a personal responsibility to keep sorrow at a distance. How does one do that? Whereas we might think of emotions as having a life of their own—grief inevitably following loss—the Balinese think that behavior, including how one forms one's face and the choice to laugh or cry, shapes the heart and channels emotions. Laughing, then, keeps sadness from welling up, and thereby keeps the person strong against murderous sorcery.

Wikan concludes that Balinese appearances of calm and joy are not due to a theater-like detachment from the world, but rather to their strong fears of sorcery and their ideas about how best to combat it. During the transition period after death, these dangers are at their highest and thus when the practices of laughing together are most required.

Wikan, then, affirms the distinctiveness of Balinese ideas and practices but sees them as responses to a universal emotion of loss and grief. Scheper-Hughes claims that the emotions of the Brazilians she studied are quite different from those experienced by middle-class families, but she does so by way of a general theory about the responses of mothers (and others) to infants and to risk. Both underscore the critical role of culturally sanctioned practices designed to shape the emotions people feel when a loved one dies. Balinese laughing and Brazilian "angel caskets" bridge the transition period between death and the reintegration of the survivors into the ordinary routines of life.

Conclusions

The three-stage model of transition rituals provides a powerful way to compare rituals across societies and across ritual types. We can analyze rituals of initiation, death rituals, and pilgrimages through the same lens. And the evidence suggests that this lens provides a very useful tool for examining rituals and then comparing them. But the debate over emotions also provides a cautionary note. Just because everyone dies and all societies organize the passage from life to death in some way, we do not know that all societies shape emotions in the same way, or that all individuals in one society experience the same emotions at deaths. There remains an important role for in-depth ethnographic study, and for expecting to find considerable variation in experience among individuals in any one society. (You would probably discover such variation in comparing your own experiences at deaths of friends and family.)

Films to See

To illustrate rites of passage quite different from those discussed here, *Kinaalda: Navajo Rite of Passage* is about the four-day event performed to guide a young girl's ascent to womanhood. The theme of passage to adulthood is of course a staple in American films. A number of films now are available about the Islamic pilgrimage; my favorite is the IMAX 2009 film *Journey to Mecca*.

Worship, Hierarchy, Conflict: Focus on Hinduism

Religious practices can be studied by focusing on particular aspects of religion, such as death rituals, and we have taken examples from several distinct religious traditions in order to highlight certain commonalities across religions. This way of studying has its advantages: It encourages us to compare, to find similarities, and to think about why we might find such similarities. But it does have one important disadvantage in that it does not allow us to approach religious life in the way that a participant does. For a practitioner of a specific religious tradition, the tradition does not come carved up into different realms, it is rather experienced as a coherent whole. Consequently, in this chapter, we take that second point of view, and explore the ritual, intellectual, and sociopolitical dimensions of one religious tradition, that of Hindus living in India. I try to give a multidimensional portrait of one religious tradition by moving from worship rituals and ideas about deities to social hierarchies and political conflicts.

SACRIFICE, OFFERINGS, AND DEITIES

In India, sacrifice, offerings, and devotions are directed toward gods, of which there are many. About 80 percent of India's 800 million people consider themselves Hindus, and most of them, daily and in countless ways (including sacrificial ways), carry out rituals of offerings and homage to the gods (Fuller 1992, 29–56).

Some gods are entirely specific to a village or district. Others may have locally specific forms, but are also manifestations of pan-Indian gods. Particularly important are Vishnu and Shiva. These two gods stand in complementary relationship to each other, Vishnu as the preserver and Shiva the destroyer, Vishnu the king and Shiva the ascetic (the renouncer of worldly pleasures), Vishnu at the center of the world and Shiva outside of it. (Brahma, not to be confused with the Brahmin caste grouping, is less prominent in worship, but is in fact the creator.) Because creation is cyclical—creation following destruction in the cycles of cosmic history—both are necessary elements in the world.

From Chapter 7 of *Religions in Practice: An Approach to the Anthropology of Religion*, 5/e. John J. Bowen.

Vishnu is usually worshiped through one of his ten incarnations, in particular as Rama or Krishna. The ancient epic of the Ramayana tells of Rama's life as the king of the northern realm of Ayodhya (later the site of intense conflict; see below). The epic represents his life as the model for a righteous king's conduct. The Ramayana is known throughout India (and in much of Southeast Asia) in various versions, some emphasizing Rama's divinity. It is read or viewed today in the form of sacred texts, popular stories, comic books, and shadow puppet plays, and during 1987–1988 it appeared as a hugely popular television series—a series that also raised popular enthusiasm for Hindu nationalist politics.

Krishna is portrayed as a warrior or as a mischievous child. His battles are recounted in another well-known epic, the Mahabharata. But he also transcends mere human warfare. In a section of the epic called the Bhagavad Gita, he counsels his cousin Arjuna to remain above the world even as he is forced to continue his battles. Krishna is also worshiped as a youth and remembered for his romance with the cowherdess Radha.

Shiva has many manifestations. He may be represented by a phallic linga statue, or as a human-looking image. Shiva has two sons, Skanda and Ganesha, the latter represented with an elephant head. Both Vishnu and Shiva may have different wives in different temples, although Vishnu is most often represented with the goddess of fortune, Lakshmi.

Both Vishnu and Shiva have followers, Vaishnavas and Shaivas, respectively, who worship them either by these names or in their local manifestations, often alongside other, lesser deities. Each temple in India is in principle unique, and each is dedicated to a particular, local form of a deity. For Shiva and Vishnu, this localization of worship means that they are addressed by a distinctive name. In the south Indian temple to Meenakshi, for example, Shiva is present as Sundareshwara, Meenakshi's consort. At a temple in Benares, Shiva's holiest site on the Ganges River in north India, he is addressed as Vishwanatha (Fuller 1992, 37–38).

Priest purifies the image of Shiva with water, Shiva temple at Yanaimangalam, Tamil Nadu state, India. (*Courtesy of Diane Mines*)

As with the Virgin Mary, one person and yet also distinct in her many manifestations in the thousands of Marian shrines, these Shivas are many and one. Indeed, some Hindus say the same of Vishnu and Shiva, that they are one, Vishnu–Shiva. Many temples have legends explaining how Shiva or Vishnu came to occupy a spot at that particular temple—after a battle, or a great deed, or to become the consort of a local deity. The one-and-yet-many conception is thus basic to Hindu religion, but at the same time a feature that at least some Hindus find requires an explanation, usually in the form of a legend.

The same unity-and-multiplicity is found with respect to the Goddess, Devi, who exists in multiple forms. As Durga, she fights off demons; as Kali or Shakti, she is power itself and is supreme over the gods, often shown trampling on Shiva. She manifests herself as not only a consort of one of the great gods but also in local forms, where she not only brings powers of heat, and sometimes disease but also fertility—all being forms of her power, shakti. In south India each local settlement has its own tutelary goddess, known by one name throughout that region. Thus, in much of Tamil Nadu (Fuller 1992, 43) the goddess is Mariyamman: Mariyamman of this place versus Mariyamman of that place—different goddesses and yet also localized forms of the single goddess.

But Hindus also have local, lesser deities, and because Vishnu and Shiva, concerned with the cosmos, are unlikely to respond to requests for assistance in everyday matters, worshipers turn to local, lesser deities, such as the god-queen Meenakshi mentioned earlier, or still lesser deities worshiped by particular castes. These deities may be ghosts who were enshrined as a means of controlling their powers, or they may be humans, who can be especially relied on to respond to human problems. A village might have dozens of these deities, worshiped by different persons or groups, or approached for particular problems.

Thus, some Hindus identify little goddesses, matas, who occupy various places in the environment—in a thorn bush, under a three-brick "altar," in a house. They are associated with the Goddess, and their festival is on her day of Navaratri, but they are distinct from her. As with the kami of Japan, these deities are many and mostly unnamed. They may enter certain men and women and possess them, and through this possession heal a child or answer a vexing question posed by a fellow-villager.

At the other end of the deity scale, modern religious and political movements have adopted specific gods as symbols for their idea of an all-Hindu India. A prominent Bengali nationalist, Bankim Chandra Chatterjee, created a form of the goddess as "Mother India," Bharat Mata (Fuller 1992, 42). In her temple at Benares, she is represented not as a personage but as a map of India—a literalistic fusion of the goddess with the nation and the state!

Do Hindus Sacrifice?

The Hindu ideology best known to the outside world is that of renouncing violence and avoiding eating meat. And yet animal sacrifice continues to be an important part of religious practice, especially, but not exclusively, in eastern and parts of southern India. Goats, pigs, fowls, and, ideally, a male buffalo are slaughtered and offered to deities—smaller animals to lesser deities and the buffalo to goddesses, and in particular to the Goddess in the form of Durga, who slew the buffalo-demon and whose victory is celebrated on Durga Puja or Navaratri (Fuller 1992, 83–105; Hiltebeitel 1985).

Woman cooking *pongal*, a dish cooked from "raw rice" and suitable for Brahmans, to be offered to the "backyard God" pictured to the left, at Yanaimangalam. (*Courtesy of Diane Mines*)

As in most religions where it is practiced, Hindu animal sacrifice is both a substitute for the giver and a gift to the god, a way of both honoring the god and transacting with him or her. Animals are often sacrificed to "hot" deities who bring violence, and particularly epidemic diseases such as smallpox. The offering appeases and honors them, asks for the disease to be removed, and for the deity to protect the sacrificer. The meat offering is a substitute for the sacrificer; it is offered, consumed by the goddess, and then taken back to be eaten as *prasada* ("blessed food," "grace") by those present, who thereby take in the grace of the deity. The deity is responsible for both the disease and the source of grace, and the twinned acts of sacrifice and consumption bring together these two functions.

Although in the term used to denote it, sacrifice (bali) is contrasted to worship with vegetable foods (puja), in ritual practice it often complements vegetable worship. Animal sacrifice may conclude a sequence of worship events, or vegetables and meat may be separately offered to two complementary deities.

How can sacrificial practices continue to coexist with the principles of nonviolence? It is not as if sacrifice is a marginal practice that has somehow escaped the attention of Brahmans. Indeed, in eastern India a Brahman priest often purifies the sacrificial animal before its slaughter (which is carried out by someone else), and the offering may take place at a major temple. One Brahman in west India told the anthropologist David Pocock (1973, 72–73), when asked about the animal sacrifices he conducted on the occasions of foundation-laying for houses, that "of course it's violence (hinsa). So what? You can't have a foundation ceremony without a blood sacrifice, it's essential and that's that." Although he was never present at the actual killing of the animal, the Brahman considered these and other sacrifices to simply be a necessary way of responding to the demands of certain deities.

Buffalo sacrifice was outlawed at independence in 1947, and from time to time the police try to break up sacrificial rituals. Stories circulate (Fuller 1992, 104) as to how officers who made these attempts were rendered blind by local goddesses until they allowed the ritual to proceed.

The Vedic Roots of Indian Sacrifice

Sacrifice once served as the mainstay of Indian religion, of what is often called the Vedic religion that preceded Buddhism and modern Hinduism. Indian religious ideology shows a change from practicing animal sacrifice to renouncing meat consumption (a change that parallels—in quite different form, of course—changes in Jewish ritual practice).

Hindus have available a large number of older sacred works, including the early texts (the Rig Veda and the Upanishads) composed over the millennium 1400–400 B.C.E. and known collectively as Veda, "knowledge"; the two later epics already mentioned, the Ramayana and Mahabharata (conventionally but controversially dated between 500 B.C.E and 400 C.E.); and subsequent treatises on law, state craft, and devotions. Evidence for early sacrifice comes from the four Sanskrit texts called the Vedas. The Vedas consist chiefly of hymns for use in sacrificial ritual; the oldest, the Rig Veda, describes how the world and its institutions were created by sacrificing Purusha ("Man"). The four exemplary, male victims—horse, bull, ram, and he-goat—served as substitutes for human sacrifice, and were killed and cooked.

Agni, the god of fire, is said in these texts to be present at all sacrifices. Fire, today as well as in antiquity, is required for sacrificing even grain and milk products—recall the clarified butter placed onto the fire in household worship, and the camphor flame used at temples. In the Vedas, Agni is described as receiving the sacrifice with his tongue of flame, and carrying it up to the other deities with his smoke. The very first hymn in the Rig Veda (1.1.1) is to Agni:

> "I pray to Agni, the household priest who is the god of the
> sacrifice,
> the one who chants and invokes and brings most treasure."

By the sixth and fifth centuries B.C.E., the older Rig Vedic religion of sacrifice was submerged by new religious ideologies. One important break with this tradition comes with the teachings of Gautama Buddha (563–483) that one must renounce violence.

Buddhist teachings became the religion of state under Asoka (r. 268–239), who constructed a new imperial state in India. Buddhism supplanted the sacrificial religion of the Vedas. But post-Rig-Vedic texts within the Hindu tradition also appeared after 500 B.C.E (in particular, the Upanishads) that deemphasized sacrifice and instead stressed the individual's obligation to adhere to a moral code, the dharma, that forms part of a universal moral and physical order. In this code, every action has its consequences according to the laws of karma, such that one's deeds in this life or in a previous life shape one's present condition. Ideally, one would be able to renounce this life and pursue the goal of liberation (moksha) from the eternal cycle of suffering and rebirth (samsara).

In the first centuries of the common era (C.E.), a new "Brahmanic religious synthesis" developed, with renunciation of violence and sacrifice at its core. Sacrifice continued as a central element in Hindu life, but now as a submerged line of practice under a quite different ideology. Animal sacrifice was now conducted alongside vegetable offerings.

Today, particularly in south India, one may find two deities, side by side, in a temple. One, the dominant one after whom the temple is usually known, receives only vegetarian offerings. The other deity requires, and receives, animal sacrifice. The vegetarian deity's image may be screened from the sacrifice as a sort of insulation. The great gods do not divide into two complementary deities in this fashion; their worship is more thoroughly shaped by the Brahmanic synthesis, in which the great god, vegetarian worship, and vegetarian Brahmans are absolutely superior to all else.

Offerings and Grace

Let us focus on the more common vegetable offerings to deities, or puja. These offerings may take the form of an informal family rite or that of a village temple festival. You may perform puja to ask a favor from a deity (usually a minor deity; greater ones tend to be above that sort of thing), or when you recite sacred Sanskrit texts about the exploits of a goddess, or when you join a group in singing devotional Hindi songs to Krishna.

A relatively simple puja might be focused on the ancestors of a joint family, of parents, sons, their wives, and children (Fuller 1992, 57–82). Here is an example: In a village in Madhya Pradesh, central India, the father regularly worships his agnatic (through males) ancestors in the home. Just before noon he bathes himself, offering some of the water to his ancestors; his wife and sons' wives meanwhile prepare an elaborate meal. He takes a plate of the food, a dish of clarified butter (ghee), and a brass pot with water from the bath, and, in the kitchen, kneels before a piece of flaming cow dung. He sprinkles water around the dung and places some of the butter on the fire. Again he sprinkles water, and this time places some of the food on the fire. After a third sprinkle, he bows before the flame, his hands pressed together, touching his forehead. He then joins his family for their meal. Because some of the food has been offered to the ancestor, all the meal now contains the "grace," prasada, of the ancestors. Homes also contain altars with images of family deities and teachers; women as well as men worship there daily or occasionally.

Here is a second example: In a village temple in the southern Indian state of Tamil Nadu, a priest is ready to honor Meenakshi, the goddess-queen of an ancient kingdom, and her consort Lord Shiva, in one of his many local manifestations. Each of the deities is represented by a two-foot-high movable image, set up in the temple complex and draped with white cloth. Musicians play, and their loud drumming signals the close of each ritual stage. A chanter recites sacred formulas (mantras). The priest purifies the images by bathing them with a series of liquids, including sesame-seed oil, milk, and water that has been infused with divine power through the chanting of mantras. The gods' images are adorned with clothes, jewelry, and flowers, and their foreheads are marked with three stripes of white ash, the mark of Shiva. Food is held out to the deities while water is sprinkled around the offering. The priest waves oil lamps and a candelabra with seven camphor flames in front of the images. People attending the ritual then

Worshiper receives from temple priest as *prasada* a garland that had been offered to Shiva, Shiva temple at Yanaimangalam. (*Courtesy of Diane Mines*)

crowd in to place their hands over the flames and touch their fingers to their eyes, and to accept white ash from the priest to place on their foreheads.

This temple ritual may be reduced or elaborated. The images may be purified with water before the ritual, and at its conclusion butter may be poured onto a flame as a final offering. More foods may be offered, and distributed to all worshipers. Or the ritual may be reduced to a presentation of one camphor flame to the deity, with a plantain on the side as an offering. The reduced ritual is still valid (it counts as puja); the elaborations are not superfluous (they add to what is accomplished).

Forms of offering vary within India and abroad. Major Hindu communities are found in Africa, Europe, and the Americas, and Hindus make up a large proportion of the populations of some Caribbean islands, Fiji, and Bali. Men and women may worship at home or in a temple, where the deity may be an incarnation of a great god, usually Vishnu or Shiva, or a local deity. Festivals all revolve around making offerings to the gods. Festivals vary across India, including the springtime Holi, celebrated in north India to mark the burning of the demonness Holika and the start of the agricultural season, and a sequence of festivals in September and October, in particular the festival of lights, Diwali, a time for welcoming, and escorting, departed ancestors. (The celebration of Diwali at my own university is one of the season's highlights, with students of all religious affiliations lining up overnight to get tickets.)

All forms of offering, simple or elaborate, involve purifying, communicating, and making offerings. Some objects are by their origin pure, such as cow products, from butter to dung to the ash of the dung, and thus can be used in rituals. You can purify something by pouring water over it, thus the importance of bathing, particularly in the Ganges, and sprinkling water at an altar.

Girl with food that she has offered and received as *prasada,* part of an annual offering she makes to fulfill a vow, temple to Murukan, son of Shiva, Pattamadai, Tamil Nadu state, India. (*Courtesy of Diane Mines*)

People and deities communicate through multiple channels: chants, music, words, and gestures. One always shows respect to the gods through the gesture called namaste or pranam, holding the hands together and touching the forehead. It, too, may be succinct or elaborated: a supplicant may merely hold up the hands to the forehead, or may bow down, even touch the feet of the deity. You also indicate respect to other people by drawing on this same repertoire of gestures, and according to how they rank in the social hierarchy relative to you. Through this gesture, you honor "that bit of god which is in every person."

We also see the deities—and they see us. We exchange darshan, "vision," just as we exchange gestures and words. A priest can attribute this power of seeing to the statue of a deity by painting eyes onto its face. This act brings up a critical point about images in India: the image is not the same as the deity, but the deity comes to be in the image, and also, at any one moment, exists in many different images throughout India. Worshipers enhance the exchange of vision by placing a light, especially a camphor flame, by the altar.

These exchanges of vision already imply the commingling of human and divine essences, but this exchange focuses on food. Whatever we do to dress a deity, sing to it, or chant over it, we must feed it. The food may be anything that people eat, but it is always offered to the deity, taken back, and distributed to those present—family, neighbors, or temple-goers. It may simply be placed before the god, or it may be put on fire—"the flame is the tongue of the gods." The consumed food becomes the embodiment of the deity's power or "grace," the literal meaning of prasada, the food offering. Anything that has been placed in contact with the deity and then returned to humans—ash, water, food, or flowers—is prasada, and conveys that divine power to the human partakers.

We can see that puja is most importantly *transaction:* something is given and something is received, and by this event the worshiper takes on something of the divine being.

Reform and Devotional Movements

Opposition to sacrifice was one element in broader movements for religious reform and national self-determination. Some of these movements were influenced by Western rationalist ideas about religion, but the movements also incorporated Brahmans' ideas about proper Hinduism. Brahmans had relegated sacrifice and meat-eating to non-Brahmans, but new movements for reform urged all Hindus to renounce meat-eating (Fuller 1992, 155–203).

Reform movements began in the early nineteenth century with Ram Mohan's Brahmo Samaj in Bengal, which claimed to have discovered a "rational" and monotheistic Hinduism in the Vedas and Upanishads. Indeed, Hindu reform movements share with many Islamic and Christian ones an emphasis on returning to the sacred texts, not as a way of escaping the present but, quite the contrary, in order to rationalize religious practice and purge it of undesirable traditions and superstitions. In the Hindu case, the practices to be discarded included most spectacularly the self-immolation of widows (sati) and the exclusion of untouchables. The still more influential Arya Samaj movement, which spread across north India after 1877, was less radical in its reform agenda, but it, too, called for an end to animal sacrifice as a barbaric incongruity in a religion dedicated to nonviolence. Arya Samaj was dedicated to universalizing the Hindu message and making it accessible to members of all caste groupings—and, indeed, to uniting Christians and Muslims under the banner of Vedic principles.

A different kind of reform comes from the proliferation of Agamic schools, designed to lead priests to memorize the important texts to be used for ritual, those thought to have been produced by Shiva for Shivaite temples (Fuller 2003). These schools produce priests who may be no more expert or adept at performing the physical acts of worship and offering, but who now know what to say during their physical acts. These schools promote the idea that one must learn the content of religions before learning to practice it—an element of reformism that we will find elsewhere as well.

Some reform movements have emphasized devotion, and these movements appeal particularly to middle-class Indians. Urban, middle-class associations bring people together to sing songs of bhakti ("devotion") to gods. Most popular are songs about the exemplary devotion of the cowherdess Radha for the god Krishna. The songs sung in their praise are erotic and religious. These associations provide new ways for urban dwellers to create social forms of religiosity, and in some cases also to maintain religious purity in an urban world of social intermingling—hence their appeal to some middle-class Brahmans.

These devotionalists joined nationalists and other reformers to oppose animal sacrifice. In Gujarat, west India, where Vaishnava (Vishnu-centered) devotionalist movements campaigned against sacrifice, many villagers have simply abandoned the goddesses who demand animal sacrifice. The convergent pressure of these movements has been to flatten out worship: All deities should be treated the same, as vegetarians. Mahatma Gandhi contributed to this pressure, raising his own Vaishya caste's vegetarian dietary code into a universal moral imperative that "Hindus shall not eat meat" (Fuller 1992, 103).

Within the collection of practices, teachings, and ideas called "Hinduism," a tension has persisted between a notion of religion as effective action, where an offering produces a result, and religion as obedience or devotion to transcendent deities. This tension has itself produced some of the diversity of practices observable in Hindu settings, whether in South Asia or elsewhere, and it invokes broader differences about what religious practice really is: obedience to a deity, or actions taken to obtain material or spiritual benefit?

BATHING AT BENARES

The Hindu pilgrim's goal is to enhance his temple experience through journey, to "exchange vision" (darshan) with deities many times in many places. Each site is called a "crossing place, ford" (tirtha) to somewhere beyond; a pilgrimage is a tirtha-yatra, a journey to a ford (Fuller 1992, 204–223).

The prototypical goal is Benares (Kashi, Varanasi) in north central India (Eck 1982). This "City of Light" lies alongside the Ganges, a river said to have descended from heaven to earth. Over seventy landings line its banks, some containing temples to Shiva, who makes Benares his earthly home. Benares has always been an earthly crossing, the place where the old trade route across northern India crossed the river Ganges. As with other places of pilgrimage, it is also a spiritual cross, one where earth and heaven meet. Here the dead may be assisted in crossing over the Ganges to the condition of moksha, liberation from rebirth, the ultimate goal of the Hindu. Here, too, the gods may descend from heaven to earth. Shiva lives not only in the city's many temples, but also in its ground and buildings: "The very stones of Kashi are Shiva," goes the popular saying.

The gods descend and pilgrims cross at many other fords throughout India. Of the thousands of places where Shiva, or the hero Rama, or the goddess Durga have emerged to split rocks or crushed enemies, a few cities are particularly favored. Some are associated with Rama, and in particular his capital at Ayodhya. Others, including several associated with Krishna, are on mountains; still others mark the four corners of India.

Benares is the most widely acclaimed of all, however. To many Hindus it is the center of the universe (as is Jerusalem to some Christians, Mecca to some Muslims, and Beijing to some Chinese), and located directly under the heavens. Benares also encapsulates worship in India: Temples in other parts of India, from the Himalayas to the southern tip of the subcontinent, have replicas in Benares. One may visit these replica temples and exchange vision with their deities without leaving the city. The city has absorbed their power. And in one new temple, the devotion is of "Mother India," Bharat Mata, represented in the form of a relief map inside the temple where the image would usually be. The map shows the major pilgrimage places, which pilgrims can view and thus "exchange vision" with all at once! But this logic of replication also goes in the reverse direction, for Benares is replicated elsewhere in hundreds of temples called "Shiva Kashi" found throughout India (Fuller 1992, 208–209). The deities are here, in this city, because gods and God, the spiritual force behind all the gods, is everywhere. One pilgrim, longing for the black stone dedicated to Shiva found near his own village, remarked: "I miss God."

Benares also attracts pilgrims to bathe in its particularly sacred waters and to cremate their dead. The pilgrim's first duty is to bathe in the river on one of its many landings. Pilgrims bathe in the Ganges to partake of its purifying powers, brown and replete with ashes and bacteria though it is. Indeed, usually they take the popular "Five Fords" trip along the riverfront, where they bathe at each of five landings (ghat). At each stop, the pilgrim recites a statement of intention, that he or she is undertaking this pilgrimage, and if the pilgrimage is made to fulfill a vow or with a goal in mind (which is not necessary), a statement to this effect is added, such as "I am making this pilgrimage in hope of bearing a son." Each stop has stories of kings and gods associated with it, and nearby are temples, or phallic linga statues devoted to Shiva, or even a mosque (Eck 1982, 211–251).

The last bath is taken at the landing of Manikarnika, at the center of the three-mile long waterfront. This bath is the most important. The site has a cremation ground and a large sacred well nearby. Shiva is in the temple, but Vishnu built the well as the world's very first tirtha. And a manifestation of the Goddess or Devi guards the well.

Manikarnika is called the "burning landing" because when seen from the river one sees the plumes of flames from the crematorium located among the temples. Those who die in Benares are cremated next to the Ganges and their ashes are scattered over the waters. Some who die elsewhere have their ashes brought, or even mailed, to Benares. When one's ashes lie on the Ganges, one's spirit crosses over from earth to liberation. But even failing this, pilgrims will say prayers for the dead to ensure that the ancestors will dwell in heaven. So important are these rites that when long-lost ashes from the cremation of Mohandas K. Gandhi's body were discovered nearly a half a century after the event, they were carried to the Ganges to be poured into the waters (*New York Times* January 31, 1997).

Corpses brought here are placed by the river's edge before being dipped into its waters for their final bath and then hoisted onto the funeral pyre. The eldest son circumambulates the pyre, lights it, and when the burning is finished, walks away without looking back. Members of an untouchable caste in charge of the cremation ground throw the ashes into the river, where they are gradually carried downstream.

The religious importance of seeing sacred places and images helps us understand why a rapid bus tour of a large number of sites makes religious sense. Pilgrimage is the major reason why Hindus travel, and they do so by the millions every year, traveling on foot, by bus, or by train. They value the journey itself: joining others in travel, making merit by giving alms, seeing many deities, getting away from normal routines, and experiencing another realm—both another part of the country and a glimpse into the beyond. Hardship may itself be felt as a proof that merit has been earned through the journey, even if it is not explicitly sought out.

Or, pilgrims may choose a bus tour that, without the hardship of journeying on foot, offers a greater number of chances for darshan with deities. The anthropologist Ann Grodzins Gold (1988, 262–298) traveled by bus with a group of pilgrims from northwestern India to the eastern coast of Orissa. The pilgrims were from different castes and came from town and village settings. The villagers included Brahmans (the order or varna associated with the priesthood), Rajputs (traditionally a warrior caste and of the second-ranking Kshatriyas order), and people from farming, gardening, and other miscellaneous castes. The pilgrimage did not erase these distinctions; indeed, the castes stayed apart; "the fact that we were sharing a pilgrimage did not act as a leveler of rank" (Gold 1988, 269).

On the road, pilgrims sang songs about the deities Ganesha and Rama, and about the Sun King, from whom a woman in the song takes darshan each morning. They stopped at one site after another. Upon reaching a tirtha-yatra, they would bathe in the waters, view the images in the temples, make gifts to priests and beggars, and occasionally perform a short offering ritual. They traversed the country where Lord Krishna had spent his childhood and observed darshan tableaux of his babyhood. They made a whirlwind tour of Benares's many temples, which left a colorful blur in their minds. The deepest and most favorable impression was made by the sea. "These Hindus had seen countless icons in their lives," remarks Gold (1988, 284) after one pilgrim, emerging from the famed temple at Puri, said with a shrug that "Well, God is God." But, she continues, they had seen "only one sea."

What did the pilgrimage mean to them? None of Gold's fellow pilgrims thought that bathing in sacred waters would cleanse them of bad deeds. Rather, and in a more diffuse way, the entire experience of getting out of everyday routines, taking many powerful darshans of gods, enduring the hardships of the road, and giving alms to beggars would be good for the soul. Hitting the road and seeing the gods lightens the pilgrim of goods and attachments and concerns, bringing her or him nearer to "the deity within himself." Approaching one's inner divinity prepares oneself for the moment, perhaps in some future life, when one will finally attain release, moksha. "Sweeping the road ahead," suggested one widow.

While some pilgrims thought that pilgrimages causally improve one's chances of eventually achieving moksha, others were more skeptical. One pilgrim told Gold (1988, 288) that traveling and bathing could not effect what God determines, although He would reward giving alms: "From what does moksha come? From his own hand, God's, that's from whom. It does not come from wandering. Whatever you give, in whatever place give it. From this comes moksha. What kind of dharma is dirtying the water? But dharma is giving-and-taking."

In scholarly debates as well, Hindus are of two minds about what pilgrimages get you. On the one hand, some commentators on the classic texts assure the pilgrim that: "Even if a man be a sinner or a rogue or irreligious, he becomes free from all sin if he goes to Benares." But others equally clearly say the opposite, that it is the inner self that must be purified through meditation. After all, observes one scholar, "Fish are born and die in the water (of tirthas); and *they* do not go to heaven."

MUSLIM–HINDU VIOLENCE

During the 1980s and 1990s there took place violent conflicts and riots pitting Hindus against Muslims. The flash point for some of these was located in the northern Indian city of Ayodhya, Rama's birthplace (van der Veer 1994). Ayodhya is a holy tirtha over the holy river Sarayu and a place for the pilgrim to "cross over" from the mundane world to make contact with Rama. Many Hindus claim that Rama was born on a site in the city where the Moghul (Muslim dynasty) ruler Babar built a mosque in the sixteenth century. Moghul rulers allowed Hindus to worship on this site, even inside the mosque compound, and the subsequent Muslim dynasty endowed Hindu temples in the city.

In the twentieth century, relations between Muslims and Hindus deteriorated as in much of South Asia. Hindus launched attacks on the Babar mosque during the celebration of the Day of Sacrifice in 1912, and again in 1934. The situation heated up further after the 1947 Partition and the flight of many Muslims to Pakistan. In 1949, a statue of Rama appeared in the mosque. Hindus and Muslims naturally interpreted this event in very different ways. For the Hindus, Rama had appeared in their midst, giving them a sign to liberate his birthplace from the Muslims. For the Muslims, their mosque had been defiled. Riots ensued, and the army was called in. The government closed the mosque, and it remained closed to both Muslims and Hindus until 1984, when national politics came to a head in the city.

By the mid-1980s there had emerged a strong Hindu nationalist party, the Bharatiya Janata Party (BJP), which garnered support from Hindu nationalist movements and in particular from the Vishva Hindu Parishad (VHP). The VHP was an attempt to create a united Hindu organization. Given India's diversity in religious practices and beliefs, creating a unified Hinduism would be a daunting task. What Hindus plausibly shared, however, was a belief in certain sacred objects and symbols. One was the sacred river the Ganges, and in 1983 the VHP organized a drive to symbolize Hindu unity based on shared water. Large trucks were sent throughout the country, each carrying enormous bronze pots with water from the Ganges. This water was given to villagers en route, and the pots were replenished with water from local sacred sources, symbolizing Hindu unity—and giving the VHP a way to firm up its local support network.

Hindu unity meant opposition to Muslims, and the VHP called for mosques to be removed from several sacred spots, including in Ayodhya. By 1989 the VHP had begun to mobilize support for building a new temple in Ayodhya. In November, just before Indian general elections, Hindus were urged to send or bring bricks for the temple, and bricks poured in—from Hindus in Europe and the United States as well as from throughout India. The VHP was eventually stopped from building the temple by the ruling Congress government, but the flames thus fanned led to massacres of Muslims, and numerous Hindu deaths as well, in northern and eastern India.

One year later, violence erupted again, this time brought on by the political party, the BJP. The BJP joined forces with the VHP in part to oppose the government's plan to reserve a greater number of jobs and positions for lower-caste people. (In its mass support and vote-getting, the BJP appeals most to urban, upper-caste people.) Despite police bans, some volunteers bent on rebuilding "Rama's temple" made it to Ayodhya, where many were killed. In December 1990, to further dramatize BJP support for the Hindu nationalist cause, the party leader L. K. Advani began a "chariot-led procession" to Ayodhya. Perhaps because the Ramayana epic had been serialized on television a few years earlier, Advani decked his party out as Rama's army. His chariot, drawn by an air-conditioned Toyota, was carved and gilded to recall Rama's chariot. He carried the bow of Rama, brandishing it to ward off his enemies. Supporters, marching alongside, were decked out in warrior garb and handed bows as well.

The procession began from a place in Gujarat, west India, widely associated with the tenth-century destruction by a Muslim ruler of Hindu temples. This choice of starting point played up anti-Muslim sentiments. The procession moved across India before being halted in the eastern state of Bihar, where Advani was arrested—an arrest which then led to the collapse of the fragile coalition government. Mass strikes and riots followed; all trains and buses that passed anywhere near Ayodhya were canceled, but nonetheless many people were killed. Then in 1992, supporters of the BJP/VHP rushed to Ayodhya and demolished the temple. The riots that ensued led to over one thousand deaths, mostly of Muslims (van der Veer 1994).

Though religious sentiments were front and center during the campaigns and riots, we would err in thinking of these conflicts as the emergence of "primordial" or traditional sentiments in opposition to the nation-state. The conflicts and riots developed out of a modern idea of a Hindu nation-state, itself with roots in colonial constructions of religious communities and postcolonial electioneering. In the nineteenth century, the British created the idea of a "Hindu majority"—and a Muslim minority—through the census. They interpreted these categories as native Hindus versus foreign Muslims. This view has had an effect on later Indian notions, promoting the idea that one's primary loyalty is as a Hindu to the "Hindu community" or as a Muslim to the "Muslim community," rather than to local communities or leaders. And it was on these notions that Advani and other Hindu nationalist leaders drew to mobilize support for Rama and anger against Muslims. Although Hindu–Muslim tensions predate colonialism and independence, the kind of violent religious nationalism exhibited in this case (and in many other places) is to a great extent a modern creation.

And for most Hindus, as for most people, anywhere, these nationalist claims have little to do with the practical bases and emotional pulls of religious practices. "Ram is supposed to dwell in our hearts, not in a temple," said one north Indian villager (quoted in Fuller 1992, 261). "We don't need to learn about our dharma from politicians seeking votes."

EXPLAINING WHERE VIOLENCE OCCURRED

If the violence just described was justified in religious terms, we still need to understand why it occurred in some places and not in others. Here we can make a more general point about how not to understand violence and how to approach an adequate account of its eruption.

All too often, when violence breaks out anywhere in the world, we look for causes in other features of those places. When, during the 1990s, Hindus and Muslims attacked each other in some cities of India, we might be tempted to say that, in general, the coexistence of Hindus and Muslims leads to conflict and violence. But in most places, most of the time, in India as elsewhere, religious and ethnic groups live side by side in relative peace. Religious or ethnic differences do not, of themselves, cause conflict (Bowen 1996; Brubaker and Laitin 1998). What we need to do, then, is to look for other features of social life that promote conflict.

Ashutosh Varshney (2002) asked precisely this question of Hindu–Muslim violence in India. Varshney begins by noting that 95 percent of the Indian population was not involved in the riots of the 1990s, that riots took place in cities, not villages, and that a handful of cities account for most of the deaths. These cities are scattered throughout India. Rioting and deaths are thus not generally true of India or even of urban India, and not of one region rather than another. To uncover the factors accounting for violence, Varshney ingeniously paired cities of similar size and religious composition, but where one member of the pair did experience violence and the other did not. He then looked for differences that consistently occurred in these pairs, differentiating the high-violence city from the low-violence city.

It turns out that the best predictor of nonviolence in Indian cities is the degree to which stable, formal civic associations, such as trade unions, professional organizations, or political parties, brought Muslims and Hindus together on a regular basis.

How did the presence of such ties lead to peace? In places with such associations, peace committees were formed at the threat of riot, and moved across communities, preventing escalations and contradicting rumors. Without them no one stopped the escalation of violence and often intra-community associations fanned the flames. Now we can understand why rural areas would be much less likely to have such conflicts: in villages, everyone already exists in a kind of civic association, with everyday encounters on a face-to-face basis and village organizations dealing with justice, farming, and politics.

Varshney's study thus emphasizes the importance of what Robert Putnam (2000) has called "bridging" social capital, meaning the networks and friendships that reach across social divisions, over "bonding" social capital, meaning networks that strengthen solidarities within social groups and which thus may harden social divisions. This analysis highlights the proximal social mechanisms that prevent or dampen down conflict between Muslims and Hindus. But one may then ask: Why did some cities develop these civic associations and others not? The answer to this question lies in a deeper history, one that refers us back to the activities of the Congress Party and other political organizations in the 1920s. Congress tried to develop such interreligious associations in India's cities, but only succeeded in those places where the major divisions in the city were along lines other than that of Hindus versus Muslims.

Let us see how these pathways developed in two cities: Calicut, a trade-oriented city in the southern state of Kerala, and Aligarh, an industrial city, known for Aligarh Muslim University, located in the northern state of Uttar Pradesh. In the early twentieth century, conflicts among Hindu castes dominated social life in Calicut, making it possible for the Congress party to create political, trade, and cultural associations that brought together Hindus and Muslims. When Hindu–Muslim violence did break out in 1921, the Malabar riots, it did not spread. In Aligarh, however, tensions between Muslims and Hindus dominated civic life and prevented the formation of civic intercommunal associations. Instead, politics replicated religious affiliations. The middle-class Hindu Arya Samaj movement developed influence within the local Congress Party, whereas the Muslim League, born of Aligarh Muslim University, championed the creation of Pakistan and thus was in opposition to Congress's ideal of pan-Indian union. During the 1990s' violence, politicians and peace committees worked across religious lines in Calicut to prevent local riots, but *within* religious communities in Aligarh to fan the flames.

The historical causal chains thus run from long-standing lines of cleavage within each city, to the political creation (or not) of crosscutting civic associations, to the contemporary activities of those associations, to the presence or absence of major Hindu–Muslim violence. One intriguing by-product of this analysis is that strong political tensions between upper-caste and lower-caste Muslims, as in Kerala, help to dampen down conflict between Muslims and Hindus. Class conflict thus promotes peace! Varshney's study reminds us that when we seek to understand conflict (or for that matter any social phenomenon), we need to look at cases where it is absent as well as those where it is present, lest we erroneously attribute causality point to a spurious variable, one that co-occurs—"innocently," we might say—with conflicts, but that also co-occurs with peace. And, to stay with our concern in this text, religious difference is one such variable. Because we often see and hear about instances of conflicts between groups of different religious affiliations, we often mistakenly think that religious difference "causes" conflict.

But if we examine a wide sample of cases for the causes of intrastate conflicts, we do not find such an association. One such analysis (Fearon and Laitin 2003) found that religious or ethnic diversity does not predict a greater likelihood of conflict. (The best explanations seem to be conditions favoring insurgency, such as rough terrain and a weak state.)

Conclusions

We have traced developments in Hindu practices, from early sacrifice, through the Axial Age transformations into a religion based on obedience to religious commands, to the complex imbrications of colonial rule, nationalism, and violence in today's India. We can usefully compare the Hindu transitions with those of Judaism. We can also draw on the analysis of religious violence to critically examine claims made about violence attached to other religions. Religion does not explain conflict, but religious allegiances may be a mobilizing force.

Films to See

I would recommend a film on Indian pilgrimages, such as *An Indian Pilgrimage: Kashi.* I also use a film on American Hindu devotions: *Puja: Expressions of Hindu devotion*

Imagery and Faith:
Focus on Worldwide
Catholicism

At least starting with Augustine of Hippo (354–430 C.E.), the Catholic Church set out to do two things that one might think near-impossible: to spread throughout the world, and to do so all the while maintaining a strict hierarchy centered on the Pope. What follows is a very specific window into this truly transnational religion, approached here through its use of imagery in promoting faith.

RELICS AND IMAGES IN CATHOLICISM

Catholic imagery has been based on different types of meanings and multiple associations in the minds of worshipers. When we think of Catholicism, we usually think of elaborate representations of saints, Jesus, and Mary. But Catholic images also draw on other kinds of symbolic meanings to become powerful, multivocalic foci for worship and social life.

A famous example is the Shroud of Turin, a cloth held in Turin, Italy, since 1578 that has on its surface an image of a bearded face, said by some to be the image of Christ. The shroud is venerated by many Catholics, not just because it is a likeness of Jesus but because they think that it was produced by direct and miraculous physical contact with his face, in a fashion similar to the process that produces a photograph; we call this an "indexical" relationship between the sign and that for which it stands. This claim of direct contact generates in many pious people a sense of direct communication between the viewer and Jesus. The arguments about the Shroud's authenticity turn exclusively on this issue of contact, not on its resemblance to Jesus. In fact, the iconic qualities of the image on the Shroud, its resemblance to conventional ideas of what Jesus looked like, are precisely what skeptics point to when they claim that it is only a painting. The relative weight of iconic and indexical meanings is thus of great importance for the Shroud's religious status.

Christianity is, after all, founded on ideas of contact and physical presence, in particular the idea of incarnation, the embodiment of godliness in tangible form as Jesus Christ. The central ritual of the Church is based on the worshiper's direct contact with Christ through eating and drinking of his body. Holy Communion enacts the miracle of the Eucharist, in which ordinary bread and wine are consecrated by a priest and, at that exact moment, turned into the body and blood of Jesus. This countlessly repeated miracle parallels the sacrifice Jesus made of himself for the sake of humanity.

The idea that Christ is in the bread and wine was popularly assumed for centuries. It was finally codified in 1215, when the Fourth Lateran Council ruled that consecration does indeed convert the ordinary substances into Christ, or, in the technical language of the Church, that "transubstantiation" takes place. The Council also ruled that Christ was whole in every particle of bread and wine "under two species." This second idea, called "concomitance," responded to the concern, evidently widespread at the time, that when one dropped crumbs of the bread on the floor one was dropping bits of Christ, that chewing the bread was chewing his bones, and so forth.

The History of Relics and the Host

Relics preserve the history of religious miracles through their own history of physical contact with sacred persons or events. They make up an important part of the history of Catholic religious objects—which is also the history of Catholic politics. Religious objects have mediated between the community and the church hierarchy, between local and universal perspectives, between religion and the state, and between cultures.

The central Church ritual, communion or the Eucharist, is based on a miracle of incarnation. In the early Church, the central ritual of communion or the Eucharist was carried out in a way that was expansive and collective. The priest said "Peace be with you"; the lay worshipers responded in kind and exchanged the "kiss of peace" with each other (men with men, women with women). Worshipers then brought forward their sacrifices of bread and wine to be consecrated by the priest. Communion was thus the Church partaking of Christ and worshipers communing with each other. Christianity drew on its Jewish roots but also broadened them. Communion widened the bounds of the Jewish seder to include the entire community beyond the realm of one's family and friends. Communion, thus, modeled socially the universal ideal and ambition of the Church (Bynum 1987, 48–69; Feeley-Harnik 1981, 107–168).

Communion recreates for a brief moment what is in effect a direct physical link to Christ. But Christian churches also relied on other kinds of sacred indexes to maintain a sense of connection among churches and among worshipers. As the Church expanded in Europe and North Africa, it created a network of churches under the control of Rome. Churches were built on shrines or as shrines, sometimes near or around cemeteries located just outside city walls, where the buried remains of saints sanctified the ground of the new church. There was a practical consideration at work as well—the belief current at the time was that on the day of Resurrection, the first bodies to be taken up to heaven would be those buried near the body of a saint (Ariès 1974).

A Christian shrine or church usually contained sacred objects, an image or relic that gave the shrine its religious status. A relic was a remnant of a saint—a bone, bit of hair, or an entire corpse—or an object that had been made sacred by contact with a saint (or Jesus). It was movable, and so separate from the place itself. Except in Ireland, where the pre-Christian Celtic veneration of places continued unabated, it was the relic, not the place, that was considered sacred.

Saints' bodies, sometimes partially or wholly mummified, have been favorite relics for churches. In the early churches they were often exhibited to worshipers and pilgrims. Today as well, the faithful consider saints' bodies to be capable of working miracles. Some bodies exude healing fluids, such as a marble sarcophagus in the French Pyrenees that accumulates clear water. Throughout the year the water is collected by individuals and used for healing, and the remainder is pumped out each July 30 at a special ceremony. Soil may be taken from the burial place of a saint and used to heal, particularly in Ireland and the Americas. A small church near Santa Fe contains such a miraculous source of earth. Bones are also used as church relics, today usually contained in elaborately sculpted boxes or reliquaries.

The logic of sacrality through contact reaches beyond body parts and sacred soil. Paintings and statues may acquire sacred status from having once been in contact with a sacred person or object. For example, some paintings of the Virgin Mary draw their religious force from their historical ties to what is called the True Icon (*Vera Icon*) of Mary: a painting said to have been made by Saint Luke and considered to be holy because he, a holy person, painted it, and not because of a property of the representation itself. Paintings that are understood as copies of the True Icon are found in Italy, Spain, and most famously in Poland. Our Lady of Czestochowa, the national icon of Poland, is a painting of a dark Madonna, and it is housed in a fourteenth-century church in the southwestern part of the country. It is the object of the major pilgrimage for Polish Catholics. It is said to derive from the Saint Luke painting. Other paintings or statues are touched to the painting in Czestochowa, and from that contact derive a special (indexical, we would say) power. Copies of the True Icon become as effective as the original in working miracles. (At least by the sixth century C.E., we find stories of paintings carried into battle to ensure victory.)

Images versus Relics

By the late fourth century, a lively traffic in saints' remains had developed across Europe. Remains were sent as gifts, sometimes stolen from crypts in Italy. This traffic was encouraged by the idea that remains could be divided up, and the saint became present in each fragment (analogous to the idea that Christ was totally present in every fragment of the consecrated bread). As Theodoret of Cyrus proclaimed: "In the divided body the grace survives undivided and the fragments, however small, have the same efficacy as the whole body" (Bynum 1987, 48–53).

During the eighth century, a rapid rise in missionary activity led the Church to develop rules for creating new churches. In 787, the Second Council of Nicaea declared that a new church had to possess a saint's relic in order to be consecrated. The new rule further increased the demand for relics. People began to scour the Roman catacombs for bone fragments that could be attributed to early Christian martyrs, and a virtual flood of these bone fragments poured forth from Rome out into northern Europe. The hunger for relics turned major discoveries of bones into momentous cultural events. In the early ninth century, Saint James' bones were discovered in northern Spain, and the site of this discovery, known thereafter as Santiago de Compostela, became the third most important Christian pilgrimage site after Rome and Jerusalem (Nolan and Nolan 1989, 160–171).

The propagation of relics not only expanded the bounds of the Church but also provided a firm spiritual foundation for the empire created by Charlemagne. From the ninth century onward, the oath administered to witnesses was taken on saints' relics, and read: "May God and the saints whose relics these are judge me that I speak the truth" (Rothkrug 1980).

During the early years of Christian expansion, there were no official procedures for evaluating relics, or indeed for canonizing saints. A local church could declare someone to have been a saint and then build a church around him or her. The remains would be disinterred and placed on an altar within the church. If the body was found to be intact, or in the language of the times, "uncorrupt," this condition was attributed to its holy qualities, which had continued to reside in the body after death. (Note that in this tradition intact bodies were signs of purity; by contrast in the Greek Orthodox practices, total disintegration of the flesh is a sign that the soul was received into heaven.)

Many of the relics were, in fact, fakes: countless pieces of wood from Christ's cross circulated throughout Europe, as did chalky stones from the Milk Grotto in Bethlehem said to be colored by milk Mary used to nurse Christ. The market pressures also encouraged theft: One Roman deacon named Deusdona contracted to steal the remains of Saint Peter and to supply them, broken down into small parts, to the Franks. As their authenticity was increasingly doubted, their value declined. (Compare with Gresham's Law in economics: "bad money drives out good.")

The Church responded in two ways. First, it began to exert authority over the status of holy man or saint. It carried out its first canonization of a saint in 993 and gradually gained control over that process. Second, the Church tried to substitute images for relics. Early Christian art (like Islamic art) had been largely decorative. Many people felt that the crafting of human figures would be tantamount to worshiping graven images, a fear inherited from Judaism. In the words of Saint Epiphanius in the fourth century C.E.: "When images are put up, the customs of the pagans do the rest." But popular use of imagery, pictures of saints, developed in the late fourth century and became widespread by the sixth. The Church came to encourage this trend in the interest of promoting universalism. Saints, after all, were many, and their stories often emphasized local miracles and military victories rather than the universal message of Christ that was central to the Church. Basing the legitimacy of a local church on relics underscored the local bases for worship rather than the Church's universalism. To the extent that the Church was able to refocus worshipers' attention toward paintings or statues or other images, it would be able to emphasize the universal figures of Mary and Christ, whose bodies were not available to be relics (Nolan and Nolan 1989, 160–171).

To meet popular objections that only relics were sacred—and the practical point that only relics would share in the resurrection—Church authorities encouraged the crafting of reliquaries: elaborately carved boxes, often with jewels and gold, or statues in the image of a saint that contained minute pieces of the saint's bones. These objects were both relics and images. Images such as paintings or ordinary statues were also said to have had direct contact with a sacred person, or, as in the case of the True Icon mentioned above, to have been painted by a saint, or to have been once physically touched to a painting that was painted by a saint, and so forth, along a historical chain of direct, sacred contact. These efforts drew on popular ideas about contact and sacrality but also promoted universal images.

A More Hierarchical Ritual

The Church's efforts to emphasize its universal message over local sacrality gained momentum in the eleventh, twelfth, and thirteenth centuries, a period of growth in the political power of the Church. What we often call the "age of faith," or, in reference to the great energies devoted to church crafting throughout Western Europe, the "age of cathedrals," also saw a shift in the relationship of people to the institution of the Catholic Church. Rome began to exercise more control over local churches, and in each church priests recast their role vis-à-vis lay persons in a more hierarchical or vertical way.

The eleventh century saw the growth of powerful monasteries, which resisted secular control, the struggle for priority in spiritual affairs over the kings, and the Crusades, which began in 1096. The church became "monumental" in several senses. Doctrine was systematically formulated, most notably by Thomas of Aquinas (1225–1274); the great cathedrals of northern Europe were built; and Rome was able to exert ever-greater control over the behavior of individual churches. It was the great age of pilgrimages to such sites as Santiago de Compostela in northern Spain, to England's Canterbury Cathedral, the site of Thomas à Beckett's assassination in 1170 (and the destination of the pilgrims in Chaucer's *Canterbury Tales*), and the first great Holy Year pilgrimage to Rome in 1300. Many religious orders that promoted pilgrimages—Dominicans, Franciscans, Carmelites—were founded during this period.

All these developments added to the general sense of a Christiandom united by movements of people, the mobilization of popular energies, and a central, controlling power lodged in Rome. In worship itself, these changes led to a great focus on the priest's role, as the representative of Rome, over and against that of the people. Communion and other aspects of liturgy became more centralized, more in the hands of priests and monks. Saint Thomas himself wrote that priests engage in the communion of Eucharist on behalf of others. Saints once had come from the popular ranks, even after canonization became a Church monopoly. Now male saints began to be drawn entirely from the ranks of priests (Bynum 1987, 53–69).

The ritual transformation that most evidently represented this change was the shift from *receiving* communion to *seeing* the Host. By the twelfth century, churches had begun to offer communion less frequently and instead to concentrate the attention of worshipers on Christ's presence in the bread and wine at the moment they were consecrated by the priest. Christ could be seen on the altar and adored there. Physical contact was downplayed in favor of, again, the image of Christ, albeit an image of the Host that had become Christ.

As priests emphasized the "adoration of the Host," other changes were made as well. Elaborate containers for the Host, reliquaries, were made and placed so all could see. Holes were made in some church walls so that even horses could commune by viewing the Host. The Host began to be raised up for general view; this practice of "elevating the Host" first occurred in Paris in 1200. Fifteen years later, Pope Innocent II declared as dogma the miracle of transubstantiation, the change of bread and wine into Christ's body and blood. In 1264, a new feast day, the feast of Corpus Christi, the "body of Christ," began to be celebrated. By the fourteenth century, a new kind of vessel called a "monstrance" ("displayer") was created to display the consecrated Host. As the historian John Bossy (1983) writes, the "socially integrative powers of the Host" were transferred from the mass to the feast of Corpus Christi.

From the twelfth century onward, receiving the Host became something priests did. Already by the eleventh century only priests could take Christ in their hands; others had to receive a wafer directly in their mouths from the priest. The priest had once carried out the consecration of the Host in full view and standing facing the worshipers—after all, in the early church it had been their bread and wine that had been brought to be consecrated. But now the priest celebrated with his back to the people. He took communion for their sake with his back turned. Special "rood screens" were constructed to seal him off from view. In these churches communion became a mystery, a miracle that touched only the priest, who was sometimes venerated precisely because of his privileged contact with Christ. In the words of Saint Francis of Assisi (1181–1226): "He touches Christ with his own hands."

The "two species" of the Eucharist were now treated differently. When communion was offered to worshipers, the consecrated cup was sometimes withheld and ordinary wine substituted. The reason given was that the church feared that a careless parishioner could spill Christ's blood. The wafer now became the focus of this longed-for ritual act. It became a strongly held symbol of the unity of the church and of fears of its being desecrated. Anti-Semitism was often voiced as an accusation that someone had defiled the wafers. Stories circulated of Hosts turning to flesh and bleeding in protest against misuse (for example, by sorcerers) or in an effort to warn churchgoers against an approaching danger (Bossy 1983; Bynum 1987, 53–69).

The Host increasingly became a symbol of the church, rather than a source of redemption for the individual person. Some people protested this church control; these protests included demands to receive the Host "in both species," that is, as consecrated wine and bread. A hunger for the chalice and communion intensified, and ordinary people, particularly women, experienced religious devotions and ecstasies as sensing and eating God.

The central objects that located or founded a church also shifted from relics of saints (with the Host as one of many relics) to the general adoration of Christ and the Virgin Mary. In 1150, the pope rejected his former title, "Vicar of Saint Peter" for the new one, "Vicar of Christ," shifting his grounds for authority from the presence of Saint Peter's body in Rome (a relic), to his direct receipt of authority from Christ.

The Church also began to desacralize relics and to replace them with images of saints. It developed the idea of the saints and Mary in the "communion of saints," or "the unity under and in Christ of the faithful on the earth, the souls in purgatory, and the blessed in heaven." Dead souls were enrolled in the new brotherhoods and orders as part of this universal community. This idea of the communion of saints allowed one soul to pray for another. Helping other souls through prayer became a major activity both in church masses and at pilgrimage sites.

Christ Incarnate

The Eucharist, as it became the focus of church activity, is best seen as Christ's incarnation—it gave the worshiper direct contact with Christ. Recall that it was only in 1215 that the Church proclaimed as dogma the eucharistic miracle of transubstantiation. The elevation and adoration of the Host began about then, and Corpus Christi followed in 1264.

These steps addressed what we can think of as the problem of Christ's relics (Nolan and Nolan 1989). After all, according to the church, Christ ascended to heaven

40 days after the Resurrection, leaving no body behind to generate relics. In popular opinion, he did leave some relics behind: his blood and the earth that was touched by it; pieces of the cross and nails from the cross; garments worn during the Passion; the Shroud of Turin. The church gradually accepted the idea that his milk teeth, foreskin, and spilled blood could, in theory, have remained on the earth even though he ascended to heaven. Popular pressure was for more relics of Christ, perhaps because of the more difficult access to Christ through communion.

The steps taken by the church in the thirteenth century to promote the worship of Christ may have been responses to this pressure. The doctrine of transubstantiation not only provided an officially sanctioned opportunity for direct contact with Christ incarnate but it also allowed numerous further miracles, at least in the popular imagination.

Sometimes the Host was said to really become flesh and blood. In at least one shrine, in Lanciano, Italy, are small pellets of blood and a strip of flesh said to have been formed from consecrated bread and water during the celebration of Mass by a doubting monk in the eighth century. Bavaria has a shrine where sacramental wine, spilled on an altar cloth in 1330, formed an image of Christ. Christ could now become real, the object of worship (and sometimes even contact) within a more hierarchical church (Clark 1967, 410–434; Nolan and Nolan 1989, 216–290).

MARY AND MARYS IN EUROPEAN SOCIETIES

The church has also promoted the adoration of Mary as Mother of God. This "cult of Mary," which undoubtedly draws on older images and ideas of a virgin mother goddess, first appeared in Turkey in 431 and expanded across the West. At some point a popular idea developed that Mary herself was conceived in her mother, Saint Ann, free from the original sin that everyone else receives by virtue of Eve and Adam's transgression in the Garden of Eden. This idea of "immaculate conception"—conception in the womb free of original sin—spread on a popular level but was not immediately accepted by the church. In the sixteenth century, the Council of Trent declared Mary free of original sin, but only in 1854 did Pope Pius IX declare as dogma that Mary indeed had experienced an immaculate conception.

Marian worship on a widespread, dominant scale dates from about the eleventh century and is due in part to the activities of the Cistercian order, all of whose churches were dedicated to Mary. The popular idea that she was bodily assumed into heaven was officially proclaimed as Roman Catholic dogma in 1950. As with Christ, this doctrine meant that very few relics could be claimed to be available: her sash and veil, a few strands of hair, pieces of milky rock white from her breast milk—slim pickings indeed. More popular were images of Mary, usually as the Pietà, holding the body of the dead Christ.

This image of Mary drew, intentionally or not, on much older notions of a virgin mother goddess who bears a child who later dies in her arms. Inanna, the Queen of Heaven in Sumerian mythology, gives up her son Dumuz to torture and death. The Egyptian Isis nurses and mourns for her son Osiris. (And as we shall see, such pre-Christian images are found in the Americas as well.) Pietà images are especially popular in German culture (70 percent of these images are found there), probably because of the long-standing tradition of imperially founded nunneries. Around 1300, Dominican nunneries began to promote the image of a suffering Mary, a representation of their own direct, personal, at times erotic relation to Christ. The pietà image generally becomes popular during times of sadness and war, because it provides an especially apt image for suffering. For example, many new pietà statues were carved after the trauma of the Thirty Years' War in the seventeenth century, and again after the First World War in our own century (Nolan and Nolan 1989, 191–209).

The numerical analysis of to whom a shrine is dedicated shows how sharp has been the change from saints, usually based on relics, to Mary, always based on a shrine image. In the period before 700 C.E., 92 percent of the shrines formed were dedicated to a saint. That percentage dropped to 20 percent in the "high medieval" period of 1100–1400, and has remained about the same since. The percentage of shrines dedicated to Mary was only 6 percent in the early period, but 73 percent in the high medieval period, and level ever since. Shrines dedicated to Christ have remained at below 10 percent throughout the common era (Nolan and Nolan 1989, 155).

Marian Apparitions and Modern Life

Over the past 150 years, Mary has taken on a new identity in the popular imagination, less as Mother of God and more as an individual who intervenes on behalf of individuals in modern, industrialized societies. She begins to appear in the sky to troubled individuals and to offer solace and instructions. Hundreds of such apparitions have occurred in the past two centuries, but seven were approved by local bishops and gained international attention; these occurred in France, Belgium, and Portugal. These visions include the apparitions of Mary at Lourdes, France, in 1858, and in Fatima, Portugal, in 1917. Both were eventually accepted by the Church; most others were not (Zimdars-Schwartz 1991).

In 1917, in Fatima, three children reported a series of appearances of Mary. One of the three, Lucia dos Santos, later discussed in her memoirs her religious upbringing as well as the events surrounding the apparitions. Lucia took her First Communion at age 6 rather than at the usual age 10. She tells of how the priest told her to kneel before the image of the Virgin and to ask Mary to take care of her heart; when she did so, she saw the statue of the Virgin smile at her, and she heard the Virgin say she would do this for her.

Lucia was 10 when, together with her friends, she saw the Virgin appear on six separate occasions. Mary spoke to the children, saying that they had come from heaven, and that she would take them to heaven. All three children reported hearing the same words. Others came to the place where the apparitions occurred. Some of these other watchers reported seeing a small cloud appear over the tree where the children saw the Virgin and the tree's branches bend.

At the time, the children reported hearing three secrets from the Virgin. In 1941, Lucia revealed two of them. The first concerned the nature of hell. The second was a prediction of war unless the world became devoted to her Immaculate Heart. Mary further specified that her followers would need to secure the consecration of Russia to her Immaculate Heart and to convert that country's people. If such steps were not taken, she warned, the world would be annihilated. Lucia wrote the third secret down, and in 1957 her note was sent to Rome. In 1977 Pope John Paul I visited her (Zimdars-Schwartz 1991, 190–219).

Other reported sightings of Mary followed in the late 1940s, and manifested the worries held by many European Catholics about the general loss of faith and the

The Pieta by Michelangelo, (Italian, 475–1564). C. 1498–99, Marble. The Metropolitan Museum of Art, John T. Johnson Collection, Funds from Various Donors, 1895, 95.40.5

coming clash with communism (Christian 1984). Marian apparitions provided a kind of collective catharsis, a general focusing and release of these tensions, and have continued unabated into the twenty-first century.

One of the more recent apparitions has been occurring frequently on a hill just outside Medjugorje, Bosnia, since June 24, 1981. Six children saw Mary on the first day; since then more than 20 million pilgrims have come for a view. The children moved the place for their visions into the church, until the bishop ordered them out. Since then some people have reported nightly appearances of Mary (Bax 1991; Zimdars-Schwartz 1991, 220–244).

Pilgrims to the site often return with stories of personal conversions and healing. One Irish woman described her visit as at first just a "holiday." But then she saw the concrete cross that had been built on the site, and saw the sun behind it turn blood red, with a small piece of the sun missing after it had moved behind the cross. On her return home she attended a funeral mass and when the priest held up the Host she saw it as "the image of the sun at Medjugorje and I really believed in the presence of Christ—the sun had been the Host with the piece missing like when the priest breaks off a piece—and I was overcome and cried."

Medjugorje spreads. An Italian family bought a white plaster statue of Mary during a visit to the site, and in February 1995 reported that tears of blood had begun running down the statue's face. Crowds began to flock around the family's home near Rome, and the local bishop had the statue removed. CAT scans of the statue showed no hidden mechanisms; laboratory tests showed the blood to be human; DNA matches with the family's blood were proposed. In the end, the bishop became a believer in the miracle (Bohlen 1995; Warner 1996).

In the United States, an American returned home to New Jersey after a visit to Medjugorje in 1988 and reported that he had been healed of a back injury and hearing loss. Mary appeared to him in his backyard six months later, stating that she had work for him to do. In August 1992, he publicly announced when the second visit would happen, and 8,000 people came to witness the event. About the same number showed up in Cold Spring, Kentucky, when a local pastor predicted an apparition (Steinfels 1992).

The Church has been ambivalent about the apparitions. On the one hand, the apparitions encourage popular faith, and their message is in keeping with the interest of the Church. On the other hand, the apparitions occur outside Church control; they challenge the hierarchy of the Church by providing an alternative source of religious enthusiasm to worship in churches. The Church has given official recognition to the apparitions at Lourdes and Fatima, but not to Medjugorje. There, the local Franciscan fathers, who for centuries functioned as the parish priests, have encouraged people to enjoy the special grace provided by the visions. But the Bishop of Mostar, whose district includes the apparition site, has forbidden worshipers to make the pilgrimage and has called the apparitions "theatrical practices." His ruling has been part of an effort, backed by Rome, to wrest control of the parishes away from the friars, and Mary, here as elsewhere, has become a key token in that struggle (Bax 1991).

Religious sentiments in Catholic Europe have always included some resentment of the power and privileges of the clergy. For those visitors to the sites of apparitions who share these anticlerical feelings, the Church's rejection of visions makes the visions even more attractive. The apparitions are usually reported from marginal regions during times of trouble—Bosnia and southern Italy in the 1990s, economically depressed parts of the United States in the 1980s, post–war Western Europe.

Spanish Shrines

As the Church increasingly came to promote Mary as an object of worship, people have made her into a local protector as well as the symbol of Church worship. In agrarian parts of northern Spain, each valley of herders and farmers contains a number of small villages. Each village parish has its own active patron, whose image is in the village shrine and who protects the village as a whole. The shrine may be an isolated chapel at the boundary of several villages or the parish church at the village center.

In the Nansa river valley studied by the ethnographer William Christian (1989) are 14 such village parishes. Of these 14, one has Christ as its patron, three have the souls in purgatory (*Las Animas*), and 10 have a particular aspect or realization of the Virgin Mary.

Thus, in one village the patron is Our Lady of the Queen's Ford; in another, Our Lady of the Light; in a third, Our Lady of the Bridge; and so forth. Each shrine, each saint, protects a particular territory, a "territory of grace," acting as patron to its inhabitants.

Some of the shrines to Mary are located at boundaries of villages or herding districts. In one district, three statues of Mary are found right at the meeting point of three villages' lands, each facing back toward "her own" village. In local stories, the Virgin is said to choose the spot where the shrine is to be built. In one case a shrine was placed at one spot, but during the next night two oxen came and moved the shrine up the hill to the place where she had desired it to be placed. The Virgin keeps the sheep at home, say local herders, and calls down divine power to protect them. William Christian calls the shrines "energy transformation stations."

One of these patron saints is Our Lady of the Queen's Ford, the patron of the village of Tudanca. The shrine is located in a chapel about five kilometers behind Tudanca. The saint's name comes from a nearby ford, but the patron is also identified as Our Lady of the Snows, an aspect of Mary recognized by Rome and given a feast day, August 5. Over the centuries, celebrations of the feast day have waxed and waned, depending both on the level of nearby economic activity and on the attitude of the parish priest toward the shrine. At present, the shrine is visited only by some Tudanca residents; in other decades, however, it has received attention from people of other villages as well. The shrines patronize and protect their own villages, but they may be appealed to by anyone, especially people from neighboring villages.

In the first week of May each year, the image is carried down from the isolated chapel to the parish church in town, where it remains for three months and is the center of church devotions. The period when the image is in the church is also the period of plowing and sowing the fields, and its presence may once have been intended to protect the crops. On the feast of Saint James, July 25, the image is carried in a procession of all the villagers, organized in the following order: children first, then lay men, priests with the image, and women. The villagers thus see themselves as a whole composed of parts. "The villagers for once in the year," writes Christian (1989, 70), "see the village as a social unit, abstracted from the buildings and the location that makes it a geographical unit."

It is the women who continue up the mountain to the shrine and re-place the image in its resting place. A woman keeps the key to the shrine, and when, on the patron's feast day of August 5, a mass is held at the mountain chapel, even the priest has to wait for her to unlock it. In other villages, too, special roles in the devotion to the patron are handed down from mother to daughter. Women are the chief worshipers at the shrines.

These patrons are firmly planted in the rural landscape. Each exists and acts on her own. Some of the names are unique, appearing nowhere else in Spain. Others do appear elsewhere, but then are given additional local tags to emphasize their individuality. A shrine to Our Lady of Carmel, for example (a common name for the Virgin Mary), will become Our Lady of Carmel of Cosio, or of another village. These shrines have existed for a long time; some may pre-date Christianity (when clearly they were known and worshiped by other names).

From the standpoint of these "localized devotions"—worship activities focused on a local manifestation of Mary or a saint—Mary appears as many distinct patrons woven together into a general community of sainthood. The Mary of the Snows is an agent distinct from the Mary of the Bridge, despite the fact that all are manifestations of the one Virgin Mary, Mother of God.

Many in One

Recall a similar feature of worship in India. In south India each local settlement has its own tutelary goddess, known by one name throughout that region. So throughout the state of Tamil Nadu, for instance, one finds Mariyamman of this place versus Mariyamman of that place, as different goddesses and yet also localized forms of the single Goddess (Fuller 1992, 43). This many-in-one is quite similar to that found in northern Spain and elsewhere in the Catholic world. Mary exists in both a highly local and a universal form at the same time in the consciousness of some Catholics, as does Mariyamman (the similarity in names is a coincidence) for Hindus.

The parallel stops at the level below Mary, however, for whereas Hindus have local, lesser deities as well as the major gods, most Catholics have only the major textually sanctioned figures to turn to—Mary, Jesus, and saints. In Catholicism the distance between God and local, reachable spiritual beings is mediated by proliferating the number of forms of Mary, and remaining entirely within a restricted pantheon.

There is an irony in the fact that the adoration of Mary was encouraged by the church as a way of unifying and centralizing devotion, but that Mary became the vehicle for differentiated devotions and representations. Of course, even in the universal language promoted by the church one has different names or "advocations" (different forms of a deity) of Mary, a variety that in part stems from the very images the church used: Mary of the Immaculate Conception, Mary the Pietà, Mary of the Assumption, and so forth. Mary is shown in different contexts, and these images become signs of different attitudes or emotions. But it may also be that relying on replicable images as the basis for Catholicism (or any other widespread religion) itself gives rise to this dual character, the "one Mary or many Marys" problem. Once the image takes on any local roots, it begins to be thought of as the image of a local individual. The very replicability of the image poses a problem: Is it one or many? If one, what are all these other objects? If many, are they different actors?

A Japanese Comparison

Just as Catholics have created "many Marys" to provide nearby, accessible images, so have Japanese men and women turned to deities called "bodhisattvas," or "Buddhas-to-be." These deities, who put off their transition to Buddha status in order to help humans, are nearer to hand when one needs help than are the distant Buddha figures.

Especially important among them is the goddess Kannon, who ensures fertility and safety in childbirth. In India, Kannon was the many-armed god Avalokitesvara, and became (via a gender change) the important Chinese goddess Kuan-Yin, and then the Japanese Kannon. The bodhisattva Kannon is capable of rescuing people from earthquakes, fires, shipwrecks, witchcraft, execution, snakes, and thunderbolts, and of giving a woman the child she wishes, son or daughter. She is sometimes depicted as associated with the waterfall because of her power; her many arms are likened to the many different streams of a fall. She also has lesser spirits called *jizo* who act as guardians of travelers and children. Travelers often set out small statues of jizos on their routes, and especially when they are embarking on a pilgrimage. But one may also set out a jizo as a concrete way to take a request to Kannon. These requests are most commonly either for forgiveness for having had an abortion or for safe delivery of a child.

Kannon is both a single goddess and many personal guardians. She can be depicted as a single protector, or as highly individuated. For example, a shrine to Kannon at Kyoto is supposed to contain "60,000" statues of Kannon, one for every face there is in the world; this way of representing her is supposed to guard all the people of the world.

A debate has arisen in Japan over the practice of buying jizo statues from a temple to atone for an abortion. Setting out the statue is thought by some to help guide the fetus across the river that separates the world of life from the world of death. These statues, called "water child jizos" (Mizuko jizo), are sold by Buddhist temples for several hundred dollars each. More than 2,000 temples now offer these statues, and temple leaflets warn that failure to appease the spirit of a dead fetus could lead to cancer, heart disease, back pain, rebellion of children against parents, and so forth—a list long enough that anyone who fails to buy the statue will surely find herself victim of the fetus's spirit. Is this service a way the temple serves people's needs or, as one magazine called it, a "business of terror"? Some women continue to visit the statues for years or even decades after the abortion, dressing them up against the cold or pouring water over them to quench their thirst (WuDunn 1996).

Generalized Devotions

Let us return to the Nansa valley of northern Spain, where shrines to Mary, each with her own distinct name, proliferate. Priests coming to Nansa have had to work with the shrines already in place, but sometimes they have tried to discourage devotions at the shrine. In most cases, devotions go dormant, reappearing a decade or more later. The priests bring with them devotional emphases of the papacy, and often of a religious order.

Jizo statues set out to atone for an abortion or to ask for safe delivery of a child, at the shrine to Kannon near Kamakura, Japan. (*Courtesy of John Renard*)

They try to refocus the devotions of villagers on universal images of Mary and Christ, rather than on her specific manifestations, what one priest called approaching "to the main doors, not the side doors" of the church.

These "generalized devotions," in William Christian's (1989) phrase, are based on the circulation and promotion of images that are highly interchangeable. In homes and in parish churches one finds paintings, lithographs, pamphlets, calendars, and rosaries. These images could be substituted easily one for the other, or replaced with a new batch, without any loss of religious significance. The images are usually of Mary as the Madonna, and sometimes of the cross, and they are used in family devotions. They often come from Rome or from the religious orders currently in papal favor, and their propagation and use is intended to underscore the universality of the Church. For example, the Dominican brotherhoods have promoted the devotion to the Holy Rosary at home using personal rosary beads. The brotherhoods teach people that saying prayers with the beads will allow one to share in all the prayers said by all members of the brotherhood throughout the world. Other orders, including Capuchins and Passionists, have provided images of saints or Mary that correspond to their particular religious emphases.

Mary has played her part in efforts to reuniversalize worship, both through her interchangeable pictures in homes, and through her role in regional and national shrines. Many villages in the Nansa valley have been visited on trips to the regional shrine to Mary, which was approved by the Vatican in 1954, on the hundredth anniversary of the papal proclamation of the Immaculate Conception.

Jesus, Mary, and the Nation–State

Of particular importance in changing local worship practices has been the devotion to the Sacred Heart of Jesus, begun in 1673 when a nun in Paris had visions of Jesus Christ in which he urged her to devote herself to his heart as a symbol of his love for humankind. But it was not entered as general feast of the church until 1856, when it quickly became an image, to which popes and rulers tried to rally the faithful. In 1899, Pope Leo XIII consecrated the world to the Sacred Heart of Jesus, and King Alfonso of Spain did the same for Spain in 1919, with the backing of a conservative government. Images of the Sacred Heart entered the Nansa valley about that time as well (Christian 1989, 84–85).

Because of its association with the political right, in the 1930s statues commemorating the Sacred Heart became symbols of the Nationalist forces, the right wing fighting under Franco to topple the government. The national monument to the Sacred Heart was frequently "executed" by the Loyalists, and pictures of the ruined monument were circulated by Franco's side to rally Catholic support.

Elsewhere too, the Sacred Heart of Jesus became a symbol of conservative governments. In late-nineteenth-century France, the relation of a largely Catholic people to a secular state (and largely secular capital city) was a continuing source of tension. In 1871, many Parisians rose up against the Thiers government, in part because of the state's capitulation to Prussian forces. The government, which had fled to Versailles, brutally suppressed the uprising, known as the *Commune,* and regained control of the city. Shortly thereafter, in an attempt to underscore the central place of the church in French life, the government constructed the magnificent church on the hills of Montmartre called Sacre Coeur—Sacred Heart. Though much loved by tourists (and many Parisians), the association between the building and the suppression lives on in the minds of many on the left. (I happened to be living in Paris in 1971, the year of the Commune's centennial, and I witnessed Sacre Coeur being pelted with tomatoes and stones.)

At the same time, images of Mary surface as symbols of national resistance. In communist Poland, the national shrine of Polish Catholicism dedicated to Our Lady of Czestochowa has for centuries been associated with national resistance against foreign conquerors. The Polish Primate under communist rule, Cardinal Wysynski, mobilized the nation around the shrine image, beginning with the rededication of the nation to this "Queen of Poland" in 1956, and following with hugely successful annual pilgrimages of the shrine to every single town in Poland.

The state's use of religious imagery underscores the changes in how the Church represents itself. In the ninth century, a person was sworn in on relics as the clear chain of direct contact to local sources of sacrality. By the late nineteenth century the state was staking its claim to loyalty on images of and devotions to Mary or, in particular, to Christ. Christ seems more immune to the differentiation process that has made Mary many. Indeed, the role of Mary in Catholicism as an emblem for emphasizing local identity goes far beyond Spain.

Conclusions

We have traced the changing religious and political roles of saints, Christ, and Mary in Europe from the beginning to now. On the one hand we have the idea of the unchanging and centralized message of the Catholic Church and on the other the changing emphases in worship and images, and conflicts between the hierarchy and local worshipers.

For Debate

In North America and Europe we often discuss religion as a matter of individual choice, but for most of Catholic history (and in different ways for other religions) priests have seen obedience as an obligation. Moreover, most churchgoing parents have not left the choice of religion up to their children, but taught them so they will follow the same faith. To what degree can and should ideas of choice play a key role in religious lives, vis-à-vis ideas of obedience and discipline? How do you see this issue in your own religious traditions; what are the moments of choice and what are the moments where choice is not available?

Films to See

The forthcoming film on the Virgin of Guadalupe by Joe Eszterhas promises to be controversial; in the meantime there is Santiago Parra's *Guadalupe*.

Transatlantic Religion

From Chapter 9 of *Religions in Practice: An Approach to the Anthropology of Religion*, 5/e. John J. Bowen. Copyright © 2011 by Pearson Education. Published by Prentice Hall. All rights reserved.

Transatlantic Religion

Although we often speak of "globalization" as a late-twentieth-century process, in fact people have been moving across long distances for centuries, carrying new ideas with them.

The history of religious innovation across the Atlantic is an important case of these often neglected trans-state socio-religious networks. Catholics in Mesoamerica appropriated the symbols of the Church into their own cultural frameworks and political struggles. Africans forcibly brought to the Americas as slaves developed new images and religious practices based on West African religions, but in the guise of Catholicism. But these peoples in turn shaped later developments of religions in Europe and Africa, just as Africans today are reshaping older churches in Europe. By looking at these phenomena as elements in a field of "transatlantic religion," we can see that religions cannot be studied only within the nation-state context.

MARY IN MESOAMERICA

The nurturing and tragic image of Mary has served as a particularly powerful figure in translating Catholicism into other cultures. Not only are there universal resonances with her story, but one also finds very specifically similar stories about a sacred and virgin birth or an assumption to heaven in other cultures.

The story of Mary in the Americas exemplifies the logic of religious syncretism, or the blending of two or more traditions. Syncretism occurs when people adopt a new religion but attempt to make it fit with older ideas and practices. The process usually involves changes in both or all of the traditions. Japanese religious history is virtually defined by syncretism, as Japanese have combined elements from Chinese Confucian political ideology, Buddhist teachings and practices, Christian ceremonies, and the older practices called Shinto. Places already sacred before Christianity became the sites of shrines to Mary. When this happened, the meanings of these sacred places changed, because now they no longer were simply local sacred spots but places that tied local worship to the broader Catholic religious tradition. In the Spanish case, for example, images of Mary in the shrines were carried to the common parish church for feast-day worship. But the meaning of Mary was also changed, in that she became locally specific and concerned with rendering assistance in local affairs, and not just a remote semi-deity. (More examples of these changes in the meaning of Mary are offered later.)

The Virgin of Guadalupe

In Mesoamerica, today's Mexico and Guatemala, the Mary of Guadalupe has served as a symbol of nation and people, sometimes in opposition to foreign rule. During and after the Spanish conquest of the region (from the mid-sixteenth through the late seventeenth century), the native Mayan people of eastern Mesoamerica organized rebellions. These rebellions soon incorporated the symbols of Catholicism, reworked in Indian terms. The insurgent movements often included figures anointed as Christ or king. In some cases, villagers were visited by the Virgin Mary, who then instructed them to start a new church organization. She would leave proof of her visit in the form of an image that she created either on cloth or as a statue (Lafaye 1976; Wolf 1958).

In the two most influential cases, both from the sixteenth century, the Virgin revealed her image to a peasant (in both cases he was named Juan Diego). The first apparition, in which Mary left her figure on a cloak, took place in 1531 in Tepeyac near Mexico City and became known as the Virgin of Guadalupe; the second, known as the Virgin of Ocotlan, occurred about 10 years later in Tlaxcala state, when Mary imprinted herself on an *ocote* tree.

The Virgin of Guadalupe was to become the master symbol of Mexico. The Mexican War of Independence was fought under her banner, and her shrine at Tepeyac became the major Mexican shrine. In the official story of the events, the Virgin addressed a Christianized Indian, Juan Diego, 10 years after the Spanish conquest of the area. The Virgin commanded him to go to the archbishop of Mexico and tell him that she wished a church built in her honor on Tepeyac Hill. Juan Diego tried twice to win the archbishop's approval, but was unsuccessful. Mary then performed a miracle. She told Juan Diego to gather roses in a dry spot where roses never grew, and then to present them to the archbishop. He did so, but when, standing before the archbishop, he unfolded his cloak, there appeared from inside, not roses, but the image of the Virgin miraculously imprinted on the cloak. The bishop immediately acknowledged the miracle, so the story goes, and ordered a shrine built on the spot where she had appeared.

This particular spot was not, however, a random choice. It had once been the site of a temple to the goddess of fertility Tonantzin. Tonantzin, Our Lady Mother, is associated with the moon, as is Guadalupe's image. Indeed, for at least the next 50 years worshipers called her Tonantzin as well as Guadalupe, and this still is the case in parts of Mexico. Stories about Tonantzin continue to be told in Mexico: In one, she intervened when God wanted to punish his children, by challenging him to try to produce milk so she could nourish her children.

These associations or "syncretism" are not unique to the New World, of course. In Spain, there probably were pre-Christian deities where now there are shrines. In Ireland, statues of the Virgin are often erected in spots formerly considered sacred because of an unusually shaped rock formation or a sacred grove. And in the Church of

Saint Germain in Paris, a black image of the Egyptian goddess Isis was displayed as the Madonna until 1514.

Guadalupe and Mexican Resistance to Spain

In later centuries, rebellions against Spanish control frequently formed around cults of the Virgin Mary. In 1721 in Cancuc (Chiapas), the Virgin appeared to a young girl and asked her to place a cross in her hamlet, build a chapel around it, and offer incense. A local Mayan leader then claimed to have ascended to heaven where he spoke with the Virgin Mary, Jesus Christ, and St. Peter, and was told that the people were to appoint their own officials and no longer needed the Spanish. This man, Sebastian Gomez, then appointed bishops and priests, all using the symbols of the Catholic Church.

Devotions in the local church had already become "localized" in the sense in which we used the word earlier: Worship focused on locally specific images of the Virgin that were understood as protecting the village. Services consisted of giving offerings and prayers to these advocations of Mary and to other localized saints, rather than addressing prayers to God. Gomez and his followers now renamed Cancuc "Jerusalem" and referred to the Spaniards as "the Jews who persecuted the Virgin Mary." Although the movement was suppressed, it illustrates the ways in which local opposition to Spanish rule was elaborated in what were once the conqueror's own images, the sacred images of Catholicism itself. By choosing Mary and the saints as key images, those local movements that did not reach the stage of open rebellion managed to insulate themselves (and popular religious practice generally) against charges of heresy. The Spanish Inquisition investigated these religious movements and looked for evidence of idolatry, in particular prayers said to images that asked them to directly heal illnesses. The Indians whom the inquisitors interrogated denied that they acted in this way, claiming that they merely appealed to the patron saints and to the Virgin Mary for help. Because the Spanish Church accepted as legitimate both the cult of the patron saint and the possibility of visitations by the Virgin, the inquisitors were unable to find solid ground to prosecute Indian religious leaders (Lafaye 1976).

Why was it the Virgin Mary (and not Christ) who became Mexico's national symbol? The answer is in part due to the way the Church itself portrays Mary and Christ, and perhaps in part due to local family dynamics. The Virgin is associated with struggle and life in Mexico, while Christ is associated with defeat and death. On the religious plane, these distinct associations stem from the crucifixion of Christ, on the one hand, and the nurturing role of the Virgin, on the other. The anthropologist Eric Wolf (1958) argues that on the family plane, the associations grow out of the distinct sentiments the child forms toward his or her mother and father, in both Indian and Mexican families. The child experiences a paradise of closeness to his or her mother, and sides with the mother in her struggle against domination by the father. Mary thus brings out a wealth of early pleasant memories; Christ, the object of struggle. Sentiments formed in the family are expressed in the culture through the symbols of the Virgin and Christ.

On the plane of politics, the Virgin Mary, in the specific form of the Virgin of Guadalupe, is associated with the struggle against Spanish military and religious colonization. Many Mexicans interpreted Guadalupe as the goddess Tonantzin who has returned to liberate Mexico. This interpretation follows an indigenous logic of cyclical history, in which gods depart only to return later. Mexico appears as a new paradise, to which came the Virgin to herald independence. In a seventeenth-century text, the Virgin of Guadalupe is linked to the woman portrayed in the Revelation of John, "arrayed with the sun, and the moon under her feet, and upon her head a crown of twelve stars," and who is to realize the prophecies of Deuteronomy. Not coincidentally, the image of the Virgin of Guadalupe in the shrine today is adorned with a sun and moon and the 12 stars.

The Virgin of Guadalupe thus links family (mother), politics (liberation), and religion (salvation). Against the background of these linkages, we can understand how it was that in 1810 the patriot Father Miguel Hidalgo y Castilla began the revolution for Independence with the cry: "Long Live the Virgin of Guadalupe and down with bad government." The political and religious associations have continued in full force into this century. In the early twentieth century, the church, trying to render more uniform the devotions of the faithful, attempted to replace the Virgin of Guadalupe with the Sacred Heart of Jesus from Rome. This attempt was perceived in Mexico as an effort to supplant a Mexican figure with a European one, and it was strongly, and successfully, resisted. And in 1996, the Bishop of Guadalupe, speaking to a reporter in Italy, declared that he considered the peasant Juan Diego to have been a mythical figure (*St. Louis Post-Dispatch*, September 7, 1996). The remark led to his immediate removal from office!

TRANSNATIONAL RELIGION: AFRICA AND BRAZIL ACROSS THE ATLANTIC

The example of Guadalupe and Tonantzin suggests that religious imagery can be effective in translating a new religion into an older cultural and religious context: Mary made sense to Mayans who already venerated Tonantzin. Sometimes this process involves a literal translation across deities. Such is the case for religions found in the Americas but derived from West African religions. In Brazil, Cuba, Haiti, and elsewhere, Catholic deities provided useful cover for slaves who wished to continue to practice their own religions, but had been forbidden to do so. As this need for subterfuge decreased, Americans have been free to explore both the African roots of the traditions and the appeal these traditions have to a wide range of Americans, including those of European descent. Known now by the names *Umbanda, Candomblé, Santeria,* and *Voudun,* these Afro-American traditions have formed a distinct religious stream alongside, though at times intermingling with, Catholicism (Murphy 1994).

Yoruba religious ideas and practices, in particular, shaped the development of Candomblé religion in Brazil, with its center at Salvador de Bahia, but Yoruba religion itself was shaped by people returning from Brazil (Matory 2005). The case of the Black Atlantic shows us that even as African images and ideas became the basis for New World religious creation, there also emerged a transatlantic network of men and women who shaped developments on both continents.

The slave trade brought large numbers of African people to the southern and central portions of the Americas as well as to the colonies in North America. Slavery lasted longer in the southern regions; until 1888 in Brazil. Many of the Africans were taken from what is today Nigeria and Bénin. In particular, Yoruba people were brought to Brazil and Cuba, and Fon people were brought to Haiti. Slave traders and slave owners tried to wipe out cultural traditions and mixed slaves from different regions, as an effort to prevent Africans from organizing rebellions (Walker 1990).

Because slave-owners prohibited the practice of African religions, some Africans translated ideas and deities of West African religions into the images and language of Catholicism. Slavers thought that they were imposing Catholicism; Africans understood that they were preserving older traditions. In Brazil, these traditions today are called Umbanda and Macumba in Rio de Janeiro and Candomblé in the northeast region of Bahia. They combine, in different proportions, African qualities, especially in Bahia, and Brazilian innovations, especially in Rio, with Catholic imagery and ideas from a Euro-Brazilian movement called Spiritism.

In Rio, a woman presides over services in a small storefront center called the Spiritist Tent of Granny Maria Antonia of the Congo, one of many places to which people come to worship and seek help from the spirits (Guillermoprieto 1990). In this center, as in many others, there is a particular "patron" spirit, Granny Maria Antonia. She is understood to be a woman who was born in Africa and was brought as a slave to Brazil, where she died. She is of a recognizable type of Afro-Brazilian spirit, the "Old Black Woman." Also exhibited at the center are statues of Christian figures: the Virgin Mary, Jesus, St. George (of dragon-slaying fame), and others. Each resembles corresponding statues in, say, European Catholic churches. But each also corresponds to an Umbanda deity called an Orisha, and can be traced back to its original in Yoruba society, West Africa. Today people freely offer the Orisha as well as the Catholic name for each image; a century ago any but the Catholic identity would have been strongly denied to outsiders.

In this schema of cross-religious translation, God is Olorun, the creator of the world. The image of Jesus is also identified as Oshala, the creator of human life. Saint George, depicted slaying a dragon, corresponds to Oshossi, the hunter god, and St. Lazarus, protector of lepers, to Omolu, a deity governing disease. Mary is identified with Yemanja, the mother of some of the other Orishas. Furthermore, and here note the parallel with our Spanish valley, other Orishas who are mothers are also identified as manifestations of Mary. These maternal deities are associated with the water and sea as well.

The lifting of the veil surrounding this momentous project of religious translation was not followed by the crafting of new, original statues. In Yoruba and Umbanda thought, the Orishas have no concrete form; they are forces and principles rather than personages. Thus, the process of rendering African deities in Catholic form added a new visual and individuating dimension to worship, and the Catholic images remain as foci for Umbanda worship. The identification extends to ritual occasions as well. People observe the Catholic feast days that apply to their "translated" deities, but do so in a way that corresponds to the Afro-Brazilian meaning of the deity. For example, Yemanja (Mary) is identified with the sea, so people flock to the sea on the Catholic feast days for Mary and once there, they offer gifts to Yemanja, wading out into the water and letting the sea carry them away.

Umbanda and Candomblé in fact bring together three religious traditions. Alongside of Catholic and Yoruba religions is the doctrine of Spiritism or Kardecism, popular among the elite in Europe and Brazil in the late nineteenth century and today adhered to by millions in Brazil, either as part of Umbanda and Candomblé or on its own. Spiritism provides a means of healing people from physical and mental afflictions. The doctrine attributes a wide range of events in the material world to the desires and actions of spirits. Sometimes spirits possess people, and when they do, they can cause the person to suffer illness. Specialists can communicate directly with these spirits, ask what their wishes are, and restore the person to health.

Afro-Brazilian Trances

In Brazil today, healers draw on these Afro-Brazilian religion traditions to carry out their art. In Macumba sessions (Richeport 1985), trance is employed in varied settings to aid in healing. In sessions involving "professional mediums," specialists sit in a separate, cordoned-off part of a room. They are dressed in white and are already in a trance. They each have special "spirit familiars" with whom they communicate. Patients deliver to the staff slips of paper containing their questions; usually the questions are about their own illnesses. The mediums then ask for answers from their spirit familiars and relay these answers back through the staff. These sessions are calm, although sometimes a supplicant will slip into trance, and in such cases he or she may be approached about becoming a medium. A second type of session involves mass trances. Dozens or hundreds of people gather together for evenings of trance, dancing and music, and consultation. These large-scale sessions also employ mediums, but they walk and dance around on the floor, mingling with other people who wish to attend. Rather than having personal spirit familiars, all the mediums cycle together through several standard spirit types during the evening. Each type represents both a familiar cultural figure of the Brazilian environment and a kind of emotion. When the mediums are possessed by the "old black slave" spirit, they sit, smoking pipes, and dispense this old man's wisdom to those attending (who are often relatives or friends). When they take on the flashily dressed woman called *Pomba Gira,* they are seductive and loose, enjoying this break from normal behavioral restrictions. When they are a child, they scamper about eating candy. (There is also an Amazonian equivalent of these sessions, in which Indians act the role of whites, drink champagne, and act terribly refined.) Use is also made of trances at clinics for the mentally ill. Patients are encouraged to enter a trance state and act out their emotions and frustrations; often they, too, take on stereotyped roles such as those mentioned previously.

Umbanda in Rio

Umbanda was in fact born as a revolt against the elitism of Spiritism in Rio (Brown 1986). By the 1920s, Spiritism had become a highly intellectualized and European-oriented set of practices. Lighter-skinned Brazilians (Brazilian color coding of individuals contains many categories, from very dark to very light, rather than a simple black/white dichotomy) controlled the séances. They were speaking with the likes of Voltaire and Plato. If an Indian spirit appeared, possessing one of their own, they would refuse to allow him to speak.

In 1920, a middle-class Rio man, Zelio de Moraes, suffered an illness that left him partially paralyzed. His father, a real estate agent, was a Spiritist and took him to his group for healing. There he was visited by the spirit of a Jesuit priest, who revealed that the illness was spiritual, and that he had a mission, which was to found a truly Brazilian religion that would be dedicated to the worship and propitiation of Brazilian spirits. These spirits included *caboclos,* spirits of Brazilian Indians, and *pretos velhos,* spirits of Africans enslaved in Brazil.

Zelio received additional messages from other spirits. The "Indian of the Seven Crossroads" told him the new religion would be called Umbanda. Zelio then did as he was told, and founded the first Umbanda center, today called the "Mother House." This center, the Spirits' Center of Our Lady of Piety, attracted a largely white and middle-class clientele. But the spirits that spoke through the participants were those of Indians and Africans, giving them the voice denied them by the Spiritists. The movement grew rapidly, attracting a diverse range of participants.

The social and political role of these movements has changed dramatically in this century. At first tolerated, it was repressed as heretical in the 1930–1950s by the Catholic Church, with support from the Brazilian state. State repressions began to loosen in the 1960s, and since 1970 people have enjoyed relative freedom to worship openly. The initial reason for this tolerance was political, as politicians seeking office sought support from the large communities of Umbanda-Candomblé followers. But the change has also been motivated by social and cultural changes (Walker 1990). In the past 30 years, many Brazilians have sought their "roots," and some, including many of lighter skin color, have found them in the links back to Africa. Many of these people, mostly of the middle class, have found these links through the experience of possession by an African spirit. In doing so, they have moved away from the Catholicism that once was virtually required of those seeking high social status. Being known as follower of Umbanda or Candomblé is no handicap to political office, and participation in the movements can be combined with a range of political and social doctrines. The Brazilian Secretary of Public Works in the 1980s, for example, called himself a "Marxist-Spiritist," believing in both reincarnation and Marxist-Leninism.

These movements have also become part of a broader popular culture in Brazil. On New Year's Day, the major newspapers in Rio run the Umbanda seers' forecasts for the next year. In Bahia state, the home of Candomblé, pop singing groups have risen to the top of the charts with songs based in Candomblé; new wave filmmakers have drawn on the Orishas for their subjects, as in the popular film *The Amulet of Ogun*. The Orisha named Esu, who controls roads and pathways, was adopted as the patron deity of all communications facilities, and a statue to him stands in front of the post office in Salvador, Bahia's capital (Murphy 1994). The urban poor are drawn to these movements. Many of Rio's poor people live in squatter settlements called *favelas*. For them, "survival calls for imaginative solutions, and Umbanda is nothing if not the triumph of imaginative thought," writes the reporter Alma Guillermoprieto (1990).

Let us return to the Granny Maria Antonia center mentioned earlier. The center is located in a two-story house located in a lower middle-class neighborhood in central Rio. A black woman named Stella Soares runs the center. Stella, a former nurse, insists that all who attend don white uniforms; this measure makes everyone more nearly equal, she says. Certain specific spirits visit the center and possess those who attend its services. They are the spirits of individual Indian and African people rather than Orishas. They include the Indian of the Seven Crossroads, the Indian of the Coral Cobra, and the "Indian who tears up tree stumps with his bare hands." They speak, they embody the local identity of black and Indian Brazilians, and through the experience of being possessed, the worshipers can experience several identities, several sides of themselves. Her clientele not only includes dozens of mainly white, middle-class initiates, who go into trance, but also many very poor black clients. "Once they have changed into their white clothes," she says, "you cannot tell the difference."

Are these religions part of Catholicism? Catholic priests call on people to abandon Umbanda, claiming that it has nothing to do with Catholicism, and some practitioners (probably an increasing number) consider themselves to be followers of Umbanda and not, or no longer, Catholics. But many other Umbanda followers claim status as

Catholics. They point to a number of close relationships between Umbanda practices and Catholicism. The images in worship are all Catholic. Some Candomblé priests require initiates to be baptized Catholics before they can join in the rituals. The story of how the first center was founded also underscores the connection with Catholicism—it was, after all, the spirit of a Jesuit priest who commanded Zelio to open up his center. Catholic feast days are observed, and many Umbanda practices reinforce the link to the Catholic Church. For example, on August 16, the feast day for Saint Lazarus, Umbanda priestesses drive by churches where the mass is held and sprinkle popcorn on all so that they will receive benefits from Omolu, the deity associated with the saint.

As we saw earlier, Catholic images, and especially the image of the Virgin Mary, have served to mediate translations of religion across vast social and cultural divides, first within Europe, and then out across seas with the expansion of the Church. But the very capacity of the image to carry multiple meanings—what we have called the multivocality of the image—has allowed subordinate groups to contest the dominant meanings. Spanish villagers insist on their own Mary's capacity to protect and nurture; Mexicans, of the Virgin of Guadalupe's role as a national symbol; Brazilians, of Yemanja/Mary's powers over the sea; Christians throughout the world, on Mary's willingness to appear to them and to deliver messages of hope and struggle. Each set of claims to Mary is asserted over and against official counterclaims that underscore the unity of Mary and Christ and the single authoritative voice of Rome.

In this example, transnational Catholicism appears not as a single set of ideas and practices, but as a set of contested images, and, in the case of Afro-Brazilian religions, as part of a contested legacy of religious survival and creativity.

THE BLACK ATLANTIC

But in the nineteenth and twentieth centuries, Brazilian-born men and women traveled to West Africa and helped shape the development of religious practices in Nigeria (Matory 2005, 46–72). Following uprisings in Brazil in the mid-nineteenth century, thousands of people were able to return to West Africa, and most of them gravitated to the now bustling seaport of Lagos. The British encouraged the immigration of these and other people into West Africa, and there they began to build up a new sense of Yoruba identity. The cultural nationalism that developed in Yorubaland at that time included a sense of the superiority of Yoruba religions, and this sense was then carried over to Brazil in the late nineteenth century. Thus, what some had thought to be "survivals" of West African ideas in Brazil in fact were brought to Brazil as part of a continual traffic across the Atlantic by African-Brazilian men and women.

The Brazilians developed a notion of religious purity that was absent from the Yoruba side of the Atlantic. Matory (2005) chronicles how by the 1930s traders working the route between Lagos and Bahia were nourishing a Brazilian appreciation for "pure African" goods (good for trade) and religion (good for prestige, and thus for trade). Afro-Brazilians began to "purify" Candomblé of what they saw as accretions from Catholic or other influences. In particular, the head of a Bahia Candomblé temple, Mãe Aninha, was able to successfully claim that her knowledge of African practices made her version of Candomblé more pure and authentic. She was able to jump to the top of the Bahia hierarchy through these claims. (A second wave of "purification" of religion came in the 1980s when Nigerian religious experts visited Bahia.)

Because of this new concern with purity, Candomblé incorporated into its central practices a concern with ritual cleansing that is not central to Yoruba practices. Contemporary Yoruba practices emphasize maintaining health through restoring the balance of elements within the body. Candomblé healing, by contrast, emphasizes expelling polluting elements from the body (Matory 2005, 128–133). The deity Esu may have been adopted as the patron saint of communications, given his position at crossroads and thresholds, as mentioned above, and he is the guardian of the centers, but because of his liminal position he is also responsible for introducing disorder, and can be bribed into bringing disease and misfortune. Cleansing an afflicted person of these misfortunes requires using products thought of as "pure African" such as kola nuts. Thus, the transatlantic production of notions of African purity has reshaped the practice of healing.

The same logic has been at the heart of ideas that link Brazilian identity to Africa. Celebration of the African roots of Candomblé was a way for Brazilian cultural leaders to oppose the dominance of the United States. And beginning in the 1980s, increased, and often state-financed, trips by Brazilian Candomblé priests to Nigeria and reciprocal visits by Nigerian priests have led to a movement to recognize the independence of Candomblé from Catholicism and its place in a transatlantic network and history of religions. As Matory (2005, 152–181) shows, these transatlantic affiliations by no means diminish attachments to nations and to territories. Brazilian nationalism increasingly is based on transatlantic memories and connections. Conversely, the houses (or "nations") of Candomblé are rooted in specific parcels of land in Brazil.

Indeed, Matory's (2005, 177) affirmation that "diaspora is therefore better described as a *pluralization* of territorial identities than as an abandonment of them" serves well in examining other transnational projects as well. With Muslims in Europe, where far from developing a deterritorialized or new sort of transnational citizenship, one sees men and women developing citizenship projects in two or more countries.

BLACK CARIB RELIGION IN AFRICA, HONDURAS, AND NEW YORK CITY

Now let us follow another story of movement, diaspora, and transformation of African religions across the Atlantic, this time centered in the Caribbean, on the Antillean island of St. Vincent (Johnson 2007). This story concerns the people now known as Garifuna, historically as Black Caribs. During the 1500s and 1600s, Africans arrived by many means on this island: some surviving shipwrecks, others fleeing slavery elsewhere in Caribbean. St. Vincent had native peoples on it already, and these "Yellow Caribs," as they were called in Western accounts, fought with and to some extent mixed with the newcomers, the "Black Caribs." The latter developed lucrative tobacco and sugar trade with French and British settlements elsewhere and resisted enslavement and colonization from either power. They fought with British forces for control over the lucrative plantation lands, but by 1800 had been defeated and deported to an island off Honduras. Spreading along the coast, they lived alongside native groups and settlements of Africans who had arrived by way of other Caribbean islands. During the first part of the twentieth century, the expanding banana economy provided work for many Garifuna, but by the 1960s, with the decline of banana production and the opening up of immigration to the United States, tens of thousands of Garifuna left the Honduras, many migrating to New York City.

Garifuna in Honduras and in New York engage in religious practices that draw in varying mixtures from Africa and the Caribbean. In Honduras, ritual focuses on fulfilling obligations to deceased members of the community. Shamans (*buyei*) lead people through a hierarchy of such rituals, starting with a burial ritual, and followed by a mass a year later (but only if the ancestral spirit requests it), the more elaborate *chugu* later on, and, only if required, a large ritual called the *dügü*, which even far-away relatives must attend. Shamans engage in divination to determine whether any or all of these higher-level rituals need to be carried out. As more and more Garifuna emigrate to the United States, *dügü*s are held more and more often, probably because they provide the best way to bring the dispersed family together.

As the ethnographer Paul Johnson (2007) points out, the Garifuna think of themselves as located in a diaspora—but with "diasporic horizons" depending on where they live. Honduran Garifuna think of St. Vincent as their origin point, and this perspective orients toward a shared sense of being Caribbean people, with much in common with other native American peoples and a memory of their struggles against the British. The thousands of Garifuna living in New York think about Honduras but they think even more about Africa as their homeland, and they find more in common with others who see themselves as of African origin.

Honduran shamans draw on a range of saint and spirit figures that resemble those we discussed for Brazil. Against the malevolent spirits they seek the aid of Catholic saints, including the Virgin Mary. But the local spirits are never thought of as coming from Africa; they are more likely to come from St. Vincent. The shamans feature figures of ships on their altars, and rest on hammocks during the major rituals—both ships and hammocks bring to mind the peaceful conditions once enjoyed on St. Vincent, by contrast to the sufferings of the deportation. Africa is absent from this repertoire of symbols. Shamans diagnose lingering illness that does not respond to other treatments as indicative of possession by ancestors, and curable only by holding a large-scale ritual, usually a dügü.

New York shamans have developed their craft in a different direction: as one member of a family of Caribbean religions that include Candomblé, Santeria, Voudun, and Cuban Palo Monte. Shamans have fit into a new semiotic niche, one in which Afro-Caribbean spirits rule the roost. Some of the Cuban or Brazilian spirits are very useful. As one Garifuna shaman in New York told Johnson (2007, 129): "The Garifuna ancestors, they're family, but they can be slow; the muertos [of Cuban Palo Monte], you have to watch out, because they eat *everything*, but they work fast." The New York shaman sees his "family" as one part of a much larger clan, all members of which are available to help out. This makes these men and women conscious of a shared African identity which links them to others who have arrived in the United States by way of Brazil, Cuba, or Haiti. Indeed, some may become initiated into one or more of the other Afro-Caribbean traditions, and always have one or more helper spirits from Africa: Kongo, or Yoruba, or even African American spirits.

These identifications take Garifuna in two directions. First, they borrow particularly from the Santería set of Afro-Caribbean ritual practices associated with Cuba. But they learn these practices mainly from Puerto Rican practitioners of Santería, mainly because there are many more Puerto Ricans living in New York City than there are other Caribbean peoples. So, much of what the Garifuna learn about African deities and rituals comes by way of Cuba, and then by way of New York Puerto Ricans!

Second, Garifuna have become black: that is, they identify with others of African descent as well as being labeled as "black" by white Americans. African identity movements in the United States have highlighted Yoruba religious traditions and in particular their deities, or Orishas. The Orishas figure in most Garifuna shamans' altars as they do in those of Cuban and Puerto Rican shamans working in New York. Now, all this might simply mean that these groups identify with the Yoruba, or with western African societies more generally, not that they identify themselves by a racial term such as "black." And yet it is very difficult for dark-skinned immigrants to the United States to avoid being classified as "black" by whites: race works as the overarching way of categorizing other peoples. Sometimes Garifuna will foreground other horizons of their identities, as when they joined 1992 protests against celebrating Columbus's arrival, and did so as Amerindians, or when they joined electoral coalitions in New York City politics as Hispanics. But on a religious plan, shamans assert their specifically Garifuna identity by highlighting their African ties, not those of Amerindian or Hispanic heritage. What the shamans emphasize is the African diaspora that joins them to Haitians, Puerto Ricans, and Cubans, but this emphasis then leads them to self-identify as black, not as Hispanic or Amerindian (or Honduran). In other words, a religious means to emphasize distinction highlights African ties, which in the race-over-all American identity framework means that they are black.

Conclusions

In this chapter, we concentrated on one transnational space and some of the religious movements and practices found therein. The Atlantic turns out to be a pretty complex space: for the Garifuna living in New York, the relevant horizons for thinking through religion and healing are a changing diasporic network involving Africa and the several major sources of religion in the Caribbean. For many Brazilians, those horizons include native peoples, Africans, and Europeans. For many Mexican Catholics, they include both Mexican history and global Catholic networks and institutions. You can easily think of other such transnational spaces: Hindu networks with their dense ties between India and Britain, and increasingly with the United States; the Jewish diaspora, and particularly the complex religious and political interactions between Israel and the United States; and some lesser-known spaces, such as that linking Somalis in Kenya, Minnesota, and Somalia.

Films to See

Several films chronicle the healing associated with Afro-Brazilian religions; I have used *Macumba: Trance and Spirit Healing*. The film *Legacy of the Spirits* traces religion and healing from Africa to Haiti to New York, and would complement well the study of the Garifuna in this chapter.

Speech and Power

It is hard to think of a religion in which set ways of speaking—spells, prayers, recitations, and so on—do not play central roles. Humans are talking animals, and we use our powers of speech to understand and shape events in both the visible and invisible worlds. Most rituals we have examined so far have had certain speech forms at their center: invocations of ancestral spirits (in Africa, Sumatra, or New Guinea), stories and spells that heal (in Japan, Panama, or the United States), and pronouncements that channel the meaning of images (in the Catholic mass).

Some religious traditions place particular emphasis on the centrality of the spoken word to religious practice. For the Navajos of the American Southwest, the world was brought into being by the Gods when they spoke and sung it into existence. Speech and song bring this creative power into the present world, for good or evil. So, too, for the Dogon of Mali, who understand the world as having been spoken into being. In Hindu, Buddhist, and Islamic traditions, the word that is spoken and heard has primacy over that which is written and read—in the latter case a direct chain of transmission is broken. It is not only in the European traditions of Moses, Plato, and Jesus that writing has been understood as secondary to speech (mistakenly so, argues the philosopher Jacques Derrida), but in other religions, of greater and smaller scale, as well. Written scripture may play an important role in these traditions—"scripture," after all, means "writing"—but it does so as the written record of what was originally an act of speech.

Certain religious movements portray their own distinctiveness by contrasting their emphasis on the spoken word to the reliance of competing faiths on images. In seventh-century Arabia, Muhammad and his followers contrasted the Word of God, which they followed, to the images of polytheists, which they condemned. Moses responding to Aaron's setting up of the golden calf, or Joseph Smith and Brigham Young leading the Mormons across the United States: both condemned the worship of "graven images" and urged their followers to focus on the Word of God. Luther chastised the Christians of his time for following the Church rather than scripture, and the "letter of the Bible" has been the watchword for Protestant movements of reform ever since. Each of these leaders has accused other faiths of forgetting or ignoring God's words.

From Chapter 10 of *Religions in Practice: An Approach to the Anthropology of Religion*, 5/e. John J. Bowen. Copyright © 2011 by Pearson Education. Published by Prentice Hall. All rights reserved.

But how can we tell if certain words come from God or some other supernatural agent, rather than from a human, or the Devil, or one's own anxieties? It could be that the speech itself is wonderful in some way, or that other signs of the divine source present themselves. When Augustine of Hippo heard commands to "take and read" coming from the other side of a wall, he took them to be God's commands to pick up Scripture. Muhammad's own illiteracy made his reports of receiving complex, poetic revelations from God all the more believable. Sometimes revelations are received in written form so as to attest to their divine quality, as with Moses and the tablets, and Joseph Smith and his tablets.

But speech, like images, can be meaningful in more than one way. When we speak, we refer to concepts and through them to things in the world. We also call up associations in the minds of our hearers, associations linked to their memories of hearing such words before, or to the style, rhythm, or voice tone of the speaker. Thus, the way in which a sermon is delivered or a hymn sung can be as meaningful to worshipers as the manifest content of the sermon or hymn. We also understand some speech as directly accomplishing something, as having force as well as meaning: a marriage vow seals a pact; a spell compels a spirit to act. Within a religious tradition, people often discuss and debate how best to understand their own speech. Is a sermon better if it is carefully crafted beforehand (as clearly a human product), or is it better if it is spontaneous (allowing the Holy Ghost to offer direct inspiration)? Can a prayer, or a mass, or the recitation of a verse work directly on the universe, or is it only a request to a deity or god?

We consider the relationship between ways of speaking and divine powers in three religious traditions: Islam, in which God's speech sets out a proper path for humans to follow; Navajo religion, in which humans draw on the creative powers of the first beings when they sing prayers of blessing or healing; and several Protestant religions, in which God reveals his word through scripture and spontaneous, inspired speaking.

QUALITY AND MEMORY

But first I want to call on a different case in order to focus on ways in which the quality of speech itself can render it sacred and sometimes powerful. In particular, the form of speech can make it "work" better as religious speech that is remembered and transmitted over time. Around the world, couplets or linked pairs of utterances seem to evoke a sense of power and sometimes bring out the desire to participate in a recitation. Consider, for example, an epic chanted by the people of Roti, an island in eastern Indonesia, as recorded by James Fox (1975):

> *The dogs form a pack*
> *and the hounds join as one*
> *They track civet*
> *and they hunt pig*
> *Deep in the woods of Kai Tio*
> *and deep in the forests of Lolo Batu*
> *The dogs corner their prey*
> *and the hounds give chase.*

Even from this brief excerpt, one can instantly grasp that dog/hounds, civet/pig, and Kai Tio/Lolo Batu form pairs, and one suspects that they will be repeated in much the same way throughout the epic. (This is indeed the case.) These pairings help the chanter remember the epic: Where there is civet, there will next be pig. Sometimes, the pairs are simple semantic equivalents, as in dogs and hounds, and sometimes their pairing carries meaning. Pigs and civets are proper objects of sacrifice, for example, when killed together; a different pair, such as cat and civet, would not be. The use of roughly equivalent verbal structures, such as "form a pack" and "join as one," allows the chanter to make two lines out of one idea.

These and other parallel forms surely help in remembering texts, but they also assist in producing new texts that are recognized as culturally appropriate. The technique is found worldwide. It is basic to the prophetic sections of the Hebrew Bible:

They shall beat their swords into ploughshares
and their spears into pruning hooks
Nation shall not lift up sword against nation
neither shall they learn war any more.

(RSV Isaiah 2:4)

Parallel forms are also used in sermons to encourage the silent or aloud participation of the congregation. Richard Bauman (1983, 76–78) studied the sermons of the Quaker leader George Fox and found that he made extensive use of parallel constructions for this purpose. In one sermon from 1674 one finds the following sort of phrasing:

This is known
as everyone hath received Christ Jesus
so walk in him
there is the gospel order that is the power of God
which was before the Devil was
which brings life and immortality to light
the power of God the gospel brings into life
now in this power in this gospel is the order
the everlasting order of the gospel
which is a mystery.

Even in this brief selection you can see clearly not only how Fox employs parallel constructions but also how he repeats familiar phrases, building up a general sense and sentiment of "gospel—life—order." He also uses these same phrases in subsequent sermons, so that those attending the services would have been ready for the phrases as they came, and they would have sensed themselves participating in them.

The use of familiar phrases, structured in parallel, thus facilitates the delivery of stories and sermons. These formal features also can help people to learn how to produce them by grasping the logic underlying each of them, so that English preachers, Hebrew prophets, or Rotinese tellers of epics could pass their repertoires on to a new generation simply by performing many times, always following the same logic. Perhaps even more importantly, the speakers and preachers bring the hearer, the worshiper, into the speech event as a coparticipant, someone who can follow along, respond, and coproduce the spoken word.

THE QUR'ÂN AS RECITATION OF GOD'S SPEECH

For Muslims, speech is sacred and powerful because God made known his commandments by speaking them, and because Muslims can obey those commandments through various ways of speaking. Muslims' sacred book is the Qur'ân, a word that comes from the Arabic root meaning "to recite." The Qur'ân is the collection of verses spoken to Muhammad by the angel Gabriel, who conveyed them from God. The revelation of these verses took place between 610 and 632 in Mecca and Medina, in Arabia. Muslims believe that the Qur'ân preexisted these revelations, that it already was God's speech, probably for eternity, before it was revealed (Graham 1987, 79–115).

These revelations were handed down orally before they were first written down, and even today Muslims consider it important to memorize and recite these words of God. In its written form, the Qur'ân is arranged as 114 chapters, each divided into verses, and arranged not in the order in which they were spoken to Muhammad but, by convention, from the longest to the shortest.

Unlike the Hebrew Bible or Christian Gospels, the Qur'ân is not a collection of long narratives. It contains brief parables and stories but mainly consists of directives and exhortations to Muhammad and his people. Muslims learn the fuller stories of the prophets and of Muhammad's life from other narratives, not from the Qur'ân itself. Much of the Qur'ân concerns about how Muslims ought to live: it sets out values, social norms, and what we generally call "law." These guidelines for living are called sharî'a, "the way." (Law in the narrower sense of enforceable jurisprudence is designated by the term *fiqh*.)

Here we consider this passage from the third chapter of the Qur'ân for the way in which several kinds of messages are typically combined. It reads:

> Say: 'God has spoken the truth; therefore follow
> the creed of Abraham, a man of pure faith and no idolater.'
> The first House established for the people
> was that at Mecca, a place holy, and a guidance to all beings.
> Therein are clear signs—the station of Abraham,
> and whosoever enters it is in security.
> It is the duty of all men towards God to come
> to the House a pilgrim, if he is able to make his way there.
> As for the unbeliever, God is All-sufficient nor needs any being.

(Qur'ân 3:90–92)

A lot is contained in this passage. Muslim children and adults will memorize it in Arabic, learn its meaning in their own language (if they are not Arabic speakers, as most Muslims are not), and then be taught the ways to understand it by a religious teacher. Most Muslim children begin to learn the Qur'ân at a young age, and as they grow up, they will likely attend Qur'ân interpretation sessions in the local prayer house or mosque.

The passage is addressed to Muhammad, as are all Qur'ânic verses. It shows him precisely how to admonish and guide the people of Arabia, some of whom had become his followers. God directs him to say a certain passage to the people, a passage that identifies Muhammad's mission as pulling people back to the true path of worship of God from which they have strayed. How that path is identified is important: it is the "creed of Abraham," the same creed delivered to Jews and later to Christians. These people had their own "messengers," similar to Muhammad: the Jews had Moses, to whom was revealed the Bible, and David, to whom was given the Psalms; Christians had Jesus, to whom was revealed the Gospels (in this, the Islamic view of Christ's mission). Jews and Christians are "people of the book," and have been accorded special treatment in Muslim-held territories. Muslims believe that Jews and Christians eventually strayed from pure monotheism (the doctrine of the Trinity is a particular target) but that people of all three faiths worship the same God. *Islam* means "submission [to God]" and is intended as a return to an old faith, not the creation of a new one.

The passage then refers to a historical event, the construction by Abraham of the Ka'ba, the large, cubic, black-draped structure in Mecca around which Muslim pilgrims process during the annual religious pilgrimage. The duty to make the pilgrimage, for those with the means to do so, is based on this passage in the Qur'ân, short though it may be, and the fact that Muhammad made such a pilgrimage in 632, the year of his death. The final sentence in the passage implies a warning to the unbelievers, those who do not yet accept God, and reminds them that God does not need them, but, it is implied, they do need to heed his call.

The Qur'ân is treated as a book that is not just to be read, memorized, and studied but also to be celebrated through song and calligraphy. Contests of Qur'ân melodic recitation are held at regular intervals throughout the Muslim world, in which the beauty of the voice control and melodic interpretation, as well as the fit of melody to content, are the basis for judging winners. (Indonesia and Malaysia, two non-Arabic speaking countries, routinely win prizes at the international finals.) Much Islamic art is based on the artistic interpretation of the form of the written Qur'ân, and intricate writings of the names "Allah" and "Muhammad" are found on almost every conceivable (and appropriate) surface in Muslim societies. Many Muslims also believe that the spoken and written words have the power to ward off evil or heal people of illness.

The Qur'ân is God's major gift to humans, analogous to the presence of Jesus among humans in Christian understanding. It is an exact replica of the words spoken to Muhammad; therefore, the forms of the spoken and written words themselves take on sacred value. It is also evidence of direct historical contact between God and Muhammad. This direct contact is crucial to Islam's religious foundation, and explains two areas of study within Islam: one that proves that Muhammad was illiterate and could not possibly have created the Qur'ân, and the other that shows the Qur'ân to be inimitable in grammar and rhetoric. These lines of investigation, taken together, prove that the Qur'ân is from God. (Contrast the lack of importance to most Christians of the original sound and shape of the Greek words in the Gospels.)

Let us consider another example, a tiny unit of Islam, the very short chapter of the Qur'ân called Sûra al-Ikhlâs. This *sûra* or chapter comes toward the end of the Qur'ân, as chapter 112—precisely because of its length. As I noted earlier, when the revelations

Islamic calligraphy in the Congregational Mosque in Isfahan, Iran. The inlaid tile design shows both cursive and geometric styles; the inscriptions include Qur'ânic passages and, in this Shi'i setting, invocations of both Muhammad and 'Ali. *(Courtesy of John Renard)*

were first collected, they were placed in order from the longest to the shortest, placing this *sûra* or chapter near the end of the Qur'ân (although it was one of the earliest to be revealed). It reads:

Qul hu wallâhu ahad   *Say, He is God, one,*
allâhu samad   *God the everlasting refuge,*
lam yalid wa lam yûlad *Neither begetting nor begotten,*
wa lam yakul lahu kufuwan ahad *and having as an equal none.*

Speech and Power

The sûra affirms the single most important value of Islam, the unity (*tawhîd*) of God. In a few short lines, it unpacks the dimensions of this unity. God is eternal as well as an indestructible refuge (the word *samad* predicated of God has both senses), and He is prior to all things, the Creator of all. He created all but is not a father, and here the verse underscores the monotheism of Islam in contrast to Christian ideas of God the Father and of the Trinity. God is without equal. This proposition places Islam in clear opposition to polytheism (*shirk*), the act of attributing divine attributes to a being other than God. Polytheism is one of the gravest sins in Islam.

The sûra begins by commanding the reciter: "Say" (*Qul*). Just as Muhammad began his career as Messenger by hearing the order to "Recite," so the worshiper begins this recitation by quoting God ordering us all to restate the fundamental truths contained in the chapter. The sûra is thus a kind of *da`wa*, a call or an outreach to other Muslims, reminding them of the bases of their religion. The title of the chapter, "Sincerity" (*ikhlâs*), adds an additional value to its message, that of sincerity, humility, and authenticity, the appropriate attitude of the worshiper before God.

Because it is one of the shortest chapters, children will learn to memorize it early in their lives as they begin to assemble their repertoires for worship (*salât*). They will also hear it explained countless times—by parents, in school, at a lesson held after morning or afternoon prayer, and sometimes with the statement that because it sums up so many key ideas, it encapsulates the entire Qur'ân. Children also hear adults in their community chant it aloud during congregational prayer, either on Fridays or on any occasion when two or more people pray together. In my own experience they will hear it chanted in a straightforward way, with little embellishment. Hearing these repeated chants gives the child a basic idea about the melody, timbre, and rhythm (through paying attention to long and short vowels) to be used in reciting from the Qur'ân.

Children also hear the very different rhythm of the *adhan*, the call to prayer that is performed prior to each prayer time. In singing out the call to prayer, whether in a field, a mosque, or over a loudspeaker to all in an urban neighborhood, the reciter typically draws out some vowels to great lengths and pronounces others quickly. He begins with repeated cries of "God is great" (*Allâhu akbar*): twice pronounced very quickly, in a rising intonation, to grab attention (and, in the morning, to wake up sleeping Muslims), and then twice with the long vowel in Allâh drawn out.

The Sûra al-Ikhlâs is recited on other occasions as well, for meditation or to achieve a practical end. And here we move from general features of Islam to observations from anthropological fieldwork, beginning with my own. When in the 1980s I lived in the highlands of the Sumatran village of Isak with my many Gayo-speaking friends and neighbors, I heard the chapter recited repeatedly after Friday worship as a way of meditating following the genre of repeated chanting called *dhikr*. I also heard it recited at ritual meals held in conjunction with Islamic feast days, or to help the spirit of the recently deceased navigate through the trials and tribulations that occur after death. (Muslims in other parts of the world chant scripture in similar ways and for similar purposes.)

Indeed, the all-night sessions of chanting verses that follow a death in that community are called *samadiyah*, from the last word in the chapter's second line: *samad*. In the sessions I attended, men and women, seated in the home of the deceased, chanted the chapter 40 or 60 times, first quickly and then slowly. (They said it more times if fewer people were present, so that the total amount of merit generated would be about the same for every deceased person.) Many of my acquaintances stated that because the chapter contained so many of the truths in the Qur'ân, it had the value of one-third of the entire Qur'ân. The assembled villagers chanted many other verses, both short, complete chapters, and segments from longer chapters, including portions of the second chapter, al-Baqarah. Verse 255 of this chapter is called the "throne verse" for its invocations of God's majesty, reminding us in part: "His Throne encompasses the heavens and the earth, and their preservation does not burden Him. He is the Most High, the Most Great." Recitations have a long history of use for power: During the revolution against the Dutch, the Gayo men would chant the Sûra al-Ikhlâs as a way of keeping bullets away from themselves; others still recite it as part of charms or spells.

The average adult in a simple Sumatran village thus has at her or his command a great deal of scripture, and knows when and how to recite it. Not everyone agrees that all of those uses are appropriate. Many Muslims find the very idea of chanting verses for the dead, a practice found across Muslim-majority societies, to contradict the reliable report (*hadîth sahîh*) that the Prophet Muhammad once said:

> Three things accompany the deceased [to the grave]: his family, his wealth, and his deeds. Two return and one remains: his family and wealth return; his deeds remain.

In other words, after death you only benefit or suffer from what you have done during life; your family cannot help you, and your wealth is for naught. When relatives gather to chant for your benefit, they are at best deceiving themselves, and at worst contravening God's explicit commands.

In the Gayo highlands, especially in the 1920s and 1930s, Muslim teachers who wished to alert people to the impropriety of many of their practices wrote and sung poems—indeed, they invented a new genre of poetry just for this purpose of religious education and correction. These poems often began with a verse from the Qur'ân or with a report from the Prophet Muhammad, and then developed the idea in the Gayo language. To discourage people from chanting for the deceased, for example, they would recite the hadîth quoted above and then expand on its meaning, concluding with the message:

> If you die and your relatives give alms (*sedekah*), the merit does not reach you.
>   Did you not hear the words of God, "a person shall have only as s/he has labored?"

By beginning with a statement attributed to the Prophet, and ending with a verse from the Qur'ân (the part in quotations, recited in Arabic), these change-oriented teachers secured their message with scriptural proofs (*dalil*). By singing Gayo-language poetry in between the hadîth and the Qur'ânic verse, they appealed to ordinary people.

Note how much ground we have covered by beginning with this small unit of knowledge, the short Qur'ânic chapter "Sincerity," and then tracing the diverse ways in which Muslims understand and use it. It functions in everyday life as a unit in worship and rituals, and as a summary of basic Islamic teachings, suitable for expanding for teaching and discussion. Its repeated recitation in the *dhikr*-chanting sessions (dhikr means "remembrance," here of God) brings men and women to a state of transcendence and nearness to God. Some people believe that the reciting transmits spiritual merit to other people, or that it converts God's blessings into bodily protection. Others disagree. Its very range of uses gives rise to further citations of verses and hadîth in commentary and debate about the proper uses of verses. Knowledge may begin with learning how to recite a small snippet of revelation, but it quickly expands to a wealth of religious and ritual activities and to a set of debates about the power and limits of religious acts.

Learning religion begins, then, in mastering the many ways to draw on God's revelations. Revelations tell you how to pray, how to carry out the pilgrimage to Mecca, and how to perform the many ordinary acts of everyday life that could be seen as having a religious dimension: how to enter and leave a mosque, how to greet other people, how to dress and eat properly (and to say the "Bismillah" before starting to eat). This knowledge is practical knowledge. Of course, there are also basic tenets to learn—the five pillars of faith, the required beliefs, and so on—but these are the easier elements of basic knowledge. God's major gift to humans is scripture; humans' major obligation to God is to follow His commands. Humans must thus begin by mastering scripture and learning how to follow those commands, before delving into the subtleties of theology, ethics, or jurisprudence. And indeed, such is how schooling progresses, from knowing how to, eventually, knowing about.

Islamic history, too, is above all a history of revelation (*tanzil*). Two methodological points follow. First, the facts of where and when God chose to send down a revelation may have theological and thus normative relevance for Muslims. When Muslims turn to the historicity of the Qur'ân, it is not to debunk it (although some non-Muslim historians have tried that) but to ask whether it makes a difference that, say, the verse permitting men to take more than one wife was revealed after wars had left a number of widows and orphans. Do these circumstances of revelation mean that polygamy is only permitted under such conditions of demographic imbalance? Or do they mean that such was an opportune moment to make believers aware of an option always available to them?

But the precise historicity of revelation also gives a high degree of religious value to the exact words used by God, through Gabriel, to speak to Muhammad. Revelation was aural, and transmission has continued to take place in an aural/oral mode. Writing was never absent (a point to which I return below), and Muslims recognize as legitimate a number of slightly differing written forms of the Qur'ân. But today, just as centuries ago, Muslims use written scriptural texts in order to learn to recite them. The precise form of recitation continues to refer back to the moment of revelation, the presence of the spoken word.

The sounds of revelation share in this value of originality. Throughout the world of Muslim-majority societies, many boys and girls, and men and women, learn not only to recite the Qur'ân but also to recite it melodically, using certain rules of pronunciation (*tajwîd*). Far from Arabic-speaking regions, Indonesians enthusiastically enter local, national, and international contests (and do quite well), and they often raise the question: Can we not use Indonesian melodies? The authoritative response has been: no, because the Qur'ân was revealed to Arabic speakers—and indeed, some Indonesian reciters practice sounds from Arabic music in order to become habituated to Arabic singing styles.

This epistemology of revelation—valuing the precise act of aural revelation and repeating the act of oral transmission—derives from the ideology of absolute and unmediated *presence* that founds the religion. Gabriel appeared and spoke directly to Muhammad, and he to others, and so on. Muhammad did not interpret the words, and as an illiterate man he could not have created them; he is a vessel of God's message.

But Muslims debate among themselves about what the implications of the Qur'ân's divine source are for everyday life. Many Gayo Muslims, for example, consider prayers (*do'a*) that include Qur'ânic verses to be directly effective in healing, or giving one invulnerability, or harming one's enemy. One of my friends, for instance, used a passage from Chapter 61 of the Qur'ân as the beginning of an invulnerability spell:

> *And He will give you another blessing which you love:*
> *help from God and present victory.*
> *Give good tidings, O Muhammad*
> *to believers.*

To which he would append a plea ending in the lines:

> *Let my blanket be from God,*
> *my cloak from God,*
> *my shawl from God.*

My friend thought that when he uttered the prayer, God gave him a cloak and shawl, as the material realization of God's promise to give "help from God and a present victory." In his own memory, these divine gifts had served him well during battles fought in the 1950s, making bullets and knives skip off his clothes as he fought. But in the 1980s, others pointed out to him that the Qur'ânic passage had been revealed to Muhammad as a message of peace, to stop fighting. One scholar objected to my friend that reciting the Qur'ân could not automatically confer any power on the reciter; that all power came from God and that He knew all that happened in the world anyway and would do as He pleased, regardless of what mumbo-jumbo ordinary men and women chose to recite. All that we can do, he said, is to live good lives and worship God, and then perhaps He will choose to reward us.

THE CREATIVE POWER OF NAVAJO SPEECH AND SONG

The view that speech directly confers power, limited within Islam to one, often criticized, view about the Qur'ân and God, flowers fully within Navajo religion. Like Muslims, Navajo place speech at the center of religion, but as the source of creative power rather than as the source of divine commands.

In Navajo tradition, the individual human being has the power to change the world through language (Witherspoon 1977). A person can do so because the world itself was created through language, when First Man sang the song known as Blessingway. Among the first creatures, the Holy People, were Long Life Boy (thought) and Happiness Girl (speech), to whom First Man said: "You two will be found among everything." Indeed, their names are found in nearly every Navajo prayer and song as signs of the powers to create. They are also the parents of the Changing (or Earth) Woman, the being who is associated with the earth's fertility.

The sung prayers known as Blessingway tell the story of creation. They also reenact creation each time they are told (Wyman 1970). They may be performed as a separate ritual—for example, to bless a house—or be incorporated into other rituals in which, by invoking the events of creation, they endow the ritual with the same creative power. Navajo sand painting also draws its powers from the story of creation. After the Holy

People built the first house, they decorated the floor with bits of shale, rock, and mineral dyes. They drew all the forms of life that they eventually were to create, depicting them in the forms of holy people. They then recited a long prayer to these holy people, and in that act created a causal pathway between sand paintings and the sacred powers of creation. Blessingway and many other prayer cycles identify and associate everyday people and conditions with the Holy People and the events of creation. Blessingway contains many lines that link powers given to the Holy People to powers desired by the speaker, such as:

> *May the power that enables you to inhale also enable me to inhale.*
>
> *Let the dark flint which arises to protect you always arise to protect me.*

Often these sections of the prayer provide long catalogues of body parts and powers, underscoring the identification of the Holy Person's body with that of the prayer reciter. These identifications are intended to transfer the properties of the Holy People to that of the person who is the object of the ceremony. For example, Navajo singers will help ensure a good birth for an expectant mother by performing a Blessingway ceremony that identifies the Holy People of the Earth, themselves associated with fertility and life, with the mother and child (Gill 1981). The singer will collect earth from a cornfield and water from a flowing stream, both nurturing life, and apply them to the woman. The prayers recited include the Earth's Prayer, which underscores these identifications through passages such as the following:

> *Earth's feet have become my feet by means of these I shall live on.*
>
> *Earth's legs have become my legs by means of these I shall live on.*
>
> *Earth's body has become my body by means of this I shall live on.*
>
> *Earth's mind has become my mind by means of this I shall live on.*
>
> *Earth's voice has become my voice by means of this I shall live on.*
>
> . . .
>
> *It is the very inner form of Earth that continues to move with me, that has risen with me, that is standing with me, that indeed remains stationary with me.*
>
> *Now it is the inner form of long life, now of happiness that continues to move with me, that has risen with me, that is standing with me, that indeed remains stationary with me, surprising, surprising.*

> *(Wyman 1970, 136)*

The pair of terms *long life* and *happiness* are the principles personified in the *Holy People Long Life Boy and Happiness Girl* (Wyman 1970, 19–46). They are linked to all the components of the earth. The effect of these pairings is to transfer to the mother and expected child these two essential qualities, long life and happiness.

Prayers such as these are used for healing when Holy People are thought to have been responsible for the illness. If a person has trespassed on a holy site, the Holy People may place a spell on that person; the Holyway ceremony is designed to induce them to remove the spell. The singer addresses a particular holy person by name and makes an offering of tobacco smoke to him. In the Holyway stories associated with the ceremonies, the holy person is sent tobacco, which he smokes, and then agrees to help cure the patient. The holy person addresses the patient as "grandson," placing himself in a relationship, in which he can be compelled to aid the ill person, his "grandson." The prayer draws on the knowledge contained in these stories by demanding, not requesting, that the holy person cure the patient:

> *This very day you must remake my feet for me,*
>
> *This very day you must remake my legs for me.*

The prayer ends by asserting that the cure has occurred:

> *With my body cooled off, I am walking about,*
>
> *with my body light in weight, I am walking about,*
>
> . . .
>
> *As one who is long life and happiness I am walking about*
>
> *Pleasant again it has become,*
>
> *Pleasant again it has become!*

(Gill 1981, 128–129)

In this, its concluding section, the prayer performs the act of bringing the patient to health. The verb is in the progressive mode—"I am walking about"—indicating that the patient will continue to enjoy health. Most importantly, the prayer identifies the patient with Long Life Boy and Happiness Girl: He or she has become "one who is long life and happiness."

SPEECH AND GRACE IN PROTESTANT CHURCHES

So far we have considered ideas about how speech relates to power; now we introduce a third concept, that of the grace of God. Ways of speaking found in many Protestant churches introduce the idea that speech by everyday people can, when accompanied by God's grace, be divinely inspired.

In the sixteenth century, several Christian scholars, notably Martin Luther (1483–1546) in Germany and John Calvin (1509–1564) in Geneva, protested against certain Church teachings, thus giving their worship movements the name "Protestant". Although differing strongly among themselves, these movements shared the dual conviction that, first, people could be saved only through faith and by the grace of God and, second, that scripture, not human institutions, was the ultimate source of religious authority. As the billboard outside the Lutheran Church near my home in St. Louis sometimes proclaims: "Only by Grace; Only by Faith; Only by Scripture."

Protestants make the claim that faith and grace connect individuals directly to God in conscious opposition to the Catholic claim that the Church, through its sacraments, creates that connection. For the Catholic, the miracle of the Eucharist means that Christ is produced in the bread and water of the Mass. For most Protestants (and, from at least the ninth century onward, for some Catholics), the objects of a mass are signs of, not the substance of, Christ. Moreover, for Protestants the ritual of the Eucharist does not automatically confer merit or salvation or grace on the individual worshiper. Nor do chants said on behalf of the dead aid the dead in their struggle through purgatory to heaven. The individual has free and direct access to God, and God may bestow grace on anyone—or may refuse to do so. The gift of the Word of God thus may reach anyone at any time and place and in unpredictable ways. Faith is all that is required (Clark 1967, 99–115).

In the wide array of movements and churches that followed Luther's break with Rome—Methodists, Baptists, Lutherans, and so on—this emphasis on universal access to God's grace and revelation of grace through speech and hearing led people to develop many and varied ways of worship. Quakers and some Baptists have stressed the universal nature of the minister's role, that anyone may be visited by the Holy Ghost and moved to preach. Charismatic and Pentecostal churches (and certain movements within Lutheranism) have encouraged worshipers to let the Holy Ghost visit them and lead them to speak in tongues, as did the apostles after the death of Jesus. But other movements denied the universal access of people to grace and salvation. John Calvin argued that God has predetermined who is to receive his grace and be saved, and who is to be condemned to hell. This doctrine of *predestination,* held by the Puritans in early North America as well as Calvin's followers in Europe, implied that one's good works had no bearing on one's fate after death.

THE LETTER AND THE SPIRIT OF SCRIPTURE

The ultimate authority on all religious matters for Protestants is scripture, and not the teachings of a church or pope. But what is "scripture"? One interpretation of the Protestant slogan "only scripture" (sola scriptura) is that the written text is paramount. Luther was indeed an outstanding biblical scholar, learned in Greek, Latin, and Hebrew, and did argue for the importance of the scholarly interpretation of the text as written. Early Protestant preaching never strayed far from the text of the Bible. What came to be called "Fundamentalist" movements, but might more correctly be called "literalist" emphases on the literal meaning of the text, follow from this focus on the written word.

For some Fundamentalist churchgoers in the United States today, literal truth resides in the 1611 King James Version of the Bible. Some of these Christians call modern translations "perversions." KJV is the Bible "as it is written" (Ammerman 1987, 53). Rather than considering the Bible as a whole, and worrying about contradictions between various parts, Fundamentalists (along with many other Christians) tend to refer to a verse or a phrase, on which they then elaborate, both in sermons and in discussing everyday life. People turn to individual verses that they have memorized, and they also use the language of some of those verses in everyday conversations, speak of their sicknesses as "suffering in beds of affliction" or having "a thorn in the flesh" (Ammerman 1987, 87).

This literalism can lead some Fundamentalists to a point at which they are nearly using the Bible for divination, as in the case of a man who decided to order a tent from Sears and Roebuck Company because he found listed among the permitted foods in 14 Deuteronomy the "roebuck" (Ammerman 1987, 54).

This interpretation of scripture can, of course, be used to underwrite claims of special authority grounded in learning. But these claims are often countered within the tradition of Luther and Calvin by appeal to a second understanding of scripture. Luther, Calvin, and other reformers looked beyond the text to the divine message it conveyed (Graham 1987, 141–154). They placed no special value on the original languages of the Hebrew Bible or the Greek Gospels, and indeed Protestant reformers have encouraged translation as the best way to spread God's word. In this respect they differ from Muslims, for whom there can be only one Qur'ân, the Arabic-language speech of God. (Indeed, most Muslims consider it impossible to "translate" the Qur'ân; English and other versions are usually called "interpretations" or "renderings.")

For the Protestant reformers, then, speech and writing was best thought of as a window to God's word, transparent to its referent. It is in the Word, not the particular words and letters, that holiness lies. The Bible as preached, translated, interpreted, and witnessed in one's life is the key to the proper understanding of God, not the scholastic analysis of the Hebrew or Greek constructions. The Word of God is thus the meaning of scripture. It can take different forms, including the presence of Christ himself in the world, as the Word made flesh. God can thus communicate his word in very different ways. Luther underscored the importance of inner communication with God, communication that did not depend on learning. He wrote that "no one can understand God or God's word rightly unless he receives it directly [literally, "without mediation"] from the Holy Spirit." And Calvin wrote that "all of scripture is to be read as if God were speaking," and that the spirit of scripture was more important than the letter of scripture. In their view, God can communicate with ordinary people through many media: the revelations recorded in scripture, the embodiment of the divine in Christ, and the visiting upon any of us of the Holy Ghost (Graham 1987, 143, 147).

Because these inner modes of communication—hearing with help from the Holy Spirit—must accompany the reading of the Bible, Luther linked speech and hearing to the central value of faith: "If you ask a Christian what work renders him worthy of the name Christian, he will not be able to give any answer at all except the hearing of the word of God, that is, faith. Therefore the ears alone are the organs of the Christian person, who is justified and judged a Christian not by the works of any member, but through faith" (in Graham 1987, 141).

The writings of Luther and others thus could be taken to give to individuals the right to hear God's word, no matter what statements were made by the authorities of a church. This radical giving of spiritual rights to individuals surfaces time and again in subsequent history.

ELECTION AND SIGNS

Most Protestant Christians would agree that God bestows his grace where he sees fit. But how and when does he see fit? Can our actions bring on grace?

The struggles over this issue within Christianity trace back to the very roots of the religion. On the one hand, Christianity drew from Judaism. It began, after all, as a sect within Judaism, where obedience to the Law determined the fate of individuals and of the universe. The idea that good works redeemed one's soul was developed by the Church into elaborate doctrines of penance, masses, and salvation. Many Protestant traditions also incorporated such a notion, Methodism among them.

But Christianity became, not a sect within Judaism, but a new religion, and did so in large part by adopting ideas from Hellenism, the world view that pervaded the Mediterranean world (Jaeger 1961). Hellenism included the idea of divine grace that is visited upon humans rather than achieved by them. This concept accorded well with the idea of an all-powerful God, and indeed with the unpredictability of the God of the Hebrew Bible. After all, if God does not need humans, he will dispense grace in ways that fit his plans, not our works.

The idea that God's grace is entirely independent of human actions finds its most eloquent exposition in Paul's letter to the Romans, in a section where Paul is distinguishing between the older idea of the Jewish "chosen people" from the Christian idea that God chooses, or elects, some people (and not others) both from among the Jews and from among the Gentiles:

> . . . [W]hen Rebecca had conceived children by one man, our forefather Isaac, though they were not yet born and had done nothing either good or bad, in order that God's purpose of election might continue, not because of works but because of his call, she was told, "the elder will serve the younger." As it is written, "Jacob I loved, but Esau I hated."
>
> What shall we say then? Is there injustice on God's part? By no means! For he says to Moses, "I will have mercy on whom I have mercy, and I will have compassion on whom I have compassion." So it depends not upon man's will or exertion, but upon God's mercy. For the scripture says to Pharaoh, "I have raised you up for the very purpose of showing my power in you, so that my name may be proclaimed in all the earth." So then he has mercy upon whomever he wills, and he hardens the heart of whomever he wills.
>
> You will say to me then, "Why does he still find fault? For who can resist his will?" But who are you, a man, to answer back to God? Will what is molded say to its molder, "Why have you made me thus?" Has the potter no right over the clay, to make out of the same lump one vessel for beauty and another for menial use?
>
> (Romans 9, 10–21)

Just as the potter may select some pots for greatness, and others for quick destruction, without the pots having the right to answer back, how can we, God's creations, question the will of God, our Creator?

The doctrine of election formed a central part of the teachings of (Saint) Augustine of Hippo in the fifth century (Burns 1994). Because original sin cost humans their free will, he wrote, all our fortune, good or ill, is due to God's grace. In the sixteenth century, John Calvin developed this argument into the idea of predestination, which became founding doctrine for the Presbyterian Church. As inscribed in the Westminster Confession of 1647, which the English Parliament accepted the following year, the doctrine was stated in the form that "some men and angels are predestined unto everlasting life, and others foreordained to everlasting death" (Weber 1958, 98–101).

This doctrine left its adherents with a radical uncertainty about their future. Calvin taught that no one can know whether he is saved (although Calvin apparently thought he was), because the damned can have all the mental states possessed by the saved except for the final state of trust in God. So, although a strong feeling of faith in God is necessary for salvation, it is insufficient as a source of reassurance about salvation.

This uncertainty has one opening, in the "doctrine of signs," that even if we cannot know with certainty about our salvation, we can see signs of it. These signs could be in one's ability to succeed in the world. Some Protestant theologians argued that one had a duty to assume that one was saved and act accordingly. Individual psychology led believers in the doctrine toward intense worldly activity in the hope that leading a rational, systematic life for the greater glory of God on earth would itself be a sign that one has been called to serve God—has been elected. Some added an additional tenet that helped close the logical circle: that only the elect had faith strong enough to keep them hewing to this path. Thus, success and profit are themselves signs of election.

Although this line of thinking brought even Calvin's heirs back to a position, in which good works counted for something on the religious plane, it was not a return to Catholic doctrine. The Calvinist still has no possibility of absolution; if he is damned, there is still nothing he can do about it. Furthermore, in the idea that a life spent for God was a sign of election, it was the whole life that mattered, and not the individual work, as in the Catholic calculus of sin and absolution.

Max Weber (1958) drew on these religious responses to develop his theory that what he called the "Protestant ethic" provided a psychological push for the development of modern capitalism in Europe. He noted that the pioneers of modern capitalism in Europe were mainly Protestant rather than Catholic, despite the fact that Protestant theologians were far more restrictive regarding what we might call the modern business necessities of interest and competitive pricing than were their Catholic counterparts. Luther, for example, wrote that "the greatest misfortune of the German nation is easily the traffic in interest. . . . The devil invented it, and the pope, by giving his sanction to it, has done untold evil throughout the world."

Weber's idea was that Protestantism spurred on the development of capitalism, not directly through its doctrine but through the psychological consequences of that doctrine. Men tormented by the unknowability of election were spurred on to succeed in the world, to build edifices of successful businesses as monuments to their worldly success. Weber called this cast of mind "worldly asceticism": denying pleasure to oneself but doing so in a life very much devoted to this world. The capitalist experienced loneliness, since no one could save him and God was distant; had a hatred of material, sensuous life, since it had no positive religious role and tempted people to idolatry; and threw himself into a social life that was solely work for the glory of God.

Weber advanced his thesis by studying the sermons and diaries of Calvinist theologians in the seventeenth and eighteenth centuries. Richard Baxter, for example, served in Cromwell's government as well as in the Puritan Church. He preached hard, methodical work as a religious labor (and opposed sports). The divine quality of this work will be "known by its fruits," he wrote. As a consequence, these men preferred specialization and the division of labor for the greater returns to labor they brought, and thus the greater indication of their own personal election.

The doctrine of election—or "particular election" as it came to be called—was by no means universally accepted by Protestants. An especially widely effective treatise written by Jacobus Arminius in 1608 and called *Declaration of Sentiments* argued that God wishes all people to be saved and gives them the means to do so. Living the good life, stated Arminius, can bring one to God's grace. This position (often called "Arminianism") implied that humans are "perfectible." This argument was taken up in the eighteenth century by John Wesley. The movement he founded was named Methodism for the methodical life he urged Christians to lead. Methodists and other movements accentuated the emotional work required to bring about certainty of salvation and to lead the person into the state of grace.

Baptists gained their distinctive position within the array of Protestant churches through their argument that only those who had gained their faith should be baptized into the church. They thus rejected infant baptism. But Baptists themselves split over the issue of election, with some teaching that Jesus died for everyone; others, that he died only for the elect. Those who held the first view were called "General Baptists" and included the group that left England for Holland in 1607, some of whom then journeyed to Plymouth, Massachusetts, in 1620. Those holding the second view, called "Particular Baptists," founded churches in England and also sent groups to America. Today, some Presbyterian and Reformed churches in Europe and the United States advocate the doctrine, but may place more or less emphasis on it.

SINGING AND CERTAINTY AMONG U.S. PRIMITIVE BAPTISTS

One group of churches that has attempted to remain faithful to Calvin are the self-styled "Primitive Baptists" of the southeastern United States. These churches are scattered throughout the Appalachian mountains, but I draw here on a study conducted in the early 1980s by James Peacock and Ruel Tyson (1989) in the Blue Ridge mountains straddling North Carolina and Virginia. In this sparsely populated region, both elders and other worshipers travel from church to church to worship, often staying Saturday nights with friends. Services include hymn singing, one or more sermons preached by elders, and large meals spread out on communal tables. The churches belong to the Mountain District Association.

The Primitive Baptists adhere to the Westminster Confession, and they actively wrestle with the difficulties the doctrine presents. They attempt to uphold election and reject the idea that we can earn our salvation or have certain knowledge of it. As one preacher put it, "every time you feel inspired, it didn't necessarily come from the Lord." But they also hold to the idea of signs of salvation that one can sense in the world. These signs include the experience of community attained through fellowship and church services, "a sweet meeting," such as one preacher recollected in a sermon in the early 1980s. "Oh, my friends, sometimes we've sung songs here that've lifted us up," he reminds them. And the beauty of their singing is a sign, a foretaste of heaven: "Beyond the little foretastes of experience now, ah, in heaven's pure world today there are angels that sing" (Peacock and Tyson 1989, 112).

"Hymns are small sermons," notes one church elder. Peacock and Tyson describe how, concerned with not overstepping the boundary between faith in their salvation and (mistaken) assurance about it, they choose their songs carefully: "Amazing Grace" and "Guide Me O Thy Great Jehovah" affirm God's absolute sovereignty and "In Sharon's Lovely Rose" expresses hope of reaching heaven, but "Blessed Assurance, Jesus Is Mine" is unacceptable because it presumptuously claims assurance of salvation. In their style, too, they express resignation and modest hope, but avoid the joy that could dangerously approach certainty. Upbeat tempos and complex harmonies are avoided; unison singing in a dignified cadence is preferred. Peacock and Tyson recall the tears running down the cheeks of the congregation while singing; their participation in the service is no less emotional than that of their more animated Pentecostal brethren, but it bespeaks a resigned, stoic attitude in the face of God's great and unknowable will (Peacock and Tyson 1989, 114–118).

Sermons pose two related dilemmas for the preacher. Does one prepare an elaborate sermon and risk the sin of pride, or wait for the Spirit to emerge inside one, and risk incoherence? Does one urge people to perform their duties as Christians and risk strengthening the erroneous idea that doing their duties will win them salvation, or refrain from any exhortations and miss the opportunity to guide them along a righteous path? Preachers do not, in fact, preach from outlines or notes. To do so would be to insult the "Spirit that bloweth where it listeth." Sermons come from the heart. "If I can't feel that power, I ain't preaching the Gospel. I may stand up there and quote scripture and so on, but it ain't the Gospel," remarked one preacher. For, as Luther and Calvin proclaimed, the Bible is the inspired word that emerges in and through humans, not the dead letter of the written book. It was the Word of God that produced the Bible and inspires people today as well. Or does not: An elder may rise to preach and after quoting scripture, sit down when he finds he has nothing to say (Peacock and Tyson 1989, 118–126).

In their sermons, preachers strive to avoid implying that religious experience is evidence of salvation or that good works can lead one to salvation. Elder Bradley used a sermon he preached in a North Carolina church to trace his own path. His experience preaching and "saving souls" had led him to think that preaching could bring a person to salvation. He realized his error after revisiting the passage in the Letter to the Romans on election. His sermon reminds us how what appears to be an obvious reason for preaching is indeed in error from the perspective of the doctrine of election, and also how the apparent gloominess of this perspective can be in fact the basis for joy:

> Finally came to the conclusion that this which I'd been taught, that salvation was dependent upon men hearing the gospel, repenting of his sins and believing on Jesus, that God was using this the preacher to reach the dead sinner, that this was totally contrary to that which was taught in the word of God, but that this salvation depended upon God's own sovereign pleasure and that he made choice of a people in a covenant before time began. And, oh what a joyful sound it was, and how beautiful it was for me then to see things in that order! To see that God planned this salvation, and if God planned something you can rest assured it's not going to come to naught. That which God has planned will be executed. God declared this salvation before men ever had being in himself. (Peacock and Tyson 1989, 122)

The "sweet meeting" that comforts the soul depends on community: Preaching, singing, and eating together makes up what these Baptists call "the visible church." But here enters a difficulty: If your group consists of both the damned and the elect, how can you construct a solid community? Two ideas of community have emerged in the Mountain District, roughly corresponding to the contrast between North Carolina and Virginia churches, and these two ideas have consequences for practices of speaking, singing, and gathering in fellowship.

Two Models of Church Authority

For reasons of topography and modes of livelihood, the churches in North Carolina are dispersed in fields and hills, whereas those in Virginia are located in villages (Peacock and Tyson 1989, 87–117). The North Carolina churches are less well attended than the latter group, and worshipers are more likely to live individualistic lives, usually as independent farmers. Charisma, or direct divine inspiration, governs the lives of the elders, and it appears in their sermons, which often recount personal experiences. Songs of stoic resignation, sermons about doctrine, moods of individualism, and antibureaucracy sentiments characterize the North Carolina churches. In contrast to this individualistic structure and attitude, the Virginia churches have created some degree of bureaucracy, and their elders emphasize organization over charisma. The lives of those attending services are more likely to involve work in government civil service or small businesses (although here, too, many farm). Sermons are more likely to dwell on duty. Singing has changed in some Virginia churches, evolving in the direction of mainline Protestant church singing, with major keys predominating and harmonies explored.

Peacock and Tyson recount how the two groups of churches have come into conflict over their differing ideas of authority and community. The North Carolina churches have favored allowing individual churches and members to go their own ways, as the Spirit moves them. Charisma, the gift of grace from God, dominates. Those in Virginia have stressed the importance of following rules and obeying duly constituted authority.

The contrast surfaced in a dispute during the 1980s about the right of a church to exclude some of its members. Churches do exclude members, and members cannot join other churches. Because members and elders rotate where they worship, they can effectively keep out the excluded. In this case, one church excluded a majority of its worshipers on grounds that they had associated with a sinner. They had shown themselves not to be of the elect and so had to be thrown out of the church—much as did the Puritan churches of seventeenth-century New England. The church is responsible for community as a whole, and must exclude sinners.

But the excluded members then formed their own church and asked to be recognized by the Mountain District. The rule-following Virginia churches supported the exclusions and refused to recognize the new church, because doing so would contradict the righteous authority of the church that had thrown them out. The North Carolina churches supported the right of the members to form a new church. They felt called to do so, and who can say they are mistaken in their calling? (Peacock and Tyson 1989, 71–85).

At issue was not just who makes the rules, but who has access to the Word of God. If the Word of God is given to anyone and everyone, at any time and place and in unpredictable ways, then the worship and preaching of anyone should be recognized and attended to. If an individual is called by God, his or her subsequent actions should be respected. But if the right to provide an authoritative interpretation of scripture is held by those persons capable of correctly reading it, then all others should obey that authority. Here the North Carolina churches stood in favor of the availability of God's word to anyone; the Virginia churches, of the importance of a duly constituted hierarchy based on knowledge and the consent of the community acting as a whole.

This tension about authority and community plagues all Christian movements that attempt to structure themselves around the ultimately unknowable grace of God. The Virginia churches have moved toward hierarchy and a "routinized" authority. The North Carolina churches have resisted this pull.

CHARISMATIC AND PENTECOSTAL CHURCHES

Other Christian churches in the same part of the United States have maintained an independent stance but have taken different positions on the question of whether we can perceive and experience signs of our own election or salvation.

Many Fundamentalists, such as those in the Northeast U.S. church studied by Nancy Ammerman (1987) doubt that everyone who claims to be saved is so, and they look for signs of salvation, most importantly some outward, noticeable change in the person's life. They should have given up smoking and drinking. They should also show confidence in the Lord; constant worries are signs they have not yet been saved.

Throughout much of the South, Holiness churches are scattered in hills and towns much as are the Primitive Baptists. Preachers and ordinary people often travel long distances to worship. The focus of worship is on the relationship between the individual and God, as in all the movements we have considered so far. But here the role of rather dramatic signs is paramount, for snake-handling is often part of the service. Surviving a snakebite, or a drink of poison, or an electric shock is a sign of God's grace. The women and men who have been bitten sit together in services as the "true believers," or the "true saints." These saints, having survived, have themselves become signs, or "charismata" that are given by the Holy Ghost. They are proofs of Jesus' power to save them; cups of strychnine are called "salvation cocktails" (Covington 1995; La Barre 1964).

One church name says it all: "The Church of Jesus Christ with Signs Following." The phrase is in reference to 16 Mark, a key chapter for worshipers at Holiness churches and for many other churchgoers throughout the South—just as the Primitive Baptists and other believers in particular election take their cue from 9 Romans. In 16 Mark, Jesus appears to his apostles and upbraids them for not believing those who said they saw him risen. He then commands them to go into the world and preach the Gospel, and says:

> He who believes and is baptized will be saved;
> but he who does not believe will be condemned.
> And these signs will accompany those who believe:
> in my name they will cast out demons;
> they will speak in new tongues;
> they will pick up serpents, and if they drink any deadly thing,
>   it will not hurt them;
> they will lay their hands on the sick,
>   and they will recover.

Mark continues to relate that these apostles did indeed go forth and do the work of the Lord, and the Lord confirmed the message "by the signs that attended it" or, in the King James Version, "with signs following." Here ends Mark, and from here derives the name of the Holiness church mentioned above.

The relation of speaking in tongues to salvation is further evidenced in 2 Acts, the second key text for Pentecostal and Charismatic churches. It relates, speaking of the apostles:

> When the day of Pentecost had come,
>   they were all together in one place.

And suddenly a sound came from heaven like the rush of a mighty wind,
*   and it filled all the house where they were sitting.*
And there appeared to them tongues as of fire,
*   distributed and resting on each one of them.*
And they were all filled with the Holy Spirit and began to speak in other tongues,
*   as the Spirit gave them utterance.*

Because these events took place on the Pentecost (the Greek name for the Jewish Feast of Weeks), religious movements that seek to experience what the apostles did are called Pentecostal, or they are called Charismatic because of the adherents' desire to receive the charismata, the gifts of grace visited upon them by the Holy Spirit. Participants in these movements believe that their own speaking in tongues and ecstatic experiences are signs that they are saved. They have renounced the doubt that plagues those who adhere to the doctrine of particular election, and they embrace the idea that anyone may be saved—and yet these signs of salvation are still required.

Perhaps it is the strong need to overcome strong doubt that explains the great lengths to which some worshipers go to prove their salvation to themselves and their fellow worshipers. Some handle snakes; others swallow poison. Snakes may have been chosen precisely for the shock the handling delivers to outsiders. "Spread the Word! We're coming down from the mountains!" announced one preacher. The Holiness churches in which snakes are handled date only from about 1900. As with the Primitive Baptists, the churches value their independence. They are usually scattered throughout rural areas and are visited by a series of preachers. They first practiced snake handling in 1909, in Tennessee. Apparently it was not until 1918 that someone died from snakebite, and he was denounced as a backslider, someone who had lost his faith, when he died (La Barre 1964).

Snakes are typically brought out in their cages partway through the service, after a sermon and singing have taken place. Sometimes music continues, usually on a guitar, and worshipers begin to dance and enter trance states, at which time someone may pick up a snake and handle it before dropping it back into the cage or passing it on to someone else. The handling may take place in a more subdued setting, the snake passed from one person to another. Women and men handle the snakes. Perhaps 20 or more people are known to have died from snakebites in Holiness meetings; some state governments have responded by forbidding the use of poisonous snakes.

The Church of Jesus Christ with Signs Following in Alabama received national attention in 1992, when the church's preacher, Glenn Summerford, was accused of attempting to murder his wife by forcing her to put her hand in a case filled with poisonous rattlesnakes. She claimed he was trying to kill her because he could not divorce her and retain his position in the church. He claimed he did it to prove her innocence and that the snake bit her because she was backsliding. He was convicted and sent to jail, and his church, lacking any institutions for succession, disbanded. Other preachers soon began to hold outdoor snake-handling services, however (Covington 1995, 1–63).

But snake handling is just the most spectacular (at least to date) of a wide range of practices intended to bear witness to the divine presence within oneself. It is itself the most visible sign of the powerful need to bear witness in a striking and public way to God's grace, to the presence of the Holy Spirit in oneself.

Much more widespread than snake handling are practices of speaking in tongues. Even the relatively staid Lutheran churches of suburban St. Paul, Minnesota (near where I grew up), have begun to encourage members to speak in tongues. Some report a sense of release and of grace as the incomprehensible words flow out of them. They do not speak of the experience as like a trance, but as an experience over which they have some control. Charismatic movements are growing within Roman Catholicism as well, and in 1981 John Paul II met with Charismatic church leaders and gave his approval to their movement. Worldwide perhaps 120 million Catholics can be considered to be Charismatic. And Pentecostal churches are growing rapidly throughout the world, particularly in South America and Southeast Asia. In Brazil, where Umbanda and Macumba had become popular as supplements or alternatives to Catholicism, many are finding that Charismatic churches that focus worship on God but offer the opportunity to speak in tongues combine the best of both worlds.

All these movements are seen by participants as bringing the divine into themselves through the mediation of the Holy Ghost. The religious experience provides a material sign that God has accepted the worshiper and that he or she can hope or know of salvation. This particular emphasis on the individual's avenue to grace through personal experience—often spoken experience—is a key characteristic of Protestantism. The individual's relation to God through the inspirited Word is markedly different from the idea that contact with God is through the miracle of the Eucharist, itself mediated by the priest. Protestantism relocated God's miracles, his charismata, signs of grace, from communion and the icons of Mary and Jesus, to the individual's ways of speaking. Doing so made possible new forms of community and authority based on those ways of speaking, of which the churches discussed here are but a few instances.

Conclusions

In the religious traditions discussed in the chapter—Islamic, Navajo, and Protestant—speech is linked to power through the individual. The speaker who speaks truly and clearly is able to do so because of a relationship with the divine. This relationship is complex and debated, but across religious traditions an idea emerges that sacred speech, in its utterance, places the speaker in contact with the divine. Reciting the Qur'ân is repeating God's own words and can confer power on the speaker. Chanting Blessingway reenacts the events of creation that accompanied the first chanting by the First People. For some Protestants, a true worship service requires speaking in a holy way—in tongues, or when called by the Holy Spirit to preach, or when reading from the Bible in a state of inspiration. This inspirited speaking is in some respects the equivalent of other worshipers' contact with an image—the drawing in of power through an "exchange of vision" with a Hindu statue is probably the closest equivalent.

Catholic, Hindu, Japanese, and other traditions also rely on prayer for worship, of course. But the traditions studied in this chapter have taken the spoken element of worship and made it into the privileged element. When this is done—and it is done in different ways in each tradition—the subjective state of the individual also becomes a matter of increased concern. If an object is the center of worship, its objective qualities—its separation from the worshiper—give the process of worship an air if not a doctrine of objectivity: the worship succeeds if certain steps are taken. The Catholic mass is objectively efficacious even if the priest or the worshipers have their minds elsewhere. But once the words uttered by the worshiper become the whole of worship, those daydreamings endanger the very idea of worship. "Thought is the inner form of speech," say the Navajo; "no actions are effective without the correct intention" echo Muslims. Speech is close to thought, or ought to be, and words uttered must be accompanied by the proper state of mind if they are to reach their destination. Subjectivity now takes center stage.

Films to See

The series of seven short documentaries called *Through Navajo Eyes* would be one way to expand that section of the chapter. On Islam, a number of films trace Muhammad's life; *The Message* (starring Anthony Quinn) is interesting because it is widely showed by Muslims. *Beyond the Veil*, though somewhat dated, is still a superb film on how women in Cairo think about veiling, while *Divorce, Iranian Style* shows how a divorce court really works in Teheran.

Authority and Leaders

f *Religions in Practice: An Approach to the Anthropology of Religion*, 5/e. John J.
2011 by Pearson Education. Published by Prentice Hall. All rights reserved.

Authority and Leaders

We may believe in some religious ideas and carry out some religious practices, but very rarely do we decide to do this on our own. Much more often, we look to parents or religious leaders or texts or some sort of socially constituted body: a congregation, an informal group, or a social movement. To the extent that we reflect back on what we believe and seek to check or change it, we look for a source of authority. Authority in religion can come from people, texts, or experiences (visions, for example).

Human authorities can derive their legitimacy from diverse sources. The sociologist Max Weber suggested three types of legitimate authority: rules, tradition, and charisma, and this classification will give us a useful way to begin thinking about why people follow leaders, religious or other. We can think of leaders as authorities with social groups or movements. Social movements have some social coherence or "groupness," with leaders and followers and collective actions. To recruit or mobilize, they may draw on social networks (friends, their friends' friends, and so forth). A network may provide the ties that lead to someone joining a movement, or allow a leader to communicate ideas. We examine modalities of authority and leadership in this chapter.

AUTHORITY FIGURES

Writing in the early twentieth century, Weber argued that people may dominate others simply by making them afraid to disobey, but when that is not the case, when domination comes with reasons, then it is "authority." When domination is authority, those who obey others can justify why they do so. Weber sorted various forms of authority into three models or "ideal types": rational-legal, traditional, and charismatic.

Weber's "rational-legal" authority is based on rules and is the type most likely to be linked to explicit forms of justification: Today, governments, private corporations, and organized religious bodies have written rules or laws. Members of these groups—citizens, shareholder, and members of the congregation—can appeal to these written rules. Modern legal institutions function on the basis of accepted explicit rules, but so do religions th rely on texts to justify actions: These religious leaders cite revealed scripture, collected wisdom, or legal interpretations in support of their opinions and actions.

Weber's "traditional authority," his second type, draws its legitimacy in part from the passage of time: We have always done things this way; we have a proud heritage or tradition; the elders tell us this is how we do things. The authority of a religious leader is often based on this type of legitimate rule: He or she comes from a long line of leaders, or was chosen following a process that we have always used. Narrated traditions are important to supporting this kind of legitimacy: People often explain why they do things by telling stories of past leaders, or of ways of worshiping, or of the people.

Finally, "charismatic authority" often appears to override the other two types of authority, as when a prophet claims to have a divine gift or a new message or new powers. We often use "charisma" to refer to cases where people follow someone because they are attracted to him in some ineffable way (beauty or great speaking gifts), but Weber urges us to look for the ways followers justify their obedience. Hypnotic attraction would not fall into the realm of "authority" for Weber, even though it might well lead people to accept the justifications offered by a leader. Of the three types (and almost by definition), the charismatic authority—the prophet, messiah, or cult leader—is the most likely to be found leading a social movement.

We can define these "ideal types," as Weber called such constructions, but of course they bleed into one another in practice. Take the first category of rules or norms. It is hard to think of a set of rules that does not give rise to competing interpretations. People who manage to win converts to their reading of the rules do so in part because they can summon other authority-producing resources: they impress people, or they seem to be inspired (thus charismatic authority), or they come from a lineage of authoritative interpreters, or can do the best job of linking up to tradition (thus, traditional authority). And think about why we accept one set of rules or laws as authoritative within a religious tradition—usually it is because we believe that there was a moment of divine inspiration: God giving Moses the tablets or revealing the Qur'ân to Muhammad, or Gautama Buddha reaching enlightenment. In religious traditions based on revelation, almost by definition, the authority of rules depends on a divine intervention sometime in the past. Nonetheless, religious figures come to occupy their positions in ways that are mapped out by Weber's typology. Some figures are exemplars or leaders because others regard them as divinely inspired, or perhaps even as divine themselves. Others are elected following rules of selection; their position is entirely due to rule-following. Still others inherit their positions from a relative, and their authority is due to a tradition—even if their family or lineage is considered to be divinely graced.

SAINTS

The beginnings of a religion often lie in the personal authority generated by an individual: a prophet, saint, or holy man who is treated as truly exceptional among humans, and whose authority we call charismatic. This term originally referred to God's gift of power as understood in Christianity and as evidenced in such gifts of the spirit as miracles, faith, and speaking in tongues.

These charismatic leaders may be powerful sorcerers, or show their literal "inspiration" by speaking in tongues or acting possessed, as do shamans. The shaman's way of acting while possessed proves that he or she is indeed visited by special spirits; this proof then also lends legitimacy to the acts of healing or divination that follow. And, most importantly, the conviction that the shaman indeed has these powers is what does bring about healing.

In some societies these healers may become community leaders. In Wana society of Indonesia, they become the poles around which people gather to form settled communities. In urban Japan, they become the nuclei for new religious organizations that meet social and psychological needs of their followers. Healing may also involve other types of internal power or access to the divine. Mary Baker Eddy's popularity and the success of her Christian Science movement rested on her claims that all humans had within them the power to heal themselves.

Charismatic authority comes in many flavors; one is the saint or holy person, who provides an example of how to live a holy, virtuous, or religiously focused life. The saint is an "exemplar" (P. Brown 1987): a model of the ideal way to live, an ideal that is appropriately reflected on by everyone, even if living it out is beyond the reach of most people. Many religious traditions have stories about such exemplary people: stories of Christian martyrs, Jewish holy people or tsaddiqim, Muslim "friends of God," and the exemplary followers of Gautama Buddha in India or of Lao Tze in China. In a broad sense, stories about virtuous ancestors in any community serve the same purpose of instructing the living on how best to live.

In some traditions, the exemplary life in fact becomes the single most important element in teaching. Christianity is in many ways about Christ's lived example; Islamic teachings rely on Muhammad's life as well as God's commands. Precisely how the religion's prime exemplar lives can be taken to define the major thrusts of the religion. Gautama Buddha's turning away from the world to find enlightenment through meditation became the paradigm for the monk and the lay person, especially in the Theravada Buddhism of South and Southeast Asia. By contrast, the exemplary life of Confucius in China is based on harmony within the community, and is defined through the relationships people have with others in their family, their immediate society, and in their relationship to the state. This ethic of harmonious worldly involvement defines the virtues for which everyone should strive.

The idea of harmony or balance is also the basis for Haitian Vodou. Karen McCarthy Brown (1987) views the ritual practices of Alourdes, a Vodou healer who lives in New York, as providing a moral exemplar to others in her community. Alourdes's role is, in the eyes of participants, passive, as the "horse" ridden by the spirits who possess her. The spirits embody conflicting aspects of life for these Haitians: courage and childishness, or caring and capriciousness. Alourdes dances among different such spirits, being possessed by one after another. Her possession performances intensify and clarify the clash of such forces in the world. For those who watch her, writes Brown (1987, 167), "the moral problem is not evil but imbalance, both within and among persons." In her tacking among different deities, Alourdes exemplifies how to maintain such a balance.

The Vodou case reminds us that spirits and deities can also serve as moral exemplars, and that as a plurality of beings they can define different points in a moral space, different aspects of the moral universe. Alourdes dramatizes this plurality of spirits and ways of acting, as does the polarity of Vishnu and Shiva in Hinduism, with Vishnu as the preserver and king; Shiva as the destroyer and ascetic. Christianity provides not only the polarity of God and Satan, but also the different kinds of examples originating from Jesus, Mary, and the saints. Muslims see the world as populated by both good and bad spirits, who live in societies resembling human societies. These spirits embody "good" and "bad" traits more definitively than do complex human beings. They also illustrate the virtues of community: The good ones cooperate and thrive; the bad ones quarrel because of jealousy and hatred.

Saints and other kinds of holy persons provide practical help as well as moral examples to ordinary people. People pray to Christian saints for help, or they place the medallions of those saints in their homes or automobiles. Muslims and Buddhists also ask the spirits of holy people to help in a variety of ways. Living saints may produce talismans or amulets, objects containing some of the saint's power, for people to take home with them. (Writing can also serve as a talisman; Jewish and Islamic scriptures may be placed in a position to guard the home.)

The power to help wielded by saints and by talismans is a secondary power, deriving from their intermediate role between a deity and an ordinary person. They are "intercessors," interceding in the relationship between the ordinary person and the divinity. Muhammad, Mary, or the healer Alourdes all serve as intercessors. Because saints do not own their power, they can distribute it to others, through prayer, talismans, or dreams. In this respect they resemble the shamanic healer who channels the power of a spirit through his body and voice.

The holy man's ability to receive and distribute power sometimes comes precisely from his personal disinterest in power. The ascetic, the individual who renounces worldly pleasure for the sake of spiritual enlightenment, is a figure in many religions, from St. Francis of Assisi, to the forest-dwelling Buddhist monk, to the Nuer prophet Ngundeng of the Sudan, discussed below. Ngundeng's trance-like behavior and eating of filth placed him outside of ordinary society and gave his words added force. Mohandas K. Gandhi further developed the Hindu tradition of saintly asceticism (Fox 1989) by drawing from international exemplars, including Jesus, St. Francis, and Tolstoy.

The holy man as "renouncer," as ascetic, illustrates how the two features of sainthood—as exemplar and as helper—can present a paradox or tension. In the Hindu and Buddhist climates of South and Southeast Asia, the saintly man cuts off contact with the mundane world in order to achieve salvation. But others flock to this saint precisely because he is powerful (Tambiah 1976). Furthermore, he comes to depend on the offerings given by these devotees. How can a world renouncer also be the leader of a movement? This paradox is even more acute today, when some of these "renouncers" attract millions of followers, not only in South Asia but also in Europe and North America. We turn to two examples of these saints: a forest-dwelling Buddhist monk in Thailand, and a Hindu "god-man" who uses jets but also urges followers to return to Hindu traditions.

Acharn Man, a Buddhist Forest Dweller

In Thailand, monks are known as either "forest dwellers" or "town dwellers," with the first specializing in meditation and the second in book-learning. (Many monks combine aspects of both the categories.) Some forest monks become known as "perfected saints" or arahants (Tambiah 1976). Although their powers come from having turned away from the world, they also bless commercially produced amulets that are distributed to the lay masses. The king and queen of Thailand, along with generals and rich bankers, seek out these forest monks to absorb some of their moral powers.

From where do these powers come? In the Buddhist teachings consulted by monks and royalty, meditating and renouncing material possessions allow the ascetic to ascend to higher than ordinary levels of consciousness and to find there superior powers, *iddhi*. These powers enable him to vanish and then reappear, to hear far-off sounds, and to recall his own past lives. But the monk must refrain from enjoying these powers, lest in his worldliness he is impeded in his quest for salvation. Here the monk recalls the efforts of Gautama Buddha to avoid worldliness and yet also help humanity.

The complex life of the saint can be illustrated through the biography of Acharn Man (1870–1943), the most famous exemplar among Thailand's contemporary monks. As with Sufi orders in Islam, and lineages of rebbes in Judaism, Buddhist monks trace their spiritual lineages, their sources of inspiration and powers, to earlier monks. Most forest monks today trace their own lineage to Acharn Man.

Man's biography shows him not only wandering alone throughout Laos and Thailand but also attracting disciples, whom he then encouraged to form small monastic cells. In a story analogous to that of Gautama Buddha, Man is portrayed as passing through periods of wandering, followed by seclusion and meditation, instructing disciples in villages, and pacifying tigers in the forest. To his disciples, Man was primarily an exemplar, but to his circle of lay followers, he was mainly a "field of merit" (Tambiah 1976, 121). Donations of food or other gifts to Man brought the donor religious merit and blessings in return. After Man's death, some of his disciples joined lay followers in promoting the cult of talismans stamped with his image. Others became forest dwellers in their own right. The talismans are metal medallions, with the image of Acharn Man on one side, and the lay person or organization that contributed funds for the medallion on the other. A follower of Man blesses the talisman by holding one end of a cord that lies on a pile of the objects, and then engaging in meditation, transferring some of his own powers to the medallion.

Acharn Man's charismatic powers thus continue to be radiated outward to the public through a chain of spiritual transfers. This chain starts from his own person and image, through his followers who themselves have gained higher powers, through their direct physical contact with the metal talismans they bless, to the consumer of the talisman. Note the similarity to the chains of direct contact created by Christian relics: the painting of the Virgin made by a saint that is associated with the city of Czestochowa, Poland, is doubly blessed for its content and saintly contact; replicas of the painting derive some of this blessing when they are touched to the original.

Sathya Sai Baba, a Jet-Age Holy Man

India's contemporary saints are of several types. Some are leaders of large devotional orders, many of them directing worship toward the god Rama. These saints inherited their leadership position from their own teachers, and so on back into time, in a fashion similar to the spiritual lineage of the Buddhist monk. The orders preserve these genealogies of teachers, which tie today's leader across the centuries to the founding saint. One Hindu order, the Ramanandis, dedicated to Rama, consists of both ascetics—some of whom renounce all worldly interests and wander, near-naked—and temple dwellers—who pursue the devotion to Rama through chanting. (These movements have played an important role in current Hindu political activity.)

While many of these devotionalist orders are centuries old and make their antiquity their warrant of legitimacy, a new kind of saint, the "god-man," makes miracles to show his power and promises salvation to today's middle class. Some of the god-men have attracted large international followings; in the United States these include Bhagwan Rajneesh and the Maharishi Mahesh Yogi. But in India, the most famous of these figures is Sathya Sai Baba. He has attracted large followings in the large cities. Some Buddhists in Sri Lanka have also become followers of Sai Baba, seeing him as the Maitreya Buddha.

Sathya Sai Baba's appeal is especially to the English-speaking middle and upper-middle classes, and he is often en route by plane or automobile to meet with his followers. As Lawrence Babb (1986, 159–201) explains, Sathya Sai Baba is worshiped as a "descent" of God to earth, an *avatâr*. Indeed, his followers refer to him as Bhagavân, "God." At 13 he underwent a prolonged seizure; emerging from it months later he explained that he was the incarnation of an earlier holy man, Sai Baba, who blended Hindu and Muslim traditions. Twenty years later he added, after another seizure, that he was also the deities Shiva and Shakti. He said that after him there would be another incarnation of Shiva—this new holy man would be his successor. (He thereby solved the problem of succession ahead of time.) His miracles also became more tightly associated with Shiva: He would materialize sacred ash, a symbol of Shiva's powers, at festivals to Shiva, or materialize lingas (phallus-shaped places of devotions to Shiva) inside his own body, which he would then eject through his mouth.

His followers frequently refer to his miracles as evidence of his divinity. He cures apparently incurable illnesses, raises the dead, accomplishes surgery from a distance, changes sand into religious books, foretells a devotee's thoughts, and, his own particular specialty, materializes objects out of thin air. He apparently can produce any object, but he most often materializes sacred ash, about one pound per day, for devotees to take away with them. He is also said to leave ash footprints in people's houses without ever having entered the premises.

This god-man's cult has no formal boundaries, no membership lists, and no centers. It is a loose collection of those who consider themselves his devotees, centered on him alone. But the trusts that exist in his name receive large amounts of donations and use the money to maintain devotional centers, publish books and magazines, and build Sathya Sai Colleges, eventually, according to plans, one in each state. The trusts also sponsor charitable activities, including feeding the poor and working as relief agents during floods or other natural disasters. None of these activities proscribe any special religious rites, and the followers include Hindus and some Muslims. At devotion sessions they sing songs devoted to Sathya Sai Baba and engage in worship at an altar; they may also purchase pictures of the holy man, recordings of the songs, or even life-sized plaster replicas of his feet.

Sathya Sai Baba has special appeal to the educated, often rather secularized urban people (and white New Agers) in the United States, and this appeal is at first glance puzzling. These people should be the first to reject magic. But, it is the people who have left many older religious and social practices behind who often feel most in need of new ways to solve personal crises. In India, these people include city dwellers who accept the new conditions of secularism and egalitarianism but worry about the loss of an older life. They find it difficult to maintain religious obligations and find older patterns of authority broken down. Those who come from high castes worry about the pollution they experience in their new lives, where they mingle with people from lower castes in what feels to them to be a disordered way.

The often disorienting conditions of modern life may have led many of these followers to discover their own cultural and religious identity in need of supplement. At times of crisis—illness, loss of employment, family discord, and so on—they may be attracted to a new kind of immediately available healing power. Sathya Sai Baba's teachings reinforce their fears at the same time that he offers remedies. He blames Western values and national disorder for much of what ails people, and urges adherents to return to the study of the older Hindu texts. As D. A. Swallow (1982) shows, Sai Baba dramatizes the continuing power of Shiva to deal with pollution and sickness, to overcome pollution and restore health. He embodies Shiva, reassuring his followers of the continuing presence of the god even in this secularized world. His devotees find a way to recover the very religiosity they have left behind, through the visible magic the holy man performs. His cult is not demanding—people can participate in the magic merely by buying a portrait, or reading a magazine—and it may offer something of their more religious past. Indeed, he claims that wealth and liberation go together. He can be experienced as combining the best of old and new: Shiva, health, wealth, and social work.

PROPHETS

Religious movements usually start with charismatic figures, of which a prophet is the emblematic figure. Some prophets are also saints; they stake out a path to enlightenment by setting an example, and it is this personal example that remains behind as their primary prophetic legacy. Such was the case for Gautama Buddha in India and for Kobo Daishi in Japan (the saint in whose name Japanese undertake the Shikoku pilgrimage). Max Weber (1978, 447–451) called this type the "exemplary prophet" and contrasted it to the "ethical prophet," whose role is based on the claim to bear specific messages from divine authority. Muhammad, prophet of Islam, and Joseph Smith, prophet of Mormonism, said they were ordinary individuals through whom God relayed a call to return to the proper ways of worship. Moses, of whom we know little, was also an "ethical prophet," revealing commands from an ethical, law-giving deity.

These distinctions are general ones, again instances of what Weber called "ideal types." In practice, followers attribute many diverse qualities to prophets. Some Muslims treat all of Muhammad's actions, from the color of his clothes to the manner in which he ate, as if they provided a divine example for humankind. This view moves the figure of Muhammad closer to the status of saint. Others take a different view, considering only certain of his actions—how he conducted the pilgrimage to Mecca, for example—to have been inspired by God and thus intended as examples or models. They emphasize his ordinary human qualities precisely in order to underscore the belief that the Qur'ân came from God, not Muhammad. Such terms as "saint," "prophet," and "charisma" can therefore only be taken as indicators of types of roles and tendencies within religious movements, not clear-cut descriptions of individual leaders.

The Problem of the Prophet's Continuity

Sathya Sai Baba's teachings emphasize a return to older scriptures. But when a prophet has a new message to deliver, how can he or she transmit the prophetic authority and message beyond immediate surrounds and to the next generation? The power of the prophet may be embodied in portable objects (such as the powerful statues found in both Japanese Buddhism and European Catholicism). The message may be transmitted and transferred through verbal reports, or even songs, as in the Nuer case discussed below.

These orally transmitted messages may be considered as more authentic than written messages. (Such is the case for religious traditions in India, North America, and in Islam, for example.) When prophetic messages are transmitted, they become subject to radical change, as in the example below of the Ghost Dance. Variant versions of the original message arise. In many religions, the fact of having many versions of "the same" sacred narrative does not pose a problem. Navajo narratives of the world's origin are told in many ways and in many contexts, and this plurality of versions suits the many uses to which the narrative is put. The story of Beautyway, for example, describes world origins and the close ties between speech and thought. Narrating the story brings to life the power of creation and the power of words, to be used in healing or blessing. Different versions of the sacred story can accomplish these goals.

In other religious traditions, however, the nature of the narrative makes such diversity problematic. If, as in Islam or Christianity, the religious message stresses the importance of conformity to divine commands by the community as a whole, then disagreement about those commands will likely lead to divisions in the community. If religious leaders perceive this danger, then they will likely act to create a single version of scripture, commit it to writing, and repress alternative versions of scripture. (They will also likely act to expel religious dissidents.) Such was the case for both the Gospels and the Qur'ân: leaders of the religious community collected one version, which they declared the authoritative one. In both cases revelations had been transmitted orally and in several versions. In the case of the Qur'ân, written copies were circulated, but when the verses were collected in an authoritative version, other written versions were ordered destroyed. In the case of the Christian Gospels, writing the narratives of Jesus happened well after his death, and in many versions. Books not included in the version of Gospels accepted by the Church were labeled "apocryphal."

This passage from the individual holy person, to multiple memories of his or her life, to an authoritative scriptural text, requires the emergence of a centralized religious authority. Authority becomes less personal, and more bureaucratic. Max Weber called the process of transforming religious authority the routinization of authority, by which he meant the creation of routine ways of arranging succession to the leadership, structuring the religious organization, and resolving disputes. Even when "routinized," most religious movements are forced to come to terms with other claims to authority, either claims within the movement or assertions of superior authority by external political institutions, especially by states.

The "routinization" of a movement is one way for religious authority to be transferred. One example of this change of authority comes from the changes in authority among seventeenth-century Quakers. The Quaker prophet George Fox had been able to keep the movement together in its early years by virtue of his personal powers of persuasion, but the very ideas that animated early Quakers worked against any centralized control. The spirit, argued the early Quakers, inspires those persons whom it would inspire, so that speaking at meetings, or other social behavior, should not be regulated. The resulting Quaker tendency to pose stark and shocking challenges to established authority—from using "impolite" speech, to refusing to take oaths of loyalty to the King, to going naked as a sign of innocence before God—led to state repression and to turmoil within the movement itself.

Quaker elders eventually came to "routinize" authority in order to preserve the movement. They established firm rules about how meetings were to be run and how individual Quakers were to speak with other people. Even ways of preaching changed, from a style that emphasized the "coproduction" of the sermon by preacher and congregation to a style that emphasized the singular authority of the preacher.

The Birth of Prophecy in the Sudan

Although the Nuer people of the southern Sudan have given rise to many types of leaders and magicians, a new type of "ethical prophet" first emerged in the late nineteenth century. His message has been preserved, transmitted, and used to diverse ends, through the media of song and radio.

Douglas Johnson (1994 calls Ngundeng Bong (d. 1906) the first prophet, the first "vessel of divinity," among the Nuer. As a young man Ngundeng began to exhibit strange behavior, including wandering alone in the bush, fasting, and eating cow dung. His relatives interpreted this behavior as evidence that he had been "seized" by a divinity—much like the way Sathya Sai Baba was "seized" in his youth. They sacrificed oxen in the hope of propitiating these divinities. After these sacrifices, Ngundeng became normal once again. He reported that he had indeed been seized by a deity, the divinity Deng. He began to teach people prayers to this deity.

Before this time, Nuer had frequently sought help from clan deities, but Ngundeng declared that Deng was a deity for all the Nuer. It was less likely that many people agreed with him because of a crisis in Nuer society, argues Johnson (1994, 327–329), or the clash with British armies—indeed, it came before the impact of colonial rule began to be felt. Johnson points instead to the general increase in mobility and dislocation in the late nineteenth century in this part of Africa. In a way similar to the effects of social mobility on religious consciousness in the first millennium B.C.E., the Axial Age, these social changes may have made the idea of a general divinity more appealing to many Nuer. The Nuer were already imputing a more active role to clan deities in causing good or bad fortune than they had before, and they were concerned about the power of magic possessed by other groups. Ngundeng's claims thus fit with general changes in religious and social consciousness.

Ngundeng built up his influence and authority through a series of successful acts of religious sacrifice. Before a critical battle with another Nuer group, Ngundeng sacrificed an ox to Deng. His side won the battle. Ngundeng soon gained a reputation for having power over life and death. Merely by looking at him, said, some, he was able to cause the death of a relative who had denied him meat. Others who refused his demands soon died, without his having to say or do anything. He was also credited with making many barren women fertile by making sacrifices to Deng. Upon the outbreak of smallpox in 1888–1889, he sacrificed oxen and urged everyone to leave their houses; the incidence of smallpox upon the people who listened to him was relatively low. (One doctor who was present at the time said that the extra meat produced by the sacrifices, together with the act of inducing people to spread out, probably did contribute to a reduction in susceptibility to the disease.)

But Ngundeng was a prophet, not a sorcerer. He was able to turn other prophets and magicians into his disciples. He mediated feuds between clans, usually through sacrifices. He was able to bring together many clans through his prophetic activities, citing messages from Deng. Soon after the smallpox outbreak, he began work on a large earthen mound, and mobilized thousands of Nuer to work on the mound for over four years. The completed mound was said to enclose all evil and disease inside it. Sacrifices at the mound were intended to benefit all Nuer, not just the particular clan who had brought the ox. The idea that a religious act or a deity could give general benefits to all Nuer was an innovation over earlier ideas and practices.

The prophet spread his message widely through the hymns and songs he recited, which he said had been created by the divinity Deng. These songs urged Nuer to reconcile with each other and with their various enemies. Even after British raids on Nuer camps in 1902, one of his, or rather Deng's, songs pleaded:

> *I reject the fight you bring*
> *Divinity and the prophet do not quarrel*

The Nuer have not enjoyed peace in recent years. Relations between the Islamic northern part of the Sudan and the non-Islamic, mainly Christian south, have been violent. Southern rebels have often sung Ngundeng's songs in support of their struggle. He was said to have predicted the wars against the north. But his songs were also sung by Nuer opponents of the rebels. In addition, some of the divisions among Nuer pitted Nuer groups against members of a neighboring group, the Dinka. In 1988, these factions finally joined forces against the north, and announced their reconciliation publicly by way of another Ngundeng song:

> *Nuer and Dinka*
> *even if you hate yourselves*
> *There will come a time when you will recognize me as your father.*

The rebel radio broadcast Ngundeng's songs right after the announcement of the reconciliation, and the legacy of his prophecy continued to animate southern resistance against the north thereafter.

MORMONS

The history of the Mormons shows both how a movement can change the nature of its authority from charismatic (in this case, prophetic) to bureaucratic, and how it adapts to demands made by an encompassing political structure (in this case, the U.S. government).

The Church of Jesus Christ of Latter-day Saints, commonly known as the Mormon Church, traces its origins to a man Mormons consider a prophet, Joseph Smith (Anderson 1942; Shipps 1985). In the 1820s, Smith received divine revelations concerning certain records that had been written on golden plates and buried near his home near

Palmyra, New York. According to his own account, Smith unearthed the plates and translated them "from Reformed Egyptian" to English with the aid of two translation stones. By 1829, two years after he found the plates, Smith had completed translating them. He had kept the plates away from the vision of others, working on one side of a curtain while his scribe—initially his wife—remained on the other. He was then given further directions through divine revelation, and in particular to begin founding a new church of Christ. In it, he would speak as a prophet and would initiate others, who would also speak God's words. The church would baptize people in a new covenant with God, augmenting the earlier covenants delivered through Moses and Jesus Christ.

Smith published the translation as the Book of Mormon in 1830. The book is written in much the same English prose style as the King James Version of the Bible, and has a similar organization into books and sections. It was thus familiar in approach to the Americans reading it for the first time. The Book of Mormon tells of a tribe of Israelites who, in about 600 B.C.E., sailed to the Americas. There they built cities and temples, and continued to obey the Law of Moses. They were visited by Jesus Christ after his death and resurrection. Christ performed miracles and organized a new church with 12 disciples. But the Israelites fought among themselves. In a reprise of Cain versus Abel, one group, the Lamanites, who had become hunters, disobeyed God's word, but it was they who prevailed over the other group, the peaceful farming Nephites. (The Lamanites' descendants are said to be today's Native Americans.) The last remaining Nephite prophet was Mormon, who wrote an account of the travels and struggles of these Israelites on gold plates and passed them on to his son, Moroni. Moroni buried the plates for discovery by the people who could restore the church that had once existed in America. It was Moroni's angel who revealed to Smith the location of the tablets. The "Latter-Day Saints" of the church are those who respond to the new direct revelations from God, the first revelations since those delivered through Christ. In the Mormon view, Christianity was misled soon after its founding. God had decided to reestablish his true church, with Smith as its prophet.

Soon after the publication of the book, Smith began to attract a small group of followers, a few of whom attested to having seen the gold tablets. The group grew over time, and eventually followed Smith out of New York. His success as a prophet must be seen in the religious context of his place and time. In the northeast United States of the 1820s, a diversity of religious faiths and movements abounded. This diversity was due in part to the intensity of the religious emotions following on the Second Great Awakening, a period of religious revival throughout the region that had begun three decades earlier. The revival encouraged religious experimentation and the questioning of established churches. (Adventism also began in this region during the same period.) Many people sought more direct forms of contact with Jesus Christ than those offered through standard liturgies. Joseph Smith himself said he was confused by the diversity of religions open to him, and his first revelation was mainly a message from a divine figure telling him not to join any of the existing churches, but to recover the authentic form of Christianity. As with Islam, Mormonism began as, and remains today, a call to return to the purity of the early worship of God.

Smith's part of New York State was also replete with Native American populations and mounds of ancient origin, and the Book of Mormon responded to a deep curiosity about the origins of Native Americans and the identities of the mound builders. (This curiosity was behind much early archeological speculation in North America.)

Smith himself already had a reputation as a person in touch with the unseen. Before he received the revelations, he had found a "seerstone," a smooth, egg-shaped stone used to locate lost objects. He and his father indeed worked as treasure hunters, benefiting from generally accepted beliefs in the powers of seers. After his first revelation, members of his family stopped attending the local Presbyterian Church, and joined him in waiting to found a new church of apostles of Christ.

Relatives and neighbors began to accept Joseph's claims, not despite his reputation as a practitioner of magical arts, but because that reputation supported his claims to have found a true treasure—in other words, his initial claims to authority were based on a sense of him as charismatic, as having received a special gift. Soon the church had 40 members, with Joseph as its Prophet, Seer, Apostle of Jesus Christ, and Elder.

In 1831, Smith moved the church to Kirtland, Ohio, which he proclaimed was on the eastern edge of Zion, the Church's ultimate destination. There he attempted to construct a communal form of economy based on sharing, the legacy of which is the tithe, one-tenth of one's income that members are expected to pay the church. Financial difficulties and local hostilities led Smith to move some of the Ohio Mormons to Missouri. Their partial economic success in Missouri, their perceived socialism, and the large numbers of immigrants they attracted led to local attacks on the Mormons (Leone 1979, 11–16). Smith at one point made explicit the parallel to Muhammad's experience of a call for religious purity followed by persecution, when he publicly proclaimed, "I will be a second Muhammad." This parallel hardly improved his image locally, and in 1838, after renewed attacks on the community, the Mormons moved back across the Mississippi to an Illinois town they renamed Nauvoo.

In Nauvoo, Smith rebuilt the church around the divine revelations he continued to receive. These instructions included the doctrine, written down privately in 1843, that God intended males to take more than one wife. This doctrine, announced publicly from Salt Lake City in 1852, was part of a new vision of the afterlife, in which marriages properly conducted by the Church would be for eternity, and a man with his wives and all his progeny would move on to rule new worlds. Taking plural wives would mean a larger retinue of progeny, and it followed the example of the Hebrew patriarchs Abraham, Isaac, and Jacob (Foster 1981, 123–80).

Smith attracted many additional adherents, most of whom, poor, had left unprofitable farmlands or poorly paid factory jobs, and were attracted by the utopian message of the Mormons. The community grew into tens of thousands, with Smith as its leader, now declared to be King of the Kingdom of God. He became increasingly concerned with controlling dissident voice and in 1844 destroyed an opposition press, an action that led to his arrest. On June 27, 1844, a mob stormed the jail where he was held and lynched him.

The New Prophet and Conflicts with the United States

As with most prophet-led movements, Smith's death found no automatic successor. Struggles for leadership produced several factions. In particular, two lines of reasoning emerged. One group argued that the Smith's descendants had inherited his right to rule. This group followed members of Smith's family back to Missouri, where they established the Reorganized Church of Latter-day Saints. This church was headquartered today in Independence, Missouri, where it since changed its name and gave rise to numerous spin-off churches. A second group, the majority, continued the leadership of Smith's church, arguing that the followers had the right to choose their leader. They chose an elder, Brigham Young, to become the new Prophet and Elder. Young led the community westward, across the Great Plains, to the Great Salt Lake in what is today Utah. (A similar debate over succession, at the break between charismatic and "routinized" authority, occurred in Islam, as we shall see in the next section.)

By 1849, Brigham Young had established an autonomous, theocratic (religion-ruled) state on the lake called Deseret. Hundreds of small communities sprung up in orbit around the lake, extending into today's Arizona, Colorado, Nevada, and California. The need for cooperation in creating irrigation provided a material base for authority in these new communities; the church held them together through an intricate hierarchy of leaders and through its ownership of numerous enterprises.

In 1850 the territory came under U.S. rule, and tensions quickly mounted between the Mormons and the U.S. government toward which Mormons had always felt uneasy. For its part, the government feared that the Mormons might refuse to acknowledge the U.S. sovereignty. During the 1850s, armed conflict occurred on several occasions between Mormons and "Gentiles" (non-Mormons), and in 1857, President James Buchanan sent an army of 5,000 troops to try and occupy Utah. Polygamy, now made public, became a symbol of the conflict, and in 1862 Congress banned the practice (Firmage 1991). In 1879, the U.S. Supreme Court upheld the U.S. statutory ban on polygamy, declaring the law not to infringe religious freedom but rather to protect a vital social institution. In 1890, the Court upheld additional severe legislation that dissolved the Mormon Church as a corporation and confiscated most major Church properties.

The Mormon Church president responded to these assaults by advising his followers not to contract plural marriage or polygamy. However, he did not characterize the directive to be a revelation, as most other important directives had been and would continue to be characterized. Some Mormons continued to practice polygamy in smaller communities. By statehood, in 1896, the church was deeply in debt. Mormons had become part of a larger economy of the Western states, characterized by industries of mining, livestock, timber, and railroad, all bankrolled from the East. But since the 1930s, the church has regenerated its wealth, building on its tithing requirement, and Mormons have become successful capitalist entrepreneurs.

Authority and History Today

The Book of Mormon continues to serve as a sacred book to today's Mormons, who in 2007 numbered over 13 million world-wide. The Mormon following expands both through extensive missionary activities and by encouraging large families—children are said to incarnate already existing spirits, and to advance one's own standing in the next world. Beginning at 12, every Mormon male passes through several grades in each of two orders of priesthood. At about 18, most men also go on a two-year mission for the church, and are rewarded by passing into the second, adult priesthood order.

Mormons are grouped into wards of about 700 persons; 10 wards make up a Stake of Zion, headed by a president. The center of Mormon activity is Salt Lake City, where the Quorom of Twelve Apostles manages the church. The senior Apostle becomes the church's president on the death of the previous president. Mormons attend local chapels, and at intervals also attend services at one of the temples found in different parts of the United States and overseas. Chapels hold Sunday services, centered on a form of communion which is quite similar to that held in Lutheran and some other Protestant churches. Lay persons preside over the service and do most of the talking. Rituals held in the larger temples are kept secret from non-Mormons, but they include services held both for the living and for deceased ancestors of living Mormons.

Mormons attach great importance to the long-term historical record. They do so in part because of their ideas about salvation, and in part because of the particular historical account provided in the Book of Mormon. First, Mormons see themselves as capable of saving the souls of deceased persons. Ancestors of Mormons who lived before the advent of Mormonism may be baptized into the church, with a living person standing in for the ancestor. These souls may then be taken through the successive temple rites that move persons up the ranks of the priesthood. These ancestors may be very far removed, and in theory those who can be aided include a large percentage of the world's people. But to do so one must establish the connection to a living Mormon. Therefore, Mormons carry out extensive research into the family trees of, in theory, everyone in the world. The resulting vast holdings of genealogical records, located in Salt Lake City, are available to non-Mormons as well as members of the church.

Second, history matters because history underlies the church's claims to authority. The Mormon Apostles see themselves as the direct heirs of God's message to humankind, through the media of the buried tablets and succeeding direct revelations to the church's Prophets. The rationale for these revelations lies in the saga of Israelites fleeing Jerusalem, founding a new community, witnessing Christ, and establishing a new covenant with God. Though the community was eventually destroyed, it left its message for the latter-day Prophet, Joseph Smith, through whom God's communication with his people was reopened.

History thus provides the rationale, the reasonable account, of why it was that Joseph Smith became a new Prophet. The historical record of continued revelations to his successors depicts them, too, as Prophets. In the eyes of the outside analyst, the charismatic authority of Joseph Smith was replaced by the bureaucracy of the church in Salt Lake City. In the eyes of the church leadership, however, Smith's successors continue to serve as Prophets, Seers, and Apostles. They continue to receive charisma, divine blessings, from God, in the form of revelations. Charismatic authority is changed, but not lost.

This historical account does, however, present Mormons with dilemmas in everyday life, especially in their attitudes toward Native Americans. Descended from the Lamanites, the ancient people who disobeyed God and wiped out the obedient Nephites, Native Americans are nonetheless also descended from Israelites. They are thus of the same origins as are Mormons, and for a group that places great emphasis on genealogy, this connection gives Native Americans a special status. They are entitled to convert and become full members of the church, a privilege long denied to African Americans. Mark Leone (1979, 174–177) describes a service in an Arizona chapel at which a missionary couple described their experience living several years at a Navajo reservation. The couple spoke from their experience in business about how Navajo were like anyone else. The couple's talk encouraged their listeners to put aside conflicting attitudes toward the Navajo, and to get on with their twin concerns of commerce and conversion.

MUSLIMS

When Joseph Smith announced that he would be "a second Muhammad," he was refer-ring to the special role played by the Prophet of Islam vis-à-vis previous religions. Muhammad, like Smith, saw himself as God's vehicle to perfect and complete the work of revelation. In the views of both men, Judaism and Christianity were indeed the results of God's revelations that had strayed from the original message.

Islam was born against a background of polytheism, however, and the statement most often pronounced by a Muslim, called the confession of faith, begins with the dictum: "there is no other deity but God." Islam began in the desert central area of the Arabian Peninsula in the seventh century C.E. Trade and social life were organized by tribes, without central authorities. Power resided in one's lineage connections. Arabs also worshiped many deities, although trade with Syria had also brought the monothe-istic ideas of Judaism and Christianity.

Muhammad's own tribe, the Quraysh, dominated the city of Mecca by its control of the caravan trade. Mecca became a religious as well as a trade center; people came to the city on pilgrimages to its shrines, which included the Ka'ba. Several verses of the Qur'ân berate the Meccans for worshiping many gods, and for letting the Ka'ba, built by the prophet Abraham, degenerate into a site of pagan worship. Monotheism remains one of the central emphases in Islam. This emphasis makes especially sensitive the appeals routinely made by many Muslims to other entities (spirits, saints, or prophets) that they intercede with God. These appeals are often branded as polytheism by other Muslims, who cite the Qur'ânic texts originally directed at the merchants of Mecca.

MUHAMMAD AS MESSENGER AND PROPHET

The second part of the confession of faith reads: "and Muhammad is his Messenger." Muhammad was born about 570 C.E. and was orphaned early in his life. He married an older woman, a trader, and managed her caravan. He began to receive revelations when he was 40, in 610 (Peters 1994). The first verse of the Qur'ân to be revealed reached Muhammad when he was in a cave. The archangel Gabriel appeared to him and said: "Recite, in the name of the Lord who created, created man from a clot." (The first word of this verse is sometimes translated as "read," and quoted as evidence that God intends people to educate themselves.)

Muhammad then began to warn the Meccan people of the errors of their polythe-istic ways. A few men followed him; most threatened him, and in 622 he fled or made the emigration, hijra, to the nearby city of Medina. The emigration marks the beginning of the (lunar) Islamic calendar. In Medina, Muhammad became the leader of the community through his skill in arbitrating between its several populations. He joined with the Jews of the city in praying in the direction of Jerusalem; verses revealed during this time stress the similarity of the two religions. (These verses include the dietary laws, for example.) Muhammad's growing group of followers engaged the Meccans in several battles, most notably those of Badr and Uhud, and his victories finally won him the right to make the pilgrimage to Mecca. He died after making the pilgrimage, in 632.

The place of Muhammad in Islam is both as the Messenger of God and as the Seal of the Prophets. As Messenger of God, Rasulullah, he brought a new collection of God's revealed word to humankind. Other messengers in the past had brought other books: Moses, the Torah; David, the Psalms; and Jesus, the Gospels. This lineage of revelation makes Jews and Christians, along with Muslims, "people of the book." (Hindus were later included in this category because of their use of sacred texts.) Because of their special status, members of these two religious communities were accorded special, protected treatment in Muslim-held territories.

As a prophet, *nabi*, Muhammad is the last in a long series of prophets, including the earlier Messengers. Among the prophets mentioned in the Qur'ân are Abraham, Noah, Hud, Salih, Lot, and Shu'ayb. Hud, Salih, and Shu'ayb do not figure in the Hebrew Bible, but appear in various stories, often as specifically Middle Eastern personages. Shu'ayb warns his people against dishonest business practices, as did Moses warn the Pharaoh against preventing the Israelites from going free.

Muhammad was thus human, a normal human being granted the role of God's mouthpiece. What is sent are words, and not Muhammad himself. Because all messengers are said to have this status, Muslims strongly deny the claim that Jesus was the son of God. Nonetheless, many Western commentators on Islam continue to make the error of presuming that the place of Muhammad in Islam is analogous to that of Jesus in Christianity. (Islam once was called "Muhammadanism" in the West.) It would be more accurate to draw an analogy between Jesus in Christianity, and the Qur'ân in Islam, in that each is held by the religion's adherent to be God's major gift to humans. Similarly, the Gospels, the accounts of the life and statements of Jesus, are best compared not to the Qur'ân but to the hadîth, the record of Muhammad's life and statements.

Who Rules after Muhammad?

Muhammad's authority in the early Muslim community came from his direct ties to God. He was a prophet, but would have to be succeeded by someone who was not a prophet. Who was to rule after his death? On what principle should he be chosen? Or in Weber's terms, how was Muhammad's charismatic authority to be converted into a routine mechanism for selecting leaders?

Muhammad had neither designated a successor nor suggested a way of doing so. He had no male heir, but even had there been one, it is not clear that this person would have succeeded him. As it happens, upon Muhammad's death in 632, his closest followers in Medina gathered and chose one among them, Abu Bakr, to be the first caliph (khalîfa), "deputy" of the Prophet. He was succeeded by another close follower, 'Umar, under whose able rule Muslim armies conquered the rest of Arabia and moved on to Egypt. 'Umar realized the need to create a regular procedure for choosing rulers, and convened a council, shûra, to select a new caliph. This action legitimated the idea of reaching decisions by council, and the process continues to be followed in the Muslim world. 'Umar's committee chose a weak candidate, 'Uthmân, an early convert to Islam, who was assassinated in his own house by dissident soldiers.

THE DEVELOPMENT OF THE SHI'I

The next caliph was 'Alî, one of the key figures in Islamic history. 'Alî was the son-in-law of the Prophet and also his cousin, and had a great deal of support because of his kin ties to Muhammad. He was the closest to an heir available to the community. But he failed to punish 'Uthmân's assassins, and he revoked some of his decrees, and thereby provoked the ire of 'Uthmân's own kinsmen, a powerful Meccan aristocratic clan called the Umayyads. Their own leader, Mu'âwiya, challenged 'Alî's leadership. He called for a new council to select a caliph, and met 'Alî in battle (the dispute was arbitrated). 'Alî's rule began to crumble and he was assassinated in 661. His son Hasan abdicated in favor of Mu'âwiya, who began a new period of Umayyad dominance. But 'Alî's other son, Husayn, grandson of the Prophet, became the champion of dissident Muslims who began to see themselves as the "party of 'Alî." In 680, there occurred an event that was to mark the Muslim world forever after: en route to the Iraqi city of Kûfa, Husayn was ambushed and his entire company massacred by Umayyad forces at a place called Karbala. His head was taken as proof of the defeat.

The Karbala massacre became the pivotal event in the emergence and identity of the "party of 'Alî." Now known as the Shî'î, "party," this group conceived of legitimate authority as being forever charismatic. The spiritual and temporal authority of the Prophet was handed down through his grandchildren to a succession of spiritually perfect leaders called imâms. Born in opposition to the regime in power, the Shî'îs or Shi'ites have continued to stress the chasm between political realities and a longed for truly Islamic world. Shiite populations, most importantly in Iran, Iraq, and Lebanon, formed communities of teaching and learning divorced from the regimes under whose control they had to live. The date of the Karbala massacre, the 10th of the month of Muharram, 680, is commemorated annually in ta'ziyas, "martyr plays" that feature the assassination of Husayn. Sometimes the events include processions of men striking themselves with chains to participate in the pain and sadness that characterize the Shiite community's historical self-understanding (Momen 1985).

By contrast, the Umayyads and their successors saw themselves as the majority party and the continuers of the Prophet's ways, calling themselves Sunnîs, after sunna, referring to the Prophet's "custom" or usual practices. Sunni conceptions of authority return to the first council that chose the caliph. The entire Muslim community or umma inherits political authority, which they then bestow on a leader through a council. This way of routinizing authority drew on Arab tribal ideas of succession and loyalty, and was also effective in incorporating new peoples as part of the umma.

Note how the split in the Muslim world over succession fell along the same lines as did that affecting the Mormon community centuries later. One party elected a leader to follow the prophet, while another chose to follow his descendants. In both cases the "kinship party" refused to lose the charismatic quality of prophetic leadership and repudiated the "routinization" of authority. In both cases, this party proved to be the minority.

MASTERS AND DISCIPLES IN SUFI ORDERS

A third type of Islamic authority, alongside those of the council and kinship, is that which binds disciples to Sufi masters. Sufi orders offer paths to greater spiritual awareness and closeness to God, through prayer, chanting, and poetry. Each such order offers a specific tarîqa, "way" or "method". The current teacher or master in the order traces his authority back along a spiritual lineage to his teacher, that teacher's teacher, and so forth, often back to one of the immediate followers of the Prophet Muhammad (Eickelman 1976).

The first Sufi order was founded by the Persian scholar Abdul Qâdir al-Jîlânî (1078–1166). Abdul Qâdir's influence as a preacher grew so large that followers established a special retreat for him, where people came to study and listen. He taught that to approach God, people would first need to divest themselves of worldly goods; that these goods acted as veils that came between them and God. As in other Sufi orders, he urged people to practice dhikr: "remembrance" of God by chanting phrases either aloud or in one's heart. Dhikr chants vary from one order to the next, but often include multiple recitations of "there is no deity but God," the first half of the confession of faith, and of praise phrases such as "glory be to God." These activities of remembrance may also be enhanced by music and dance, such as those performed by members of a Turkish order called the Mevlevi (dedicated to the Persian poet Rûmî), and known in the West as "whirling dervishes" (Schimmel 1973).

After Abdul Qâdir's death, people began to ascribe miracles to him, and to consider him a saint. His sons, and their sons, and so on, succeeded him as heads of the Qâdirî order. As the order spread throughout Asia and North Africa, it gave rise to suborders, each linking back to the founder. These orders were an effective way of converting people to Islam, offering as they did spiritual activities and a well-organized religious structure. Each present-day local order has its own spiritual genealogy, detailing the transmission of knowledge back to Abdul Qâdir. These spiritual genealogies connect Muslims in South and Southeast Asia, the Middle East, northern and western Africa, and Europe into an international network of Sufi practice and worship.

Conclusions

Of course, Islam became the main religion of many countries throughout the world, while the Mormon faith, though equally universalistic, has remained geographically centered on one region of the United States. But in their beginnings, the two faiths resembled each other remarkably. In both cases, a charismatic leader received new scriptures that built on, and corrected, previous revelations, and did so by renewing the call to monotheism and universalism. In their early days, both movements were persecuted and had to flee their birthplaces. Ironically, the more successful of the two, Islam, also faced the more severe crisis of succession, a split over differences in theories of authority that continues to plague the Muslim world. The Church of Latter-Day Saints, by contrast, was able to preserve a unified theory and practice of succession—perhaps because of its isolation and persecution within the United States.

Weber's initial model of authority types remains a useful starting point for studying religious authority because it leads us to ask important questions: Why did people follow a new leader? How was succession handled, and how did the movement get "routinized"? Can we see internal disputes as regarding the conflict between two distinct theories of authority? You might extend this analysis to new religious movements in the United States, and see where these questions lead you.

Index

Page references followed by "f" indicate illustrated figures or photographs; followed by "t" indicates a table.

Toolmaking and tool use
   bronze, 81
   spears, 115
Tools
   stone, 60
Totem, 21
Trances, 107
Turner, Victor, 28, 52

U
Unilineal descent groups/systems
   clans, 19, 147
   moieties, 21
Upper Paleolithic art
   decorative, 88
Upper Paleolithic culture
   end of, 11
   Europe, 32, 63, 81, 109
   in Europe, 14, 63, 81

V
Varna, 79
Violence
   family, 74
   individual, 46, 63

W
Weber, Max, 15, 128, 138
Wolf, Eric, 104
Women
   in warfare, 62
Work, relative contributions to
   overall, 6, 38, 55
World War II, 33-34

Y
Yorùbá people of West Africa
   religion, 1-5, 9-10, 31, 49, 69, 85-86, 101-105, 113,
         137